EARWORM+EVENT

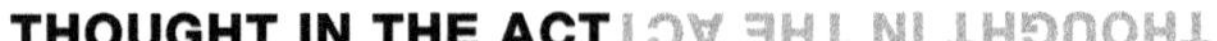

A series edited by Brian Massumi and Erin Manning

ELDRITCH PRIEST

EARWORM EVENT

MUSIC, DAYDREAMS, AND OTHER IMAGINARY REFRAINS

Duke University Press · Durham and London · 2022

Project editor: Lisa Lawley
Designed by Matthew Tauch
Typeset in Garamond Premier Pro by Copperline Book Services

Library of Congress Cataloging-in-Publication Data
Names: Priest, Eldritch, author.
Title: Earworm and event : music, daydreams, and other imaginary refrains / Eldritch Priest.
Other titles: Thought in the act.
Description: Durham : Duke University Press, 2022. | Series: Thought in the act | Includes bibliographical references and index.
Identifiers: LCCN 2021022847 (print)
LCCN 2021022848 (ebook)
ISBN 9781478015369 (hardcover)
ISBN 9781478017981 (paperback)
ISBN 9781478022596 (ebook)
Subjects: LCSH: Music—Philosophy and aesthetics. | Music—Psychological aspects. | Upstream color (Motion picture) | BISAC: MUSIC / Essays | ART / Criticism & Theory
Classification: LCC ML3800 .P84 2022 (print) | LCC ML3800 (ebook) | DDC 780.1—dc23
LC record available at https://lccn.loc.gov/2021022847
LC ebook record available at https://lccn.loc.gov/2021022848

Cover art: Eric Blum, *Pattern N° 077*, 2013. Archival pigment print. 30 × 30 in. Courtesy of the artist and RULE Gallery.

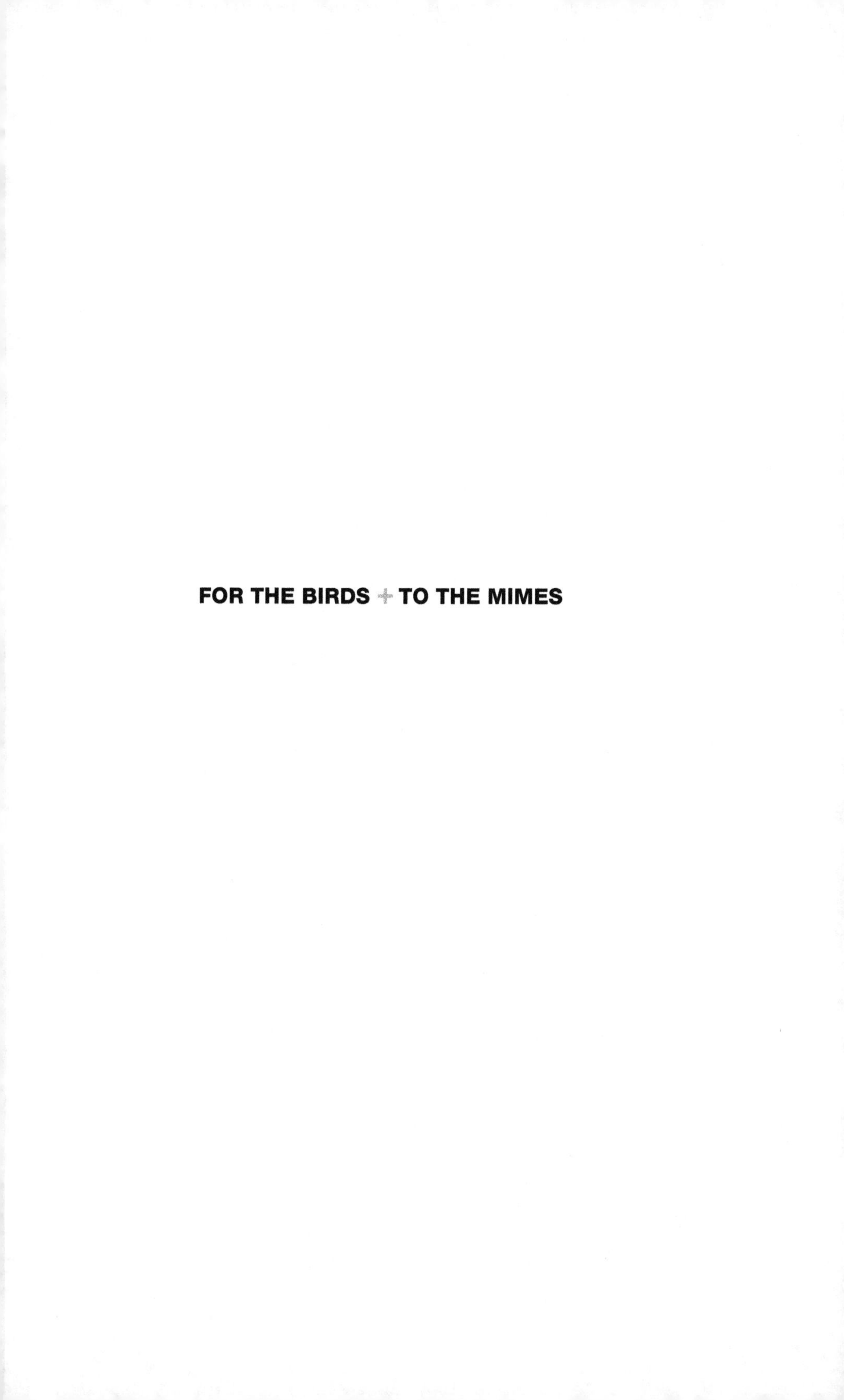

FOR THE BIRDS + TO THE MIMES

Contents

ACKNOWLEDGMENTS ix

INTRODUCTION · Earworm 1

ONE · Felt as Thought 7

TWO · Earworms, Daydreams, and the Fate of Useless Thinking 28

THREE · The Worm Refrain (or, Does Nature Get Earworms?) 53

NOTES 69 · WORKS CITED 77 · INDEX 83

Acknowledgments

I worked on this book for the better part of a decade, hemming and hawing about its need to be written and wondering, if were to be written, whether I'd be the one to do it. That you have the book in your hands and that my name appears on it is because I was privileged to share its content, in a variety of guises, with friends and colleagues along the way who both encouraged the project and enriched my thinking about what I think it means to think with earworms, daydreams, and other imaginary refrains. A sincere thank-you goes, then, to Sanem Güvenç, Saygin Salgirli, T'ai Smith, Margret Grebowicz, Deborah Kapchan, Carla Nappi, the anonymous readers of the manuscript, and especially Claudette Lauzon, all of whom took the time to be the kind of intellectual companions we dream of having when sailing uncertain waters. Thanks go as well to Jonathan Adjeman for his incisive copyediting, and to Josh Rutner for the incredible indexes. I would also like to thank Brian Massumi and Erin Manning for inviting me to publish this work in their wonderful series, and Ken Wissoker, as well as Ryan Kendall along with the design team at Duke University Press, for supporting and helping me bring this project to light. The other members of The Occulture—David Cecchetto, Marc Couroux, Ted Hiebert, Rebekah Sheldon—and everyone who attended Tuning Speculation over the years should be thanked as well, for it is with them that I was able to conjure the context that sustained the experimental thrust of this project. I want to express my gratitude to Jack Rachman, Maureen Whittal, and Kyle Burns for helping me learn to think differently about thinking. And thanks to Rocket for keeping me on my toes, and for my favorite French coat.

An earlier version of "Felt as Thought" was previously published in *Sound, Music, Affect: Theorizing Sonic Experience*, edited by Marie

Thompson and Ian Biddle (London: Bloomsbury, 2013), 45–63. "Earworms, Daydreams, and the Fate of Useless Thinking" has been expanded from a version published as "Earworms, Daydreams and Cognitive Capitalism," *Theory, Culture and Society* 35, no. 1 (2018): 141–62.

This work was supported in part by funding from the Social Sciences and Humanities Research Council and Simon Fraser University.

Introduction

EARWORM

Unbidden, uninvited, and always smack in the middle of things. Starting again and again without ending, which is to say, without clearly beginning, I hear a song, though less a song than scraps of a song, and these scraps are not really *heard* so much as they are *felt*, like an idea, or, better, like a suspicion or an inkling, an abstract feeling that cleaves to the spins and stalls of the virtual commotion called "thinking." What I'm describing is what it's like to have a song "stuck in your head," to have an earworm. There are other, punnier terms for this experience, like "humbug," "aneurhythm," "repetinnitis," "humsickness." And then there are the descriptive expressions such as "involuntary musical imagery" and "intrusive song phenomenon" favored by psychologists and cognitive neuroscientists. But like the thing it describes, "earworm," a literal translation from the German *Ohrwurm*, seems to have stuck.

This phenomenon, however, isn't new, nor is it rare. Accounts of earworms appear *avant la lettre* in literature before the twentieth century. Edgar Allan Poe, for instance, writes of the experience in his short story of 1845, "The Imp of the Perverse," in which his unnamed narrator says, "I could scarcely get rid of it for an instant. It is quite a common thing to be thus annoyed with the ringing in our ears, or rather in our memories, of the burthen of some ordinary song, or some unimpressive snatches from an opera" (3). And before Poe, a passing note on music's propensity to lodge itself in the mind is made by Immanuel

Kant in his 1790 *Critique of Judgment*. Contrasting musical and visual arts, he asserts that where the latter produce lasting impressions that sustain and entertain the imagination, the former produce only fleeting impressions that "are extinguished entirely or, *if the imagination involuntarily repeats them*, they are more likely to be irksome to us than agreeable" (1987, 200; my emphasis).

While these fleeting descriptions of music's imaginary repetition are uncommon (at least in English sources), the experience, is not. Anecdotally, this is simple to verify. Ask the next few people you meet what song is playing in their head, and you'll likely receive an answer rather than a blank stare. But several recent empirical studies have also confirmed this and suggest that the prevalence of earworms can be accounted for owing to factors such as recency of exposure to a music source and cortical thickness.[1]

These studies are interesting in their own right, but they are also notable for the fact that they represent a field of research into earworms that has developed only in the past twenty years or so. The vast majority of this scholarship, however, falls into research conducted in cognitive sciences and experimental psychology. While this gives earworms an empirical purchase beyond the shared complaints about how this or that tune has been plaguing one for days on end, the earworm has largely been treated as a pathology, and efforts are made to either determine the memory systems and brain networks implicated in their production and maintenance or make statistical correlations between variables such as the frequency of the event and the degree of musical training the subject/sufferer has. But this study, the one you have in your hands now, is decidedly philosophical and speculative in orientation, meaning that it takes the earworm as a point of entry into thinking about broader theoretical concerns regarding the nature of thought and perception today.

This book treats the earworm as an event that offers insight into not only how human brains process musical experiences but how lived abstractions and the imagination play key roles in the composition and expression of our contemporary social assemblages and more-than-human milieus. I propose, then, to consider earworms in two ways. First, I situate the earworm as a by-product of human-technology couplings that indexes the way techniques of listening and habits of thought are implicated in and transformed by a world of automated hyperattention. We are all acutely aware of how our world is saturated with electronic media. But this saturation is not without its tics. As

Elizabeth Margulis notes, the ubiquity of audio technologies brings forth "a degree and pervasiveness of repetition that was previously unheard of" (2013, 77), such that we are primed to contract the type of refrains that nurture earworms. It is partly this pervasiveness that gives earworms their purported catchiness. But it is also this pervasiveness that, I suggest, gives audition and thinking a peculiar functional autonomy that both aids and confounds contemporary capitalism's effort to draw value from involuntary nervous activities. Second, I treat the earworm as a conceit or a performative model expressive of how our broader powers of abstraction can be made to bend in on themselves and assimilate other imaginary refrains to a recursive logic. In this respect, I approach the idea of a song stuck in one's head from a point of view that takes it not as a cognitive anomaly but as a trope—an abstract lure for thinking, even—that promotes a recursive form of thought and simulates the schizoid style of being a contemporary subject of infinite distraction. Thus, in the *Earworm* side, I take up earworms as a technical affair, while the *Event* side engages with the phenomenon figuratively and (at times) ironically.

The tête-bêche binding reflects this organization and can itself be taken as a device that intensifies these two approaches. Therefore, the (mostly) straightforward scholarly approach of this side of the book, whose chapters are organized around particular themes, expresses a methodological contrast to the (mostly) experimental episodes of the flip side. Furthermore, the arrangement of the book produces a type of theory in action, to the extent that together the two sides perform a schizo-analytical act that honors the earworm, and thinking more generally, as a process characterized by flows and breaks. The binding can be thought, then, to carry out at the level of form a gesture similar to that which composes an earworm's intrusive refrain. In other words, the break-flow introduced by the binding scheme is continuous with the compositional logic of the earworm that runs throughout both sides of this book.

Ultimately, this means that you can start here or there. However, if you start here, you might want to take note of a little phrase—"felt as thought"—that appears again and again. This phrase is borrowed from Susanne Langer, who devised it as a way to reconceptualize the notion that organic processes somehow convert their goings-on into sentient experience. In her words, "If, instead of 'converted into thought,' we say, 'felt as thought,' the investigation of mental function is shifted from the realm of mysterious transubstantiation to that of physiological processes" (1962, 18). This means that, for Langer, sentience can be explained as "a phase of vital process itself, a strictly intraorganic phase" wherein an organism "feels its own actions" (17). This also means that feeling "in the broad sense of whatever is felt in any way, as sensory stimulus or inward tension, pain, emotion or intent, is the mark of mentality" (1967, 4). Thus, what is felt is thought.[2]

In this book I use the expression a little differently than Langer does, deploying it instead to bring attention to the way in which processes of abstraction and cognition are continuous with processes of feeling. Although I follow Langer's reasoning, I also allow the phrase to become a refrain, and as such I make it function as more than a shorthand for how vital processes feel their own activities. As a refrain the phrase encourages "interactions between elements devoid of so-called natural affinity" (Deleuze and Guattari 1987, 349) such that domains as disparate as music, daydreaming, animal mentality, and imaginary technics come in this work to occupy and transform each other's territory.

A NOTE ON METHOD

In March 2020 a study was published that examined the cultural evolution of song variants in white-throated sparrows (see Otter et al. 2020). In this study it was found that a particular variant—a doublet-ending song—that was heard first in western Canada has been taken up by male sparrows across the continent to replace the original song that ends with a triplet. Using geotracking devices and examining field recordings made over two decades across North America, researchers propose that the rapid spread and nearly wholesale adoption of this otherwise-rare regional variant is due to a mechanism linked to a species preference favoring the introduction of novelty into the repertoire. The precise nature of this mechanism is still hypothetical and, as might be expected given that this research was conducted by biologists, largely assumes that this preference for novelty is in service to biological needs—that is, for attracting mates. But what if the spread of this doublet-terminating tune is not merely a biological matter? What if this song is just catchier? What if these sparrows are all singing "twee-tweeee twee t-twee t-twee t-twee t-twee" because they have an earworm? It might indeed just be the case that the tune catches on because there is some biological reward to novelty—successful procreation—

and it may be entirely prudent to pursue such a hypothesis given that bird song is indisputably tied to behavioral functions in a way that a catchy tune for us is not. But it might also be the case that asking if birds get earworms opens thought up to other paths that take us on a very different adventure.

The aim of this side of the book is to consider that adventure, not exactly from a bird's-ear view (that's for the flip side), but from a position that draws from thinking about earworms a line of questioning that helps us consider a number of other issues, such as what it means for something to be felt as thought, for thinking to be a form of labor, and for a sense of self to be distributed among humans, worms, pigs, and flowers.

⁂

The first chapter builds on Susanne Langer's concept of semblance and draws from the model of feeling that she develops in her later work on the biological origins of mind, to develop a notion of sonic abstraction that sees the imagination as a speculative organ in which material powers and conceptual force converge as mood to impinge on our organism's affectivity. In particular, I ask what abstraction means in relation to the brand of virtuality that belongs to music by extrapolating from the latter's traditional meaning a concept of abstraction that resembles pure potentiality. Like Langer's in her pivotal *Philosophy in a New Key* (1942), the arguments I make about thought and abstraction follow from an analysis of musical experience that can be generalized to the wider field of perception and thought—aesthetic or otherwise. However, I reach beyond Langer's conclusion that art's semblances are cognitive tools for developing our ability to "make form expressive for us wherever we confront it" (1967, 87). Instead, I make the arguably more radical claim that under certain circumstances, such as those staged by John Cage's *4′33″*, wherein percepts and concepts fuse without becoming confused, sound is felt as thought more than it is listened to and so approaches the condition of a daydream.

Earworms are targeted more directly in the second chapter, where they are treated as an exceptionally thoughtful kind of feeling, one that realizes a tendency inherent in musical technics to be, as Brian Massumi says of every technique of existence, as "absolutely felt as it can experienceably be" (2011, 151). Although the cognitive neurosciences are currently conducting research to determine the brain networks that are implicated in the production of earworms, in this chapter I address what I see as the technical nature of these abstract parasites. Intensified by the accelerating industrialized exteriorization of the mind (Stiegler 2010a, 9) that redoubles music's technique of existence, I suggest that a mutant form of listening has developed that gives music a fatal tendency to be felt as thought more than listened to. Drawing on a number of thinkers such as Bernard Stiegler, Paolo Virno, Vilém Flusser, and Jean Baudrillard, I argue that to the extent that musical abstractions are felt as thought, they are easily channeled into circuits of continuous nascent attention where they come to function, on the one hand, as a type of virtuosic labor but also, on the other, as a strange affirmation of the feeling of thinking, or, as I suggest, the expression of our onto-power.

As already noted, the earworm is an event whose comings and goings can be helpful for thinking about social assemblages. But it can also be helpful for thinking about imaginary ones and more-than-human rhythmic processes. By transposing the earworm's refrain into the fictional life cycle of a mesmeric parasite, chapter 3 turns to a pataphysical discussion of discontinuity and repetition as seen through the lens of a single film that makes of humans, pigs, worms, and flowers an elaborately lived abstraction. The film, *Upstream Color* (2013), by the American filmmaker Shane Carruth, is an impressionistic and nonlinear existential drama that sees various actors—human and nonhuman—struggling to overcome an inexplicable sense of loss that at the same time brings each of them either literally, metaphorically, or preternaturally together. Because the work is an experimental film that relies largely on music and sound design as much as editing techniques to present a vision of a sutured life, it doesn't lend itself readily to *any* kind of exegesis. In this respect, I explore the film's primary refrain of dis/continuity dis/continuously by composing a textual form that takes after Theodor Adorno's concept of the essay, a form that "constructs a complex of concepts interconnected in the same way it imagines them to be interconnected in the object" (1993, 23). The result is a text that in its performance rehearses the way experiential incoherence is itself, like the worm refrain found in the film, felt abstractly as a bizarre form of connection. Configured as such, the book comes to an end in a way that makes thought felt in the act of its speculative share, that starts again and again without ending, which is to say, without clearly beginning.

One

FELT AS THOUGHT

As Plato noted and Muzak exploited, musical sound has a peculiar effect on us, one that we feel as feeling. Yet it's not that music actually is a feeling; it just feels that way. And although music is clearly not a feeling, something about it is so indisputably *like* a feeling that its likeness often substitutes for a temper or a mood. Just as reveries and daydreams can occasionally be proxy to living life, listening to music can be proxy to feeling it. But what exactly does it mean to think a feeling, or for a feeling to be like itself? If a semblance of feeling wrought in tones, time, and timbre is not what it appears to be, then what is it, and how can it possibly affect the way we feel feelings and think thoughts?

Susanne Langer suggests that music already provides the answer, but this answer involves seeing music not as a feeling but as a symbol of feeling. Although deeply indebted to both Alfred North Whitehead's and Ernst Cassirer's work, Langer's approach to the life of feeling, in its several and varied modes, takes its conceptual cues and logical form from the processes and experience of music. In fact, Langer generalizes her insights into the virtuality of musical experience (albeit using a very narrow example of what counts as music) to form an entire philosophy of art in which feeling is the central measure. In this chapter I want to reassess Langer's theory of virtuality and claim from her late work on the philosophy of mind a sense of the imagination that shows it to be a measure of our affectivity.

A MODE OF FEELING

While Langer's theory of art is typically taken to revolve around the formal properties of an artwork, her philosophy is grounded on the premise that human perception is characterized by a fundamental need to transform the flux of experience into abstractions that express "its immediate effect on our sensibility" (1967, 59). For Langer, the human organism not only possesses a capacity to abstract a qualitative-relational value from sensory particulars but develops a capacity to live *in* and *through* these abstractions, which are expressive of an import that doubles sensation with a likeness—semblance—"entirely congruent with forms of mentality and vital experience" (67). This is to say that perception is, for Langer, fashioned of livable abstractions, or what in her peculiar sense of the term are symbols wherein "the factor of significance . . . is felt as a quality rather than recognized as a function" (1953, 32).

Although the argument that human perception is composed of symbolic forms abstracted from patterns in the experiential field is not entirely novel (one need only cite Sigmund Freud's or Ludwig Wittgenstein's views on the symbolic nature of human psychic life), Langer's assertion that abstractions are *a mode of feeling* continuous with the vital activities that course across and though the organism is. Feeling, which Langer defines as "whatever is felt in any way, as sensory stimulus or inward tension, pain, emotion or intent," is not separable from mentality but in fact "is the mark of mentality" (1967, 4). The abstractions in which we feel significance, quality, or value are a *phase* of organic processes by which vital activities cross a threshold of complexity and intensity to be felt as thought, felt abstractly. On this view, feeling marks a continuity between material powers and conceptual force. And it is for this reason that art features so prominently in Langer's philosophy. Aesthetic experience is exemplary of how our organism perceives something nonsensuous in sensuous assemblies and how in this it becomes liberated "from the finitude of actuality" and open to "the endless reaches of potentiality" (1930, 51).

The idea of abstraction as a mode of access to the domain of potentiality is intriguing in that it shows experience to be composed of a speculative dimension that is entered once it is felt, or, rather, felt as thought. The arts play a major role in exemplifying this dimension, for in their created semblances—their sheer appearing as forms of feeling dissociated "from the physical and causal order" (1953, 47)—they show themselves as elaborate techniques of abstraction and vehicles *for* speculation. What the arts speculate on, however, is not the status of a truth or fact but what it feels like to feel oneself affecting and being affected by and as an occasion of experience. While all artworks exemplify forms of feeling by virtue of the way their techniques of abstraction figure forth a semblance particular to the relational manner in which certain factors become elements immanent to their signature ways of appearing, Langer considers musical abstraction especially significant because its explicit patterns of tension and resolution are "exemplified in all art, and also in all emotive responses" (1942, 227). She writes that "all art is but a projection of [these patterns] from one domain of sense to another" (227). Music, in its characteristic appearance as soundly moving forms that create a nonsensuous (abstract) perception of locomotion, shows itself to be exemplary of the way art forms make "the sameness of logical structure in experientially different loci" (1967, 105) apprehensible, if not comprehensible. In other words, musical phenomena exemplify what Langer calls the logical expression of feeling experienced as a qualitative-relational order *in its mode of being felt as thought*. For Langer, art's illusions (semblances) are not excessive by-products of perception's virtual depths so much as they are exaggerations of a fundamentally spontaneous activity by which the human organism generates from experiential data analogies of form that allow for the indirect perception of said form's past and future occasions. In short, art (but music especially) shows us that we "symbol-mongering" (1942, 43) organisms live a double life composed of abstract likenesses and sensuous particulars.

Langer's sense of abstraction as elementary to organic processes can, I think, be taken to expand the sense of what musical embodiment means. Although I understand the impulse to employ tropes of embodiment in order to wrest the *idea* of music from its perceived cognitive foundations, I think it's a rhetorical mistake to take the overt activities associated with its reception as a sign of music's bodily priority. Whether dubstep, a piece by Morton Feldman, or even an advertising jingle, the perception of all music entails some form of somatic comportment. That some musical practices encourage dancing or toe tapping and implicate these activities into their field of (musical) relevance does not, however, make them more embodied; it just makes that dimension of their experience manifest. Musical cultures that conduct their engagement around less overt actions, such as sitting quietly and being motionless, are no less bodily. As Langer argues, "No living mechanism is ever doing absolutely nothing" (1972, 30). If overt action is inhibited, "something is [still] covertly going on, there are changes in the maturing, proliferating, or perhaps aging processes of the surrounding tissues; the inhibited complex is waiting, and waiting is a physiological activity" (30).

In other words, the still body is still a body doing. It is acting and being acted on just as the body moved to dance (to/with music) is acting and reacting. Its doings simply take place at another level of activity, a level of incipient or inchoate activity that is, as I'll discuss later on, what is called "thinking" or "ideation." The point is that the experience of music, any and all music, entails a nervous response that implicates itself into the matrix of abstractions or symbolic assembly through which the organism experiences its own vital activity. Whether pulsed or meandering, danced to or stilled to, music presents a fabric of tensions—a tensity—that bears an isomorphy to the processes characteristic of vital activity. What matters is that in taking up this abstract similarity between musical forms and other forms of vitality (or feeling), one gains an understanding of one's capacity to feel the *possibility* of feelings, to imagine "the plenum of potential tensities, with several [indeterminate] gradients developing at the same time in different directions" (1967, 162).

If there is, to borrow a phrase from Langer, a commanding form, a matrix of envisaged sense to be made and expressed here, it is that musical abstraction is not merely a discursive construct or a cognitive by-product but the experience of sound being felt as thought. Here thought is the activity of nascent acts or suspended impulses initiated by vibratory impressions that one feels as thinking. In Langer's terms, thinking is a phase in physiological processes that terminate not in overt behavior but in the sheer expression of ideas, an event relieved of the necessity to ground itself in the sensuous side of experience. In other words, musical abstraction concerns the virtual or, as I prefer, the imaginary experience of music.

ACTIVITIES AND WHAT IS FELT

Langer's universe is a universe of activities. Like her teacher, Alfred North Whitehead, she sees processes and not substances as primary, and these processes describe regions of activity in which feelings develop. Feelings are, for Langer, neither epiphenomena arising mysteriously from physical events as an enigmatic additive nor a psychic term for the same empirical fact that another equivalent logical language would denote as "physical" (1967, 6–7). Instead, feelings denote a phase in physiological processes wherein they obtain an awareness of their own occurring. Like the red glow that appears in a bar of iron when it is heated to a critical degree, feelings are emergent phenomena. Redness, in other words, is not added to the iron; it is a phase in the activity of its heating (21). Similarly, feelings are not added to vital processes; they are a phase in "vital activities of great complexity and high intensity" (21). This psychic phase is "a mode of appearance, and not an added factor" (21). It can be said, then, that feelings are the appearance of vital activities in their occasion of being felt, and this occasion, Langer argues, includes "aspects of sensibility, awareness, excitement, gratification or suffering" (4). As a phase rather than a product of organic rhythms, the activity of feeling divests itself of the metaphysical ambiguity responsible for the problem of the ghost in the machine, or what Shakespeare called our glassy essence, and it becomes the foundation for understanding the entire field of psychological experience as "a vast and branching development of feeling" (23). This does not mean, however, that all forms of sentience are at root fundamentally emotional. It means that the center of activity that an organism experiences intraorganically as feeling comprises various modifications and transformations to a diffused tonus.

How a feeling is felt, how an activity is taken account of, depends on where and how it occurs in the organism's activities. Taking from Whitehead the idea that organisms are centers of activity, Langer distinguishes between exogenous and autogenous feelings. How one activity acquires either profile is a matter of how the organism manages "the exigencies of contact with the plenum of external events" (1967, 27) and how these contacts transition into acts that terminate in either a rapid reaction or a gradual change. In other words, activities phase one way or the other depending on whether they "carry, however vaguely, some indication of an impingement"—these are exogenous feelings, or sensation—or whether they arise from "a background of general body feeling and a texture of emotive tensions" (28), in which case they are autogenous activities, or from mentation. If an activity occurs at the periphery of the organism, where responses are managed quickly and improvisationally, it will carry an exogenous indication. And if it rises to "the level of being felt," it will be "felt as impact" (27). But if an activity obtains a psychic phase without a specifiable origin or stimulus, its indication is autogenous, and it will be felt as a mental state.

Apart from these two distinctions, feeling-tone is another important aspect of this model, for it points to the way in which vital activities felt as thought are continuously modulated by an entire field of unfelt, unconscious processes. As Langer notes, many processes go unfelt: "the whole dynamic rounds of metabolism, digestions, circulation, and endocrine actions" (1967, 22) are labile elements composing a fabric of unfelt nervous tensions. However, these processes are not irrelevant, as they "interact with others which have strong and specialized psychical character" (1962, 21). In this context the dimension of the unfelt parallels Freud's unconscious, yet Langer's unconscious differs from Freud's in that its activities compose no systematic field of psychic interactions. The unfelt makes an appearance in the life of the organism not as slips or jokes but as a feeling-tone. More precisely, the unfelt is given to feeling as a potentiality, an unspecified and continuously shifting background intensity that both donates and acquires a potential semiotic and emotional vector to/from the activity in which it is implicitly taken up. Basically, this background of feeling-tone is what we commonly call "mood," and it plays a role in modulating the intensity and conceptual valence of activities that are felt as thought.

To describe the unfelt as "feeling-tone" obviously strains the very definition of feeling that Langer establishes. To say that the unfelt is experienced at all, even as a background tonus, seems to contradict the premise that only vital processes of a certain complexity and intensity become felt. But to identify the unfelt with feeling-tone is not to say that the former is felt. While only certain processes attaining a psychic phase are felt, how the intensity of these activities is felt is a matter of how they are informed by the wider "dynamic pattern[s] of nervous activities playing freely across the limen of sentience" (1967, 22). The tone of these dynamic patterns, which mark the tonus of organic life, can be characterized as a commotion of preconscious acts. While they do not exactly describe a mode of being felt, they nevertheless communicate to perception something of the organism's current force of existing. This is to say that the unfelt conveys what Brian Massumi describes as "changes in the body's degree and mode of enablement in and toward its total situation or life environment" (2015, 71). Not only does the organism feel the dynamism of its own activities, but the feeling of those acts reaching a psychic phase is characterized by the way a more general rise and fall in enablement adjusts the organism's abstractive powers, its capacity to formulate relations and potential paths of action in and beyond actual experience. Feelings are, in a sense, inspired by the unfelt; they are *given (in) a mood*. As such, "the transformation of experience into concepts" (Langer 1942, 127) is mediated by feeling-tone.

This means that there is something about how unfelt activities affect our power of envisagement. If the form of unfelt activities—what could be called the matrix of "advancing acts that have already arisen from previous situations" (Langer 1967, 281)—constitutes the mood of a feeling, and if this mood shapes the kind of conceptual moves that can be made in an occasion of feeling, then this dimension of organic activity should be regarded as a structured and structuring ground that determines the kind of abstractions or abstractive tendencies that can take place within it—without, however, determining the characteristics of these abstractions. To put it another way, every feeling has a conceptual or imaginative valence, and in this respect its mood functions like a medium of abstraction. Thus, the envisagement of forms of feeling is influenced by the way a feeling-tone, and not just the selectivity of the sense organs, restricts the kind of abstractions that an organism may formulate in its current ambient, its current phase of vital goings-on.[1] When one is hungry, for example, the unfelt but continually ongoing acts of digestion and metabolism generate a mood that imperceptibly modulates the conceptual valence of the imagination so that expressive forms more conducive to acts terminating in eating will have a greater chance of being articulated.[2] More punctual acts that, owing to their intensity, rapidly ascend to being felt, such as being cut, also have a mood that determines the organism's imaginary valence. However, in these situations the mood is not felt as such. The flow of feelings and vital activity coincide in an immediate alteration of the organism's situation such that the mood, the feeling-tone, *is* the activity. In being cut, what Langer calls the act form, a form marked by incipience, acceleration, consummation, and, finally, cadence, becomes the shape of the organism's actional matrix (1967, 288–89). In this respect, act and what is felt as thought—felt-thought—are one.[3]

ABSTRACTION

We talk about music affecting us emotionally, but Langer's theory of semblance suggests that emotion is only part of the significance of musical experience and, in some ways, not even the most significant part. What is significant about music, says Langer, is its symbolism: the way its semblance of a lived or living time gives logical expression to forms of feeling. But semantic potential is not the only significant feature of music's semblance. Semblance as an abstraction of what it's like to feel feelings in a certain way carries a manner of feeling-thinking into the imagination that gives thought a sense of connectivity it does not otherwise have, a conceptual connectivity flush with a sense of vital import.

The reason for this is that the perception of a semblance permits the imagination to indulge in the semblance's sheer appearance. Citing Friedrich Schiller's notion of *Schein*, Langer argues that a semblance allows for "the contemplation of sensory qualities without their usual meanings" (1953, 49). In other words, a semblance is taken as something dissociated from the practical relays in which perceptions are experienced. Although art's significance lies in making semblances evident and putting them to symbolic use, semblance is not exclusive to art. Langer's reason for focusing on aesthetic experience is that she sees it as exemplary (or an exaggeration) of a basic organic impulse to draw out qualitative-relational implications from an experiential flow of sense impressions. A semblance is, in some sense, this act of abstraction. And while an artwork exhibits a much more sophisticated and overt form of semblance-abstraction, all perceptions, all feelings—whether of an itch or an artwork—are suffused with abstractions whose expressions, while "clothed in different integuments of sensation" (Langer 1942, 71), are not bound to their objectively articulable sensory order. Massumi draws out the implications of a permanent realm of semblances to suggest that the abstraction of form that a semblance is is "the way a whole set of active, embodied potentials appears in present experience" (2011, 42). In every present experience, a likeness to past and future occasions of its singular impression appears. The difference between art's semblances and everyday appearances is, says Massumi, "a question of emphasis" (45). He writes that each moment of perception "is always passing through its own potential" (45). This is true for mundane impressions as much as aesthetic appearances. What sets each off from the other is its participation in "an economy of foregrounding and backgrounding of dimensions of experience that always occur together"

(45). "Art," Massumi writes, "foregrounds the dynamic, ongoingly relational pole. Everyday experience foregrounds the object-oriented, action-reaction, instrumental pole" (45). The point here is not that art is more abstract than ordinary perception but that perception itself always has a virtual dimension to it, a nonsensuous dimension whose qualitative autonomy gives thought its characteristic feelings as something happening apart from material processes.

Abstractions are by nature nonsensuous perceptions, and insofar as they are perceived, they are felt as thought. As Massumi states, "What is felt abstractly is *thought*" (2011, 109). An actual itch is not felt as thought, for its feeling is dominated by the action-reaction pole of perception. But the idea of itching is an abstraction that can be felt as thought apart from any actual occasion of itching. That the present participle "itching" may be immediately linked to a nose or an ear, or to allergic reactions and even inopportunity, shows thinking to be an intensive activity, meaning that the articulation of abstractions like itching is not, as William James puts it, slowed by the "tardy consecution of things in themselves" (1996a, 64). In a very real sense, thinking is life lived abstractly. "When we pause to think," writes Massumi, "this is what we're doing: continuing life abstractly" (2011, 118). When "nonsensuous perception is exonerated from having to move with the actual displacements of the ongoing event matrix that is the body"—when it is taken up by language, for instance—then an "infinitely rapidly permutating flow of words removes all limits" (117–18) on the articulation of things. Thinking is life being felt abstractly, life being felt in and through the abstractions that in their detachment from the integuments of sensory particulars produce patterns of conceptual activity whose experience is characterized by logical, associative, and affective articulations "accumulating in a qualitative universe all [its] own" (110).

Massumi's example of language as a vehicle for the experience of abstraction—"open-range abstraction" (116)—is helpful for it clarifies how it is that we live abstractions to their edge, their virtual edge. Thought in its form of language "takes up the thought-felt abstraction of nonsensuous experience into its own movement" in a way that "intensifies the autonomy of nonsensuous perception by incalculably increasing the range of its potential yoking between extremely diverse events" (116). But all abstractions and symbolic forms, not just language, do exactly this. Art, too, can be regarded as a technique for intensifying "the autonomy of nonsensuous perception" (116). Through silencing rituals, architectural arrangements, and more immanent forms of spectacle, artworks dampen the exigencies of the present moment to open perception to a virtual dimension wherein its forms can be related and articulated in ways that exceed those possible in the objective sensory order of things. Language is an exceedingly good technique for stripping symbols of their sensible demonstration, and for this reason it can easily become lost in its play of difference and speculative jaunts. Music, too, participates in this open-range abstraction, yet differently than language does. Music's abstractions, its semblances, *show* forms of vitality rather than *say* them, and in this regard music is able to articulate and set forth relations that language cannot—namely, relations that are revelatory rather than explanatory. This is a consequence of a difference in modes of abstraction. But I don't want to pit language and music against each other. Dwelling on their different abstractive modes will lead the discussion astray from the more pressing point I want to make about the intensity of abstraction. In this respect, I think it's more instructive to compare music's abstraction with that exemplified by abstract painting.

Massumi cites abstract art (painting specifically) as exemplary of work in which seeing sees itself seeing. For instance, in writing about a color-field painting, he notes, "It's not an animation of anything. It's a pure animateness, a vitality affect that comes from nothing and nowhere in particular" (2011, 69). What is being perceived in the absence of a figure that would otherwise locate the painting's movement-effects and animateness are the relational dynamics productive of the act of seeing itself. However, the objectless dynamism that Massumi ascribes to abstract painting is just as evident, maybe more so, in music. Yet it is not so-called abstract or absolute music as represented by certain canonical works of the nineteenth-century Western concert tradition that exemplifies this kind of abstraction. The works of Ludwig van Beethoven or Johannes Brahms are (as I'll explain later on) not abstract enough. To the extent that abstraction is a process of extracting potential and relaying it from one occasion to another, medieval organum, the fantasias of seventeenth-century English consort music, and the ambient works of Brian Eno, as well as works indebted to the lyrical meanderings of Erik Satie and the chance-derived principles of John Cage, are more representative of abstract music. In many respects, it is the characteristically unthematic and asyntactic forms of these musical styles that excel at relaying the sheer potential of abstraction.[4]

As something whose very being may be said to define and express the idea that change has a shape or a quality, it should be axiomatic that music is rife with what Daniel Stern calls "vitality affects," a concept that figures prominently in Massumi's work. Stern, who draws elements of his own theory from Langer's philosophy, actually goes so far as to suggest that musical phenomena epitomize "the expressiveness of vitality affects" (1985, 56). While all music displays vitality affects in that its various genres exhibit dynamic forms of "'surging,' 'fading away,' 'fleeting,' 'explosive,' 'crescendo,' 'decrescendo,' 'bursting,' 'drawing out'" (54), these are arguably more pronounced in musical works that suppress, as much as possible, its figurative elements. Music that inhibits the articulation of strong gestalt forms—that is, themes and variations—in effect raises its abstraction to a higher power. It is in this sense that the music of Beethoven and Brahms is not sufficiently abstract: their music works hard to ensure that its sensible wholes become figures or discernible semiotic units in their own right, much in the way that Wassily Kandinsky's contrasting colors and floating geometric shapes become figures in a semblance of abstraction. A music of themes, variations, developments, modulations, counterpoint, and cadences, while self-referential, is not, ironically, as abstract as it could be. A focus on the extensional implications afforded by treating dynamic events as simple musical atoms on which to build complex forms generates a rhetorical force that manipulates the listener's affectivity to effect a range of responses that "are not spontaneous emotional [expressive] outlets but prescribed modes of participation and assent" (Langer 1942, 163). This management and organization of feeling eclipses the felt significance of music as a technology for abstracting and envisaging something that, strictly speaking, it is not. A more radical form of abstraction would be achieved by a work whose expressions are made to return listening not to the extensional but to the intensional implications of variation. This, in effect, is to return listening "to its movement-potential [vitality affect] while refusing to give that potential an actual outlet feeding it into other existing formations" (Massumi 2011, 70). The moment when listening listens to itself listen as it is "intensely going nowhere" (70) becomes the moment when an interest in the purely expressive value of sounds in their suchness, their quality that Charles Sanders Peirce describes as a "mere maybe" (1955, 81), trumps an interest in their use.

Abstraction of this sort returns perception to its fundamental dynamic ground. This is the point of transition where organic processes enter a psychic phase to adumbrate a realm of *articulable* expressions that, for Langer, is "the starting point of all intellection" (1942, 42) and the mark of human mentality. Although these abstractions form a constant stream of ideation, it does not mean that they always develop into or terminate in some overt form of behavior. Indeed, as William James writes, the greater part of our expressive life is lived virtually as a continuous expression of our abstractions that are "unterminated perceptually" (1996a, 69). In a sense, to live abstractly, virtually, is to live in the "*sheer expression of ideas*" (Langer 1942, 43). Here the expression itself, or, rather, express*ing* as such, is an auto-affective event that "is always passing through its own potential" (Massumi 2011, 45) and thereby constantly modulating its own capacities.

For Langer, the life-abstract belongs as much to the range of ordinary activities that found human mentality as to those exceptional events we call art: the life of the mind is "the constant stream of cerebral activities which are essentially subjective, having no perceptible overt phases, but terminate as images, thoughts, recollections, often elaborate figments, entirely within the organism in which they take rise" (Langer 1967, 229). What Langer means is that mind is the totality of those phases in nervous activity that are felt as thought, felt as a flow of images. In other words, mind is the imagination broadly construed. And insofar as "all vital action, whether of the organism as a whole in its surroundings or of an organ internal to it, is interaction, transaction" (26), the imagination is an expression of an individual's affectivity. The flow of abstractions and feeling-tone experienced as mind expresses how the individual's force of existing modulates with the welter of actions and activities, both endogenous and exogenous, that constitute the body's moment-to-moment situation. But the imagination is not only expressive of an organism's habits of abstraction. The expressions of the imagination, although exempt from sensuous obligations, are taken up as nonsensuous elements of an evolving ambient. This means that while ideas might not directly influence how the individual meets and responds to the world, because they enter into the coming experience as one of its constitutive elements, they affect the composition and selection of the impulses that function as potential acts. In a sense, the organism advances itself through its abstract expressions.

THE SEMBLANCE OF AFFECT

How, then, do musical events participate in this creative advance? As already noted, Langer's position is that, like all art forms, musical experience entails the apprehension of an illusion (semblance) whose complexly layered fabric of tensions and rhythms is expressive of "the pattern of life itself, as it is felt and directly known" (1953, 31). Music is therefore revelatory, and it is revelatory of the *sense* of feelings. It neither causes nor evokes any specific affect or emotion but presents dynamic forms whose "resulting gestalt 'is and is not' its avowed object" (Langer 1967, 170). "The imagination that responds to music," writes Langer, "is personal and associative and logical, tinged with affect, tinged with bodily rhythm, tinged with dream, but *concerned* with a wealth of formulations for its wealth of wordless knowledge, its whole knowledge of emotional and organic experience, of vital impulse, balance, conflict, the *ways* of living and dying and feeling" (1942, 244). In presenting forms of feeling, music is not articulating any particular affective state so much as it is an event by which one may get a sense of how the world could be felt in its qualitative-relational order. In other words, music gives "knowledge of 'how feelings [may] go'" (244). That music has effects on us that are strongly allied to the emotional life of a person is indisputable; however, what music offers to and for the speculative organ of the imagination is not a causal formula but an occasion to "*make things conceivable* rather than to store up propositions" (244) or, rather, to nonsensuously model how we *could* feel the world.

What musical semblances make specifically conceivable—which is to say, imaginable—is our affectivity. A work's patterns of activity, its vitality affects, do not invite reflection on how we feel but on how we *may* feel, how a world may be felt rather than how it is or how it must be experienced. Forms of feeling connote and reveal ideas about how an experience *may yet come to have been affected*. Additionally, because these virtual affections are suffused with a sensible intensity, musical semblances function as a veritable lure that draws each coming moment into the intensity of its next effect. "Its message," writes Langer, "is not an immutable abstraction, a bare, unambiguous, fixed concept, as a lesson in the higher mathematics of feeling should be. [The semblance] is always new, no matter how well or how long we have known it, or it loses its meaning; it is not transparent but iridescent. Its values crowd each other, its symbols are inexhaustible" (1942, 239).

But how music makes our affectivity imaginable and makes us able to envisage it otherwise than it is, contrary to Langer's insistence, is not solely a matter of symbolization. There is something about music's semblance of vitality that affects the way the imagination flows, the way its fluid abstractions move and articulate with one another.

All acts terminate either in the fulfillment of an organic function (scratching an itch) or in expression (having an idea about itching). As they are articulated with one another, acts of the imagination terminate in the emergence of a concept, and a concept, as Massumi describes, is the expression of "the rhythm of arrival and departure in the flow of thought" (2002, 20). This means that a concept "is defined less by its semantic content than by the regularities of connection that have been established between it and other concepts" (20). And as an image of arrivals and departures in sound, a musical semblance creates interference and resonance patterns in the stream of thought that cannot help but affect the way the imagination establishes its regularity of connections.

Thus, the occasion of music's being heard—or unheard, as when musical semblances are backgrounded and only occasionally rise to the threshold of sentience—donates its lifelike effects to the full movement of mind. Abstractions that are not strictly musical in origin are, we could say, inspired by music's vitality affects. In breathing spirit into thinking, the "aliveness" of music becomes "fusionally ingredient" (Massumi 2011, 146) to other symbolic processes of articulation, generating speculative feeling-concepts that "ninety-nine times out of a hundred" (James 1996a, 69) never find their way into actual sensory conduct. As long as the music and its being heard lasts, the imagination will be animated in a way that promotes certain, let's say, "musical" types of linkage (i.e., melodic, rhythmic) between ideas, many of which are founded on what Langer describes as "the sameness of logical structure in experientially different loci" (1967, 105), or, again, what Massumi more simply calls a "nonsensuous similarity," a similarity wherein "nothing actually given to our senses corresponds to what our bodies and the heavens have imitably in common" (2011, 105). What heavens, bodies, and ideas will have in common is symbolically conceived, abstractly felt. And by virtue of a musically endowed onflow of envisagement, the constellation of abstractly felt symbolic forms is given the semblance of a viability that makes them seem real, makes them feel truer, or, pragmatically speaking, more effective, for a feelingful idea cannot help but give the impression of being truer (more viable) owing to the fact that what registers directly in and as feeling is for the organism truly the reality of the situation. Furnished with a set of virtual, nonsensuous affects in its taking up of musical forms of feeling, the musicalized imagination's concepts become seductive forms that are alluring in their "staging of aesthetic events that speculate on life, emanating a lived quality that might resonate elsewhere [or elsewhen], to unpredictable affect and effect" (80).

This seduction of the vital elsewhere/elsewhen of nonsensuous affects makes the ideas of a musically inflected imagination "good-enough substitute[s]" (120) for actual life. Ideas charged with the semblance of an abstract aliveness cannot help but be felt-thought as meaningful, as filled with import, and their "truth" somehow already—virtually—fulfilled or demonstrated. "Relieved of the immediate imperative to terminate in the world sensuously" (121), the abstract vitality of the musicalized imagination risks taking its own activities, its own "rhythm of arrival and departure in the flow of thought," as sufficient expressions of a life lived out when in fact it is the case of a life lived in, all too in. The nonsensuous charge that musical forms of feeling give to the flow of ideation inclines the imagination toward delusion, not only because its semblances reveal a life whose virtual feelings can be taken as good enough, but because music, as Langer argues, is an "implicit symbolism" (1942, 245). Unlike language, whose arbitrarily assigned signs make its symbolic function explicit, music is not typically regarded in a way that distinguishes its meanings from its figures, its import from its ideas. As Langer writes, "Until symbolic forms are consciously abstracted, they are regularly confused with the things they symbolize" (245). But this confusion, while problematic for musical aesthetics, is, it turns out, part of music's experiential charm.

A VEGETATIVE STATE

The confusion of the symbol for the symbolized that makes music's expressions a "myth of the inner life" is the reason, for Langer, that music's abstract dimension is "still in its 'vegetative growth'" (1942, 245) and is perhaps a little misleading. Langer wants to call music a myth not to diminish its expressive sophistication but to suggest that its symbolic/

abstract technologies are not typically recognized *as such*, and in this respect, where its effects "are so much *like* feelings that we mistake them for the latter" (245), music elicits a mode of thinking that is structurally closer to mythical consciousness. Following Ernst Cassirer's philosophy of symbolic forms, which posits that human perception, in its most basic occasion, finds sensation and meaning (physiognomic or affective in kind) to be coincident aspects of the same unfolding existential context, Langer identifies in music's typical reception a mode of awareness that makes no I-It or thing-attribute distinction. Where thinking is characterized by a flow of felt significance, there are no things, only subjects: I-Thou. What Cassirer (1957) calls the expressive function (*Ausdrucksfunktion*) of cognition is the basis of mythical consciousness and is responsible for the way that we see the world as alive, animated, or, in the terms I've been circulating here, composed of fleeting semblances—vitality affects—bound together by their affective affiliations and physiognomic characteristics rather than by their participation in a structural differential.[5] That music often spurs or rekindles a mythical consciousness is ultimately, for Langer, an underperformance of what music offers: the revelation and contemplation of forms of feeling that go *beyond* actual experience. In essence, mythical consciousness seems inconducive to the enhancement of the imagination's expressive and conceptual powers, for it appears not to recognize the transcendental potency of abstraction.

Music, however, is inescapably mythical and cannot help but evoke a mythical attitude—to some degree. If the sensory particulars of sound are to have a *musical* effect—that is, a qualitative-relational feel—the organism must perpetuate the identity (confusion) of symbol and sense to give sonorous forms their semblance of felt life. Until one applies a technique for isolating the abstractions that, as Langer (1953, 375) argues, arise spontaneously as a natural dimension of perception, it's almost impossible to dissociate the semblance-abstraction from its sensory garment in a way that would realize a musical work as an explicit symbol. This is perhaps not even something that is, for most listeners, particularly desirable. The confusion of symbol and symbolized in musical experience is what permits and sustains a mythology of feelings wherein there is no essential difference in efficacy between musical semblances (abstractions) and activities felt as thought. But quite apart from the argument that organic processes and somatic states are necessary conditions for experiencing sound as musical and are charged with a semblance of vitality (see note 5), this mythology is not only ineluctable but attractive: mythical thinking, as a mode of thought completely unconcerned with the distinction between appearance and reality, is a highly effective way to organize and intensify, perhaps to the point of delusion, a qualitative-relational universe of lived abstraction. To live mythically is, in a sense, a way to live abstractly, but it is a form of experience that suffers the intoxicating effects of its own enchantment, its own self-possessed drive to assimilate more of the world to its affective imaginary.

Although enchantment by a world teeming with semblances of vitality is not exclusive to musical experience, it is particularly prompt and powerful. Certain architectural spaces, like cathedrals and museums, embrace and harmonize what dwells within them so that, as Langer writes, "everything said or done in such places seems to be augmented by the vastness of the living space and dramatized by its atmosphere" (1953, 167). But this sense of exhilaration is reserved only for architecture's "greatest effects, whereas music exerts this power at almost all times" (167). Because "aural impressions reach us without demanding our conscious attention," music is unparalleled in its power to "absorb and utilize phenomena that do not belong to its normal material" (167). This act of swallowing things that are not strictly part of the "the 'aesthetic surface' of tones in their relational orders" (167) Langer calls the principle of assimilation, and it accounts for how "anything that gives the sounds a different appearance of motion, conflict, repose, emphasis, etc., is a musical element" (150). That is: whatever "affects the illusion" (151) becomes a musical power. Enchantment is thereby redoubled under music's spell. First, because musical perception already entails a mode of awareness wherein the medium (the semblance and not the sensory matter) and the elements of signification that it creates from affective states of awareness (abstractions) necessarily coincide to confuse its symbolic forms with the things they symbolize. And, second, because music's illusion cuts such a wide swath that anything that assures "its dissociation from actual experience, or stressing its vital import, or furnishing genuine structural factors" becomes a virtual element "in a realm of purely musical imagination" (152). This is not to say that cigarettes or power plugs are transformed into tones and rhythms. They're not. But to the extent that they somehow lend their appearance to the "illusion of a many-dimensional time in passage" (150), music's signature semblance, they *become* implicated in a mythology of feeling.[6]

SWALLOWING REVERIE

Curiously, despite the strength of music's aesthetic valence, everything that may be taken up by and as music is itself swallowed by the simple drift of reverie. This can be heard-felt perhaps most readily in John Cage's infamous work *4′33″* (1952), whose conceptual gesture assimilates, in abstraction, the most heterogeneous elements to music but at the same time delivers their abstractions directly to daydream. How such a powerful abstraction as music is subsumed by something so insubstantial as daydreaming rests on the accomplishment of a tendency shared by all organic activity—but especially by aesthetic activity—to strive toward the limits of expression, "to take a technique of existence to the expressive limit of what it can do" (Massumi 2011, 151).[7] There is a tendency of self-enjoyment that inheres in the very activity of expression to do more of what it does. Activities aspire to become more expressive, not in the sense of multiplying the number of things expressed, but in their manner of intensifying the particular mode of their own characteristic occurring.

Music is paradigmatic of this aspiration, for its semblances possess an unusual capacity to be apprehended apart from the circumstances from which they emerge and experientially detach. As Massumi observes, "Music does not have to use the body as local sign. Its local signs are *incorporeal*: sound waves" (2011, 145). It is the peculiar capacity of sound that has been organized in some way, whether through elaborate internal pitch relations or something as simple as a conceptual conceit, to dissociate or pull away from the objects and events that condition its expression.[8] The mediation of sound that, in a sense, music *is* deprives sound, to a certain degree, of its characteristic tendency to immediately stir overt action. Musical semblances are in this regard in usufruct to the physical property of sound, although under the right conditions their form of feeling can be contemplated (felt as thought) apart from their material conditions. While this artificial autonomy is not exclusive to music, it explains how music's appearance easily effects a decoupling from its practical provenance and semantic relays to do more of what it does: express its abstractions of felt life.

In a sense, music's semblances are not simply abstractions of vital activity being felt as thought but "universal attractor[s] of experience" (Massumi 2011, 151). As Massumi writes, "Every technique of existence has an expressive appetite for pushing nonsensuous similarity [logical expression] as far as it can go, carrying it to its highest degree of abstractive intensity, making it as absolutely felt as it can experienceably be" (151). Where music is able to dispel, frustrate, or overwhelm the specificity of its abstraction to include the most disparate elements into its semblance of vitality, it effectively voids "the event of expression of all content other than its own occurrence" (151). Such music is, paradoxically, a music composed of impassive acts whose intense expressions are ultimately inexpressive. As music begins to advance toward the horizon of its in/expressive limit to do what it does "better than any other technique of existence" (139), which is to give sound an immediate meaning in and of itself, it surprisingly begins to go silent. At its most pure, its most abstract, music appropriates to its semblance not only all sounds but all forms of dynamic alteration. As such, the conspicuous strangeness of its appearance grows faint among the bustle of so-called extramusical elements that it virtually becomes.

Massumi (2011, 156–58) hears Gustav Mahler's music behaving this way and says that its musical semblances, in being so vivid, so seemingly full of vitality, so *affected*, de-limit the imagistic tendencies vying for expression as content in the experience of the work's unfolding. This imagistic excess has the effect of despecifying any and all image intimations, making the music an intensely in/expressive event of nothing but its own tendency to de-limit its expressive force (151–52). Although Mahler's work may satisfy the expressive appetite of his particular musical genre for absolute expression, a more striking example of this expressive in/expressivity is Cage's *4′33″*, in which listening itself—the abstractive process directed by audition—is "so excessively included" in the event of expression that it not only "becomes-immanent to the expressive force of the event" (157) but also becomes its own speculative content. Or, more accurately, the *idea* of listening becomes content. Unlike Mahler's hyperimagistic music, *4′33″* doesn't encourage "a certain modality of content growth" (157). Where there ought to be a singular modality of experience "out-treating sources for the adventitious or parasitic growth of content affecting music" (157), there is none, or, rather, there is none in particular—experience is multiple and many. As such, *4′33″* is intensely expressive, but expressive of its own idea. While vision, in its nonsensuous or logical similarity to heard, seen, and proprioceived feelings, is overemphasized and overextended in Mahler's music to render its experience "excessively non-specific" (157) and thereby intensely impassive, the idea of *4′33″* as an occasion of listening, an occasion *to experience*, makes its idea excessively nonspecific. *4′33″* is an auditory cipher that makes anything felt abstractly as thought *speculatively absolute music*. And where music is felt so absolutely abstractly, its expression coincides with its thought, its imagining.

It is music's technique of making sounds sound more musical, more like music than not-music (whatever this "music" may be), that leads it to the heights of abstraction: conceptualism. In accomplishing this limit of expression, music becomes not only "our myth of the inner life" but a veritable figment. But Langer (1953, 168) notes that daydreaming—reverie—easily absorbs music into its remit. Although reverie is not a work of art, it nevertheless obeys the same law of abstraction and principle of assimilation, such that it, too, transfigures whatever affects its appearance into an element of daydreaming. That is, anything that can enter into the patterns of conceptual activity is potentially an element of reverie's semblance, and in a manner of speaking this could be anything and everything. Reverie's technique of existence swallows even more extra-oneiric elements than a music emptied "of any symbolic evocations or metaphorical associations" (Massumi 2011, 139) swallows extramusical elements. Musical semblances, from their most abstract to their most referential, are absorbed into reverie's conceptual flow as a feeling-tone that alters and "change[s] the 'set' or 'mood' of the responding organism" (Langer 1972, 264). Music, particularly in the quasi-passive act of listening distractedly, where its tonal perceptions are not so discernible from other background perceptions, becomes an element in the daydreamer's virtual experience. For the hyperabstract work such as *4′33″*, whose technique of existence essentially extends the semblance of vitality to anything and everything, there is even less distinction between its conceptual conceit and reverie's speculative wanderings.

Both reverie and the kind of conceptual music that *4′33″* represents approach the condition of pure expression. The daydream seems as close as we symbol-mongering creatures can come to sheer expression, to expression sustained by an abstract inertia that keeps its speculative goings-on going on. Its stream of ideas, sometimes vague and sometimes vivid, is under no obligation to terminate in or consummate its ideas in activities perceived locally with the senses. At most, reverie's ideas are expressive of a "vicarious completion of impulses" (Langer 1972, 263) engendered by a constant onflow of sensory impressions and perceptions that, instead of "elicit[ing] overt reactions" (263), modulate the mood or affectivity of the organism-individual. Background music, in which perception flits back and forth between the poles of semblance and sensation, gives to the reverie that absorbs it its own semblance—a metasemblance, or, in Langer's words, a "secondary illusion" that simulates, in its presentation of a lively ambient, "a semblance of the empirically real" (Massumi 2011, 128). But a hypermusic whose ideas (forms) of feeling are rendered "as absolutely felt as [they] can experienceably be" (151) will be indistinguishable from the abstractions that compose reverie's imaginary ambient. Yet, strangely, this does not make the hyperabstract musical work any less musical. Its ideas are still about feeling, about an intensive time of alteration that is characteristic of music's peculiar technique of existence. However, these ideas find expression not in music's customary objective conditions—tonal and rhythmic relations—but in conceptualization, in a manner of thinking that abstracts forms of feeling from "a heterogeneity of factors in a signature species of semblance" (143). In other words, *4′33″* is music but only in your (day)dreams.

Two

EARWORMS, DAYDREAMS, AND THE FATE OF USELESS THINKING

THE IDEOSONIC

Almost all of us know what it's like to have a song stuck in our head—or, more accurately, we know what it's like to have the refrain of a melodic shard or lyrical splinter spread to the finer tissues of feeling that we call thinking and gently take us hostage with our fondness for patterns, flair for obsession, and fundamental distractibility. Far from extraordinary, these repetitive musical thoughts, which have acquired the odd but agreeable handle "earworms," nevertheless not only have a peculiar psychological status but seem to occupy a strange ontological station. In many ways they are like hallucinations: real experiences without actual sense impressions. But earworms are also like daydreams: unprompted and aimless figments that seem to have you more than you have them. Yet no one with an earworm mistakes its phantasmic spasms for an actual broadcast or performance, and where daydreams shuffle off our mortal coil (one can only hope), earworms bring us back again and again to the bustle in which at times they play a leading part.

Perhaps what makes earworms peculiar, besides the fact that they're not really hallucinations or dreams, is that something about them feels like they're not first-person thoughts, as though they are thoughts that you're thinking from outside of your mind. But if earworms are not in the mind, then where are they? Or, alternatively, if they are in the mind, whose mind are they in?

Research in experimental psychology and the neurosciences is currently underway to determine the memory systems and brain networks that are implicated in the production and maintenance of earworms. But my aim here is to address the technical nature of these abstract parasites, to hear their spontaneous irruption in thought as both a product and a source of contemporary capitalism's goal to draw value from involuntary nervous activities. In this respect, I approach the earworm from a deliberately speculative perspective in order to conceptualize its appearance not as a mere neurological anomaly but as a technical matter expressive of the way historically useless thinking—the kind of thinking we associate with reverie and brooding—is being rhetorically and imaginatively recuperated as a passive technology of the self. The earworm, however, is a strange case of useless thinking, because its redundancy not only implicates it in this process of recuperation but seems also to realize a fatal tendency in sonic technics in ways that at once rely on, advance, and disturb the progressive encroachment of capital on human cognitive capacities.

From this perspective, earworms do not represent a pathological brain state but are instead signs of an involuntary disposition or a fatalistic tendency intrinsic to contemporary capitalism's nonstop appropriation of attention driven by "the imposition of a machinic model of duration and efficiency onto the human body" (Crary 2013, 3). This is to say that there is something strangely logical about the appearance of earworms, and the correlative disappearance of musical sounds in them, that is proper to the accelerated functioning of capitalism. As a system for treating any registerable difference as a potential resource from which a surplus might be extracted, it makes a certain sense that capitalism would target the ears; as we like to remind ourselves, we are never *not* listening, and therefore listening is never not productive at some scale. The ears are always on, and the body is always vibrating, always doing something. What better way to exploit such a reserve than to listen to everything, all the time, everywhere and at once? Leave no sound unheard, or, better still, no sound unthought.

Although it seems fantastic, it's really not difficult to imagine the history of sound production and listening as a gestation period of sorts, a veritable education of the larval intelligence that is growing in our ears. First, instruments, with their acoustic refinement of sound, taught our ears to hear symbolically, to hear something in sound that is not indexical but internally relational. Then recording technologies tutored us in the materiality of sound, its vibrational nature and acoustic reality—a nature that would later, through the manipulation of its wax-vinyl-magnetic-digital trace, be understood as plastic and thus, in a sense, artificial. More recently, we have begun to receive training in listening to "unsound," to the infra- and ultrasonic ranges of acoustic reality that lie beyond the ear's physiological limits. For example, Oliver M. Lowery's silent subliminal presentation system (SSPS), which describes a method that uses what Lowery terms "nonaural carriers" (infra- and ultrasonic vibrations) to deliver messages of affirmation (or whatever message the sender desires) directly into the brain, shows us the nonconscious side of listening.[1] Perhaps most enigmatically, by capturing lightning-generated radio-wave emissions that occur at audio frequencies (1–30 kHz), Alvin Lucier's work *Sferics* (1981) exercises the ear's capacity to listen to electromagnetic radiation, which is to listen to what is essentially light.

But what of sounds that we can't hear not because they're too quiet or lie outside our range of hearing but because they're virtual, or, more exactly, because they are thought? The phonograph was a great first step, and the amplifier a good follow-up, but there is still the matter of the imaginary, of mind, of the ideosonic. Perhaps Lowery's SSPS brings us closest to answering this question, for using infra- and ultrasonic sound to transmit propositions directly to the brain turns unsound into something approaching thought. However, because the "affirmation" deposited in the brain by the SSPS—despite being delivered acoustically—is linguistically composed, its perception is indistinguishable from the internal chatter that we tend to qualify as thinking. A more decidedly sonorous thinking (as odd as that sounds) might, however, be found at the start of the ears' education—the point where listening becomes technical. Like Martin Heidegger's hammer, instruments and their performing protocols are a type of enframing and thus a technology that reveals a world in which their material forms get lost as sound and becomes a collection of musical things. By adapting to these instrumental technics, the ear learns about the "dissonance" and "consonance" of sounds, the "tension" and "resolution" of tonal forms, and, importantly, the symbolic affordance of (more and less) organized sonorous events. In short, instrumental technics—or perhaps we should say musical technics—direct the ear toward an intensive dimension of sonic activity whose expression is not so much heard as felt, felt in sound as a quality of aliveness or abstraction of feeling that philosopher Susanne Langer (1953) calls a semblance of vital activity. This is key, for abstractions, insofar as they are perceivable, are felt. And as Brian Massumi notes, "What is felt abstractly is *thought*" (2011, 110). But also, if what technologies and techniques produce are abstractions, and music is a kind of technology that produces an abstraction of feeling, then what is felt in music as the thought of feeling is *nonsound*, an extrasonorous semblance of aliveness that appears in sound through a technical mode of listening.

While this stages an argument for the technogenesis of all musical audition, in this study I want to focus only on how musical technics have become integrated into our daily perceptual routines through the proliferation of recording technologies, such that the distinctive thinking-feeling of nonsound we identify with listening to music has become a type of habit. More specifically, I want to consider how the techniques that give sound its profile as music have been taken up in thought as a kind of second nature and how the psychic events that we've given the name "earworms" function as a limit case of this technology of lived abstraction and its fatal end.[2] Additionally, I suggest that earworms, whose prevalence is noted in several recent studies, are symptomatic of a cultural addiction to offloading music's technical mode of listening onto external devices.[3] However, like all addictions, indulgences come at a cost, and the cost of offloading listening is paid out in the currency of attention. What we used to buy with iPods, whose immense storage capacity promised to outsource more than twenty-four hours of listening potential, and what we now rent with smartphones and their infinite streaming platforms is not greater mindfulness but greater distraction.

As I'll discuss, some have argued that offloading certain cognitive routines onto external media is not inherently detrimental to the species. For example, offloading tasks associated with memory to technological devices is thought to allow us to focus on the otherwise-overlooked possibilities of present demands as well as to indulge in certain types of nonfunctional thinking (of which the earworm is a contentious representative) that are not only pleasant but essential for mental health. Yet the celebration of nonfunctional thinking is not exclusively the purview of dropouts and dreamers. A recent trend in neuroscience has begun to develop an account of the self that is characterized by states of absentmindedness—that is, nonfunctional thinking.[4] Daydreaming, rumination, reminiscence, and mind-wandering—cognitive capacities typically gathered under the sign of distraction and idleness—are being reconfigured according to a language of productivity that regards these psychic events not as trifling states but as expressions of creativity and curiosity, generic capacities through which the sense of a human self appears to potentiate an otherwise-inactive present. In other words, the historical inutility of daydreaming turns out to be not really inutilious at all.[5] However, the language of productivity that recalibrates "that which was previously inscribed as and through negativity" (Callard and Margulies 2010, 342)—namely, the apparent distraction that daydreaming is—formally resembles neoliberal capitalism's conception of labor, which reconfigures our always-available general intellect and social skills as a form of work that we are, so to speak, never not doing. For both neuroscience and neoliberal capitalism, thought is no longer simply idle. A wandering mind "consolidate[s] past experience in ways that are adaptive for our future needs" (Buckner, Andrews-Hanna, and Schacter 2008, 31) and in this sense is a kind of nondescript labor whose value lies in the ongoing production of an unspecified future producer.

But earworms, as daydreams used to be, are also "inscribed as and through negativity." Their soundless intrusion offends the intentionality of thought, spoils our autonomy, and annoys us greatly. Yet does this dysfunctional thinking have a veiled use? Can the earworm's importunate refrains be put to work, like a broken record's repeating phrase, for keeping time, for hearing what would otherwise go unnoticed, for learning a language? Perhaps.[6] But the recursive form of earworms complicates the image of endlessly productive thought. Unlike a wandering mind, whose obliquities give it an inspired profile, the earworm's autism purges it of value or function, for it can only be exchanged for another iteration of itself. And as Jean Baudrillard notes, when things are relieved of their value, they are "free to circulate without passing through exchange and the abstraction of exchange" (2001, 121). Freed of curiosity, of forecasting tomorrow and contemplating yesterday, unburdened by knowing or caring, the thought that an earworm is becomes free to be useless, free to deploy itself as radical thought, to be more of what thinking is—"understanding without hope, but a happy form" (Baudrillard 1995, 60).

Although earworms may escape the destiny of daydreams and so become a properly nonfunctional form of thinking, it may be that in the end that begins over and over again, begins over again, again, begins again and over again, all they have to show is what human thinking that is free to lead nowhere thinks like.[7]

OFFLOAD

Before the twentieth century, there are very few reports describing the experience of an earworm. Edgar Allan Poe (1845) hints at an analogous experience in his story "The Imp of the Perverse," which likens a harassing thought to "the ringing in our ears, or rather in our memories, of the burden of some ordinary song, or some unimpressive snatches from the opera" (3). Mark Twain's 1876 short story "A Literary Nightmare!" is a more sustained account, for in this work Twain recounts his own possession by a short rhyme—what he calls a jingle—that he came across in an edition of the *New York Tribune*.[8] Yet, as Oliver Sacks notes in *Musicophilia* (2007), it's likely we were being haunted by stuck songs well before Twain resolved to write about his experience.

It can't be the case that melodies are significantly catchier now than they were, say, three hundred years ago or that we simply remember things better than we used to. In fact, owing to their sheer abundance and utter ubiquity, and to the fact that we have smartphones and other devices to remember how they go for us, tunes should be *less* catchy. Why exercise the memory when we can simply hit repeat or catch the same song on another station—or, more likely, just make do with another song that basically does all the same musical and psychological things that made the previous song (and the one before that one, and the one before that, etc.) desirable? In short, why not offload listening to the "collaborative online filters, consumer preference algorithms and networked knowledge" that David Brooks (2007) describes as our "external cognitive servants"?

According to Bernard Stiegler, this suggestion to offload our thinking to external devices is anachronistic. And insofar as the suggestion assumes a simple freeing up of cognitive powers that belong to an individual, it is also misdirected. As Stiegler contends, human being has *always* been constituted by its prosthetic relationship to machinic externalities, what he refers to as "organized inorganic beings" (1998a, 17). Stiegler argues that, unlike other animals, whose genetic traits primarily determine their species-specific prerogatives, the human animal's organismic entitlements are extragenetically derived.[9] Human being distinguishes itself from nonhuman animal life by exteriorizing its know-how in a network of artificial memory aids that it uses to accumulate and transport a species intelligence across successive generations. These mnemonic devices, which include tools, artifacts, language, and various other recording media, as well as performative techniques for recollection, grammatize the flux of experience by breaking an otherwise-fluid activity—speaking or listening—into discrete and iterable elements that permit its future recollection and reactivation.

Basically, Stiegler contends that human being is a technical achievement realized in the act of overcoming a "retentional finitude" (1998a, 267) with supplements—mnemotechniques and mnemotechnologies—of various kinds that externalize, objectify, and represent its store of knowledge. From a certain perspective, this makes human being a phylogenetic cipher for an anterior technological evolution, but, more interestingly, it makes technological evolution something essential to human thought. It should be noted, however, that Stiegler's account of human being as a technical matter doesn't simply rehearse the argument of *homo faber* (that human being is defined by a capacity to make tools and manipulate the environment). Instead, the technogenesis of human being suggests that the very capacity to make the distinction between human and nonhuman being derives from how the tools and techniques we make and use invent a form of awareness that undermines the animalistic myopia of the here and now.[10] Being able to think about "life by means other than life" (Stiegler 1998a, 17) means being able to attend not only to what is here and now but to what was then and what will be; it means contemplating traces (symbols) of past events in order to envisage future states. This is all to say that the idea of giving our thoughts over to "external cognitive servants" is not a choice we've made recently but an originary conceit of human being qua human.[11]

In a sense, there is nothing particularly novel about outsourcing attention and memory to external devices, and this would seem to sanction Walter Benjamin's (1968a) cautious enlisting of technological reproducibility in the development of suppler forms of perception and experience. However, where Benjamin's reinvention of perception and experience through technology hopes for a matching rearticulation of the task of thinking, those like *Wired* writer Clive Thompson (2007) suggest less a cognitive metamorphosis than a wish that "by offloading data onto silicon, we free our own gray matter for more germanely 'human' tasks like brainstorming and daydreaming." Thompson is not advocating that we give our intelligence over to machines for the tranquil activity of woolgathering but that we recognize the symbiotic and augmented nature of human intelligence. For Thompson, how we think and what we think about are shaped by the tools we use to supplement memory and attention, to the extent that certain types of thinking happen in alliance with a certain type of organon. For example, Thompson suggests that the chess master Garry Kasparov's collaboration with a computer after his defeat by Deep Blue in 1996 enhanced his understanding of the game by freeing him "from the need to rely exclusively on his memory" such that "he was able to focus more on the creative texture of his play" (2013, 4). Rather than vitiate Kasparov's game, the computer's superior processing power and enhanced retention of chess history augmented it. Kasparov's knowledge and ability to play chess, arguably, advanced to a new level of competence and sophistication.

Now, this is not inconsistent with Stiegler's position that there is no properly human mentality without its technical exteriorization or, in his more optimistic mood, that mnemotechnologies may expand our cognitive capacities to reason and imagine. Daydreaming and brainstorming *are* human tasks, but their human character is a function of a nonhuman organization of memory and attention that not only regulates the things that we can recollect, anticipate, contemplate, and even forget but ultimately governs what counts as thinking. The problem with Thompson's argument is not its call to hive off cognitive functions to algorithmic processors and mnemotechnical equipment. The problem is that it misjudges how thinking, which is technologically accomplished by collaborating with smartphones or computers, is implicated in what Stiegler describes as "a combat for a politics of memory" (2010b, 69). As "we exteriorize ever more cognitive functions in contemporary mnemotechnical equipment," writes Stiegler, "we delegate more and more knowledge to apparatuses and to the service industries that network them, control them, formalize them, model them, and perhaps even destroy them" (68). Although our cognitive activities have never not been bound up with processes of exteriorization, their distribution in mnemotechnical organs on an industrial scale has changed the game.

What's different about how we think with technical supports now, and how this will help earworms to be seen as a technical affair, is that our mnemotechnical milieu—the field of technological retentions through which we are afforded a complex psychic life and the very idea of the mental—is saturated with *industrial* memories, particularly audiovisual ones. For Stiegler, this is significant because consciousness, he argues, has an essentially cinematographic structure that cannot but coincide with the flux of the temporal objects that audiovisual media produce. As Stiegler writes, "The coincidence between the film's flow and that of the film spectator's consciousness, linked by phonographic flux, initiates the mechanics of a complete adoption of the film's time with that of the spectator's consciousness—which, since it is itself a flux, is captured and 'channeled' by the flow of images" (2011, 12).

Temporal objects are lures for consciousness, and the industrialization of this luring marks a distinctive shift in the history of mnemonic exteriorization. The mass production and global dissemination of time-based media not only are historically unprecedented but threaten to undermine what Stiegler sees as the necessary production of singular or nonstandard experience. By industrializing memory, particularly memories "concretized in the generalization of the production of industrial temporal objects (phonograms, films, radio and television programs, etc.)" (Stiegler 1998b, 106), we effectively synchronize individual consciousnesses. This does not mean that everyone is thinking the same thing at the same time so much as that the industrialization of temporal objects preempts the kind of collective psychic differentiation through which knowledge can evolve by increasing its points of exteriorization and supplementation. But the synchronization of thought and memory is not the only consequence of this industrialization. Perception and attention, too, are being shaped not only to reflect but also to intensify the production and proliferation of contemporary psychotechnologies.

As a counterpoint to Stiegler's model, which largely assumes the passive reception of media and unintentional synchronization of psychic activity, Jonathan Crary suggests that the reflex activity of attention is being remade into a repetitive and compulsory action by virtue of the way current media stage themselves and their flow of content "as resources to be *actively* managed and manipulated, exchanged, reviewed, archived, recommended, 'followed'" (2013, 52; my emphasis). These, along with other industries of electronic media such as "online gambling, internet pornography, and video-gaming" (52), work, Crary writes, to effect a "generalized inscription of human life into duration without breaks," a time that is "defined by a principle of continuous functioning" (43). Yet, more than simply being subjected to an economy of permanent expenditure supported by a technical array that is never not on, the life of the mind is becoming defined by compulsions to multiply choices and options. To the extent that capitalism's "logic of displacement" (a logic that figures obsolescence as novelty) has become "conjoined with a broadening and diversifying of the processes and flows to which an individual becomes effectively linked" (43), it can be said that our psychic life is dominated less by acts of contemplation and more by instances of pulverization. Because the accelerating tempo of novelty production (or its simulation) "prevents any significant period of time elapsing in which the use of a given product, or assemblage of them, could become familiar enough to constitute merely the background elements of one's life," thinking is becoming synonymous with "patterns of acquiring and discarding" (44–45). A general aesthetic equivalence among media content not only "circulates to habituate and validate one's immersion in the exigencies of twenty-first-century capitalism" (52) but also promotes a form of attention that is characterized by its flitting from one budding occasion of awareness to the next.[12] While attention of this sort often goes favorably by the name of "multitasking," it is more accurately described as thought in the mode of distraction: thought as wandering attention.

For Crary, the concern is that (pace Thompson) such a mode of thought doesn't expand our perception and cognitive capacities but instead calibrates them to "the calculated maintenance of an ongoing state of transition" (2013, 37). In other words, the proliferation of attention that Crary registers as "a qualitative dilation of one's accommodation to and dependence on 24/7 routines" (43) is the true consequence of a technosocial apparatus not only bent on finding ways to "eliminate the useless time of reflection and contemplation" but resolved to preclude a sense of protracted time that might "sustain even a nebulous anticipation of a future distinct from contemporary reality" (40–41). Thus, to manufacture a state of continuous transition is to place undue emphasis on the experience of discontinuity, such that the relations of disjunction that compose a world of 24/7 routines cannot help but forestall the articulation of longer cycles of experience that could yield transindividual interests and responsibilities.

But as real as Crary's worries are, they overstate on an experiential level something that I think cannot be sustained from a processual point of view, a view that Crary himself strives to show is being systematically controlled and contoured by an apparatus whose "purpose is directing its user to an ever more efficient fulfillment of its own routine tasks and functions" (2013, 44). Processually speaking, continuity and discontinuity cannot be disassociated from each other. Each is a matter of relative emphasis in a flow of experience. As such, the 24/7 semblance of continuity is in fact only an alibi for a functioning technical discontinuity sustained by a ramified autonomic impulse to tag and track changes in the cognitive and perceptual field, which shuffles the punctuality of experience to the background. This is to say that the logic of displacement operates perceptually as well as economically. The technicity of the global apparatus of distraction not only swaps obsolescence for novelty but stages the conditions whereby one moment uneventfully supersedes the next by drawing the force of awareness that would otherwise bring a currently perceived change to punctual attention into the next moment, and then the next, and the next, and so on. Accordingly, distraction is a technologically displaced continuity, and our 24/7 routines are a technique of attention that abstracts from the flow of experience a veritable distraction span.

Interestingly, attention does not entirely disappear in this regime; in fact, it is preserved, albeit in a very strange form, by the most unlikely of events. If the 24/7 world is composed of distraction spans that substitute a variation of nextnesses for a variation of nows, then earworms appear in the "succession of groundless points of temporary focus and shifting alertness" (Crary 2013, 127) *not* as a distraction but as a concentration.[13] By this I mean that the periodic intrusions that earworms make into the texturally feeble cascade of transitions we call "being distracted" produce a rhythm, a contour in the flow of activity that we register—though more often only with irritation or surprise than wholehearted delight—as an affectively laced contextual transition. In other words, the intermittent appearance of earworms is the provenance of a thinking-feeling emerging from distraction. In this respect, the earworm, which is simply the thought of music—the chronic thought of a vital rhythm in its most abstract—demonstrates something technical regarding the nature of musical form and its powers of abstraction.

MUSIC: TECHNIQUE OF EXISTENCE

If earworms have something to do with offloading memory to cognitive surrogates that channel psychic energies into circuits of continuous nascent attention, then how we experience music as a thought, as an earworm, might be a matter of how the technics of our techniques of existence are modulated by these surrogates. Perhaps it helps first of all to understand our senses as a kind of technology. As Massumi explains, the senses are themselves "prostheses of the body" that work "to detach from their objective (organic) functioning events of lived abstraction" (2011, 147). Basically, a lived abstraction is "an effective virtual vision of the shape of [an] event," but it is also "the form in which potential is relayed from one experience to another" (15, 17). These virtual yet livable forms of relationality are technical products insofar as they refer to experience as that which results from the execution or performance of certain techniques—techniques of existence.

From here we can think about music, in the most general sense of the term, as a technique of existence that humans have developed to achieve an abstraction characterized by the appearance in sound of fluctuating "tensities"—to-ing and fro-ing, rising and falling—that effect the appearance of multidimensional motion, which is almost impossible not to perceive as a simulacrum of aliveness.[14] This semblance of vital activity, which detaches or lifts off from the objective combinations of things (tones, rhythms, lungs, lips, fingers, mood, etc.) that make up its occasion, is an animateness virtually yet directly perceived (or not) in the ongoing relational involvements of its contributory elements. However, there's something peculiar about the technique of existence of music that sets it apart from the way moving bodies host a dance or the manner in which an arrangement of pigments, canvas, and frame hosts a painting. Music, as Massumi notes, "does not have to use the body as a local sign. Its local signs are *incorporeal*" (2011, 145). Music is hosted by sound waves that belong to no body in particular, and, as such, the quality of aliveness perceived as a properly "musical" effect is something that goes wherever sound waves go—which is virtually everywhere.

This is all to say that audio technologies do not introduce abstraction into musical experience—music is already a lived abstraction. The coupling of a music's operative constraints (its techniques of abstraction) with recording technology does not further abstract sound so much as it works to multiply, disseminate, and "impel [musical] techniques of existence into evolutions, and speciations" (Massumi 2011, 146). In other words, musical recordings spread an "abstractive manner of appearing" (148) to places and times beyond an initial occasion of production, where new relational involvements and individuation of existential events can be invented. Playback technologies—our external audile servants—literally invent new involvements that initiate a phase shift in audition.

One of the possible reasons, then, for the prevalence of earworms may extend from the fact that audio technology has invented a new involvement that affords unprecedented repeatability and new ways of attending to sound. In *On Repeat*, Elizabeth Margulis notes that audio technology not only has generated "a degree and pervasiveness of repetition that was previously unheard of" but wrests from an otherwise-ephemeral event an occasion in which "sound could be contemplated and attended to for its own fundamental characteristics" (2013, 80). Playback means that sound can be listened to again and, as such, becomes something that could be listened to *otherwise*, could be heard (as the history of twentieth-century compositional practices might attest to) as something to emphasize or to eliminate. But the technological affordance of playback also brings to present effect another type of involvement—namely, a way of listening that could perhaps be described as a way of *not* listening.

At this point in history, musical sounds are most often heard through some form of audio technology, and this technology redistributes music's involvements in a way that affects how its abstractions might be paid attention to—or not. For example, recordings give passing musical events a semblance of fixity so that they can be attended to again. Their coupling with headphones gives audition an intensive and private form, as well as giving listening a mode of intimacy, that it did not have beforehand. The splitting of sound from its original source also has a psychological effect that R. Murray Schafer (1969) named "schizophonia," a condition that describes both the event of decoupling and the sense of disorientation that a sound heard out of context can produce. However, what schizophonia identifies is not simply a nervous state, as Schafer would have it understood, but a phase shift in musical technics whereby a latent relationship between the technical object of music and the affect of nervous systems is concretized as a complementary function. Walk into any coffee shop and you'll know exactly what I mean: the sound of recorded music playing in the background is an occasion of how audio technologies have concretized a tendency to perceive an aliveness in the semblance of vital activity that musical objects create. Although any music shuttled to the background will express this function, audio technology makes this function a more stable and coherent part of music's technics and, by extension, a more integral part of our psychic life.[15] In other words, the abstract aliveness we hear in the technical object of music (e.g., a melody, a chord progression, a song) is given by the mechanization of its expression (technological playback) a functional autonomy.

Recording's schizophonic moment points to a new technical disparity through which attention and stimulus are paradoxically brought into productive effect through a relation of indifference that is passive in form but active in meaning—much in the way that dying is both something that happens to us and something we do. Simply put, the technological redoubling of the technique of existence of music that speciates its technical objects makes this profile that is passive in form but active in meaning not simply articulate but exceptionally functional. Just as a computer mouse makes our body's potential to suffer repetitive strain injury a functional phase of our prehensile dealings with a technological milieu, so, too, do recordings make listening distractedly—that is, listening nonlisteningly to the technologically occasioned abstractions of vital activity—a functional phase of our evolving auricular relations with the world.

Despite its oxymoronic formulation, which suggests a dysfunctional condition, listening nonlisteningly is nevertheless productive. Because distracted listening takes place largely alongside bodily and neurological routines that carry us through our day-to-day activities, its expression will be submerged among habits and other automatic sequences of conduct that are tributary to what we call mood. As Massumi notes, the "launching of music into everyday movement can be expected to become powerfully immanent to how the technique of existence of music can make itself felt, and what expressively it can do" (2011, 146). The concretization of musical technics as an autonomous feature of the technological environment, and thus its occurrence as something taken up quasi-passively (like a habit), will be felt not as something heard but as something occurring at a point of indistinction from vital activity, specifically from that vital activity that is felt as thought—namely, mind.

WORMLIKE

Why music felt as thought should exhibit the kind of repetition that seems characteristic of obsessive-compulsive disorder or Tourette's syndrome is not exactly clear.[16] However, from the point of view that I've been developing, the repetitive persistence of the earworm is linked to the workings of a technosocial apparatus that aims to desynchronize and scatter attention across what Crary describes as "fabricated microworlds of affect and symbols" (2013, 53).[17] Writing nearly thirty years before Crary, when the 24/7 world was just getting its legs, media theorist Vilém Flusser saw an emerging apparatus producing a program of what he termed "entertainment," a program of sustained diversion that not only served the interests of capitalism but also functioned as a technique for relaxing "*the dialectic tension* that characterizes human consciousness" (2013, 108). For Flusser, entertainment is "a motion that runs perpendicular to the plane of the dialectic of consciousness," where it carries attention along "an intermediary ground . . . of *immediate sensations*" to figure the mutually alienating I-world coordinates of thought "as specters that circle concrete experience" (108–9). "Sensation is more primitive than consciousness," he writes; "it is anterior to the alienation between man and world" (109) and so presents, at the order of our body's reflex workings, an image of immediacy that diverts consciousness from its intrinsically strained and unhappy concern to know itself and/or to know the world. However, "entertainment as a search for sensations"—their production and accumulation, specifically—has led to the construal that our society is "the digestive apparatus of a producing apparatus" (109). But as Flusser notes, this is a *mis*construal, for "that which entertains itself . . . is characterized precisely by its lack of memory, by its incapacity to digest what has been eaten" (109). The entertainment apparatus, by virtue of design, diverts energy from the chronic sadness that afflicts being's attempt to orient itself such that it affords no memory and thereby perpetrates no sense of interiority wherein sensation might get lost and become thought, become an idea. Our society is therefore not a digestive system—a contemplation complex—but "a channel through which sensations flow, in order to be eliminated without being digested" (110). Entertainment's diversion is the systematic bracketing of the hesitation that consciousness is, and this bracketing is how "sensation passes without obstacles" (110). Sensation of this sort, the free-flowing sort, is essentially pure "information"—or, more accurately, it is a *sheer fluctuation* in the force of existing that refuses to take expression in anything more elaborate than the experience of its own occurring. For this reason, Flusser contends that ours "is a society of [sensation] channels that are more primitive than worms: in worms there are digestive functions" (110).

Where there is simply input and output—sensation as information—there is only swallowing and shitting: no memory, no digestion, no gathering up of awareness in a difference that makes a difference. A worm, because it has no apparatus for diversion, loses the purity of sensation to the bureaucracy of its living organism. For a worm, sensation enters into an advancing matrix of vital activity and tendencies, where it feeds into already-established circuits with more or less apparent functionality.[18] In other words, sheer fluctuation for a worm becomes tributary to a new phase in the evolving activity of its vermicular ecology. Our diversions, which have no bureaucracy apart from their vying for increasingly refined forms of immediacy, render sensation nothing but a direct, concrete, and fleeting fluctuation of being that supports nothing but the next immediacy. However, the retentionlessness of "pure" sensation, the perpetual immediacy of sheer fluctuation, is not an organic phenomenon. Pure sensation is a technological achievement effected by the way the entertainment apparatus continually focuses our energies and attention toward a fractalized specious present, a now that is really a next that signifies "a now" over and over again. Or in more familiar (and more lurid) Freudian terms: forgetting sensation is the entertainment apparatus's program to direct libidinal forces toward the mouth and anus, a program that makes pure sensation "a counter-revolution of the *anal and oral libido* against the genital one" (Flusser 2013, 110). Coded in this way, where "only the oral and anal apparatus function," sensations become reusable. This means that we distract ourselves, via the apparatus of entertainment, from the unhappiness of consciousness by recycling sensations that "have already been eliminated" (110). We are in effect used by our own apparatus for feedback: "*We are channels for eternal repetition*" (111).

But the very nature of the feedback loop that habituates us to sensation's eternal return—making sensation all the more indigestible and concrete—contains within it the conditions of digestion, for repetition is a kind of immanent bureaucracy in which subsists an ineliminable form of contemplation. Flusser mentions the "'worm-like' feeling, by which we are sometimes taken over," and refers to it as "an optimistic sensation" (110). By this he means that "despite our programming to be channels of feedback, there still persist in us some remains of interiority" (111). The very cyclicality of entertainment that feeds us shit cannot help but at the same time stir it.

In this sense, earworms are aptly named, for the writhing returns of a melody are surely our vermicular selves insisting on the red tape of organic existence. Not unlike Gilles Deleuze's "larval selves," the vermiform eddies that bend our stream of awareness speak to an ancient part of our organism that cannot help but contract repeated sensations into habits and produce what amounts to a primitive and obscure kind of intelligence.[19] Flusser qualifies these wormlike feelings as "optimistic sensations" because the very apparatus that assembles our nervous system into spiraling circuits of mouth-anus-mouth-anus-mouth-anus . . . -∞ makes us think and behave cyclically. As Flusser writes, "Such cyclical thought and action are symptoms of a semi-conscious interiority" (2013, 111). With this semiconscious interiority, we then have a worm's-ear view of the tension that grips consciousness at its core, which is to say that the wormlike feeling of the haunting melody, the convulsively recurrent abstract squirming of music felt as thought, is how the bureaucratic organism stirs the shit of pure sensation. Earworms—psychic coprophilia.

OF WORMS, BRAINS, AND VIRTUOSITY

So earworms are not simply anomalous cognitive processes. In fact, they are expressive of how a technological movement is "immanent to the continuing self-constitution of techniques of existence" (Massumi 2011, 146–47). The matter of outsourcing or exteriorizing music to external cognitive devices does not "denature techniques of existence" so much as it "var[ies] their events" and "boost[s] the natural dynamic of self-differing inherent to experiential dynamics" (145). However, this does not mean that earworms have no cognitive profile. To the contrary: as far as contemporary capitalism is concerned, earworms have not only a distinct (if somewhat elusive) cognitive purchase but a calculable and exploitable one.

The industry of popular music, for instance, relies on the memorability and auto-inculcation of melodic material that it calls "hooks" in order to sustain the semblance of a desire for its products. In fact, the formal elements that characterize a pop hit—its common "verse-verse-chorus-verse-chorus-bridge-chorus" shape (with some variations), along with certain harmonic, melodic, timbral (think of Auto-Tune), and rhythmic/tempo conventions—can be understood as a cognitive formula, a literal procedure for thinking-feeling-consuming music. The field of sonic or audio branding, too, treats sound effects and jingles—musical slogans—as a psychological matter critical in the management of perception, recollection, and the flow of desire. T-Mobile and Coca-Cola, for example, both use distinct melodic sequences in their advertisements that function as a symbol for the consistency of the brand's identity as well as the experiences it promises. But a sonic logo is not merely a sign, for its re/iteration works to forge ideational and neurological associations with a brand that will bind the perception of the logo to an affective state, where ideally the latter will become so closely linked to the former that the affective experience will on its own call forth a desire for the brand's signature species of experience.[20] But perhaps the most unabashed example of the earworm's cognitive appeal is Earworms MBT, a tool that instrumentalizes the peculiar way in which music can be felt as thought to induce rapid language acquisition by setting common phrases in different languages to (bad) music.[21] Essentially, in these recordings we hear two voices speaking one after the other in time (sort of) to the groove of a musical soundtrack. The music used is always in a midtempo 4/4 meter, harmonically static, and with little to no melodic or timbral variation, much like the acid jazz you might hear when placed on hold during a phone call or when a radio station goes off air during a technical difficulty. The basic claim of Earworms MBT is that assimilating cognitive events to the highly efficient and robust mnemonic force of musical repetition will impart to these events a similar memorability.

In each of these examples, the functionalization of music's catchiness is representative of contemporary capitalism's ongoing reconfiguration of labor to draw surplus value directly from the activity of human psychic and affective faculties. Although these faculties have always played a productive (if not directly remunerative) role in society, as Paolo Virno argues, it is only recently that they have been made public—that is, that basic sentience and know-how have become calculable forces that can be put to work and made "a pillar of the production of surplus-value" (2004, 66). What the terms "cognitive," "cultural," and "creative capitalism," or "immaterial" and "affective labor," characterize is essentially a shift in how patterns of production and consumption have become organized less around the exploitation of raw, physical labor and more around our general species capacity to analyze, communicate, recollect, contemplate, invent, and relate to one another (virtually or actually).[22] In other words, the life of the mind—or, the goings-on of our general intellectual and social faculties—has become a significant source of labor power, and the industrialization of its exercise a means of generating wealth. It should come as no surprise, then, that a psychic peculiarity like the earworm should be targeted as a form of labor power, for there is nothing more potentially productive, more "virtuosic" as Virno would say, than that which demonstrates its own powers.

Virno (2004, 52), after Aristotle, defines virtuosity as an activity without an end product, an action whose purpose is the event of its own occurring. Such an activity would typically be indistinguishable from servile (waged) labor in that neither the virtuoso's nor, for instance, the custodian's labor produces a surplus. The work of each entails expenditure. However, the custodian still produces a product—cleanliness and hygiene—and does so without putting on a show of it. Thus, as "productive labour, in its totality, appropriates the special characteristics of the performing artist" (54), virtuosity as an action without an end product, more than custodial competence, becomes the new locus of value. Contemporary capitalism's models of production are virtuosic, then, precisely because labor has been organized around activities that simultaneously demonstrate and affirm a capacity to perform, communicate, and relate their own expenditure. In essence, that which affirms its own potential force in its doing is virtuosic, and the virtuosic is a demonstration of a potential for producing—a potential that has value not because it can be used to produce objects but because it can service the production (and control) of social relations and, by extension, the production of subjectivity.

To the extent that "for an ever-increasing number of professional tasks, the fulfillment of an action is internal to the action itself" (Virno 2004, 61), the psychic activity of the earworm is virtuosic precisely because it is its own spectacle and fulfills nothing but the demonstration of what the mind can do. In this regard, the experience of an earworm is a highly proficient performance of a certain type of cognitive talent—namely, a talent to remember but also to think alongside other activities. But the virtuosity displayed by an earworm's occasion is, paradoxically, unruly. Unlike the performance of speech, for example, whose regulability signifies a degree of agency or volition and embodies a sense of self-control, the earworm's performance of memory is always suffered. It is a habitual virtuosity, an automatic competence that befalls the performer. Like making phatic utterances—"What's up?," or "Uh-huh"—which issue from us automatically to establish and sustain the mood and sociability of a conversation rather than express information or spur contemplation, getting songs stuck in our head is something we're so skilled at doing that it seems to *happen* to us.

Curiously, the earworm may be the psychic equivalent of a phatic utterance. If we apply Bronisław Malinowski's formula for phatic speech—"speech in which ties of [social] union are created by a mere exchange of words"—to those instances of thinking that are "neither the result of intellectual reflection, nor do they necessarily arouse reflection in the [thinker]" (1972, 151), then earworms, being perfectly useless mental events, establish mental bonds between one thought and another in order to affirm and preserve the impression of an interiority, that is, the mind. The analogy can be worked out like this: earworms are to mind as phatic expressions are to sociability. Both are ways of keeping the channels open for thinking and communication, respectively. My point here is that some modes of virtuosity reach such levels of wizardry that their performance becomes second nature, which is to say that their technique of existence acquires the status of a reflex or bare nervous activity—call it an automatic virtuosity. Because it is an *involuntary* activity but also because it is a private performance whose product, as Karl Marx formulated it, "is not separable from the act of producing" (1991, 1048), the earworm's unruly mode of virtuosity has difficulty affirming itself as a dimension of labor power. Instead, its private performance finds purpose in affirming the feeling of thinking. The potential that a habitual virtuosity makes conspicuous, then, is our capacity to feel ourselves existing *in potential*, in abstraction—in thought. And, in this respect, as strange as it may sound, an earworm's performance is an expression less of labor power and more of onto-power—a power to be rather than to not be.

Another example of such virtuosity, one that shares the technique of spontaneity with earworms, is the performance of daydreaming or mind-wandering—what in cognitive psychology and cognitive neuroscience is referred to as "self-generated thought." This form of virtuosity develops from what is currently understood as resting-state research, an emerging model in cognitive neuroscience that asks whether there is "an organized mode of brain function that is present as a baseline or default state and is suspended during specific goal-directed behaviours"

(Gusnard et al. 2001, 4259). What neuroscientists have observed is that the resting brain—the brain not currently engaged in a goal-directed task—exhibits a network system that is rife with endogenous activity that researchers classify variously as mind-wandering, free association, self-focused attention, and introspection. In other words, the resting brain is not resting at all but is extremely active, more active, in fact (which for neuroscientists means more lighted brain regions are seen during fMRI tests), than it is during task-related activities (Greicius et al. 2003). The implication that most of the field has run with is that the so-called default-mode network is evidence of a neural system in which "endogenous dynamics would be meaningful and not simply unconstrained noise"—meaningful precisely in the sense that the system describes "a matrix that is constituted as perpetually productive, as intrinsically creative, and as thrown toward the future" (Callard and Margulies 2010, 334, 337).

However, as Felicity Callard and Daniel Margulies (2010) suggest, the rhetoric used by cognitive neuroscientists to interpret the activity of the resting brain draws many of its tropes from the same generalized concept of productivity that Virno contends is guiding contemporary capitalism's erasure of the distinction between labor and nonlabor. The resting brain, like the subject of contemporary capitalism, or what some call "cognitive capitalism," is never *not* working. Just as a nondescript form of work based on the generic potential to think at all times invades leisure time to effectively make the latter an unremunerated version of the former, neuroscience's focus on unconstrained mental activity as productive cognitive activity creates an image of thought in which *all* cerebration is rendered purposeful, useful—that is, valuable. As Callard and Margulies suggest, daydreaming and mind-wandering have lost their marginal status as useless—"amateur"—cerebration through neuroscientists' adoption of a rhetoric of productivity that favors eccentric, distributed, and highly flexible/irregular labor, a rhetoric that converts neoliberalism's aims, rarifying the accumulation of capital into epistemological and ontological claims. Daydreams and woolgathering are, then, private performances in the same way that earworms are: the spontaneous occurrence of absentmindedness demonstrates a potential to think and thus a power to be, a power to do. As such, daydreaming and other goalless attentions are another form of automatic virtuosity in the sense that they produce our ability to feel ourselves existing in the potential of a thinking-doing.

But there is something that distinguishes the virtuosity of earworms from that demonstrated by daydreams. My sense is that the former's technical origins and repetitive character make them less available for recuperation than the divagations of the latter. Although unruly in their general aimlessness, daydreams lend their virtuosity to contemporary capitalism's speculative investment in cognitive activity, since their digressive yet narrative-esque form exemplifies the type of creative obliquity valued by the successful entrepreneur. Whether or not the resting brain is in fact essential for maintaining "a coherent neuronal representation of the 'self'" (Fransson 2006, 2844), daydreaming's associative mechanics, speculative thrusts, and lateral articulations that spontaneously plot out lines of flight are an indisputable boon to a system that thrives on the production of difference (or at least the simulation of difference)—especially a system whose points of operation, control, and forms of labor make the drifts and wanderings of existence integral to its functioning.

The earworm, however, is a little more peculiar. As I wrote above, music is itself a technology of abstraction, whose coupling with recording technologies has spread its abstractive manner of appearing not only to other places and times but to other registers of expression and experience. Via a techno-entertainment apparatus whose ubiquity short-circuits sensation in order to avoid the dialectical tension of consciousness, musical abstractions are taken up over and over again as information that is eliminated without being digested. This makes the automatic virtuosity that an earworm stands for an excrescent feature of an apparatus inclined toward constant change. Unlike daydreams, whose affair with counterfactuals and anticipated futures makes their streamy content rife with narrative coordinates and trajectories that can be continually exchanged for possibilities and alternatives, earworms just twist and turn. The earworm's loopy performance, in which its ending is at the same time its beginning, cannot be exchanged for anything but itself, and as such the change or difference that it is and demonstrates is nothing but an *ex*-change—a change beyond change. Having, as Peter Szendy writes, "nothing to say beyond the naked exposition of this structure of interchangeability, general equivalence, and circulation" (2012, 69), earworms realize the entertainment apparatus's desire for sensation that "passes without obstacles" (Flusser 2013, 110).[23] Earworms are, then, expressive of a sheer fluctuation, a lived abstraction, or a pure sign of variation that epitomizes entertainment's principle of indigestion. But at the same time, earworms mark the limits and fate of indigestion. Their play of appearance and disappearance short-circuits the bureaucracy of the organism in a way that brings the latter's power of variation and capacity to perform, communicate, and relate to a place "where things reach their end without passing through their means" (Baudrillard 2008, 192). This is to say that earworms are the destiny of musical technics taken up in an apparatus of distraction, the destiny of indigestion where music "attains [its] effects without passing through causes" (192): a something doing becoming thought that is becoming something doing.

FATAL STRATEGIES OF LIVED ABSTRACTION

To end, I want to return to the speculation that began this chapter by considering what it might mean that the earworm's ideosonic persistence is indicative of capitalism's alien intelligence, and how this intelligence is not exactly alien so much as it is mad and fatalistic. Clearly, there is something about the proliferation of earworms that lends itself to capitalism's inhuman acceleration. However, while it may not be strictly human, there is nothing alien about a system's fate. From Baudrillard's perspective, systems are driven by an immanent compulsion to maximize their particular forms of exchange and techniques of organization (see Baudrillard 1996, 2001). Although nonconscious, this vector of excess is a form of intelligence—a madness—that, for Baudrillard, tends toward the implosion of a system's terms and, ultimately, a reversal of its functions. But this mad intelligence is not essentially negative. It is better understood as a process of intensification—hyperfication if we want to stay with Baudrillard's poetics—that inheres in any and all efforts to integrate a heterogeneity of elements. Baudrillard's infamous formula of "more *x* than *x*" is, therefore, not a fundamentally negative formula but marks instead a qualitative shift in a system that seduces itself into doing more of what it does and thus lures itself not toward its end but to a transition point, what we could justifiably nominate as "an event." Strange as it may be, this means that a body overrun with hypervitality, what we'd typically call "cancer," might be understood as a system transitioning to an event called "death." In other words, death is the fate of an excessive cellular enthusiasm.

Curiously, techniques of existence are also fatalistic, but affirmatively so. Insofar as their performance is a process, and "approaching the expressive limit is what process never ceases to do," techniques of existence are driven by a certain self-enjoyment to accomplish more of what they do—to maximize their "abstractive intensity" (Massumi 2011, 151). The qualitative change that techniques of existence effect is no less fatalistic than that of systems whose activities have multiplication as their object. It's just that whereas Baudrillard sees *madness* in fatal systems that terminate in events of reversal, in techniques of existence an immanent and irresistible *appetition* leads to occasions of novelty. So, then, whither the earworm? To madness or appetition? Reversal or novelty?

As an achievement of music's techniques of existence, the earworm is a novelty and is expressive of an appetite to carry abstractions to their most intensely perceptually felt occasion. The earworm is in this respect a limit case of perceivable abstractions in sound—which is to say, it is thought. However, as a technical artifact supplementing the musical technics that audio technology now makes ubiquitous, the earworm is a reversal and product of madness. Recall Flusser's contention that our society is governed by a system of pure sensation that "spill[s] itself over the world as method" (2013, 108). The metastasis of musical technics is the outgrowth of an extreme effort to make music's abstractions always available, an excrescence that obscures not only the categorical distinction between background and foreground music but the perceptual difference between figure and ground.[24] In their ubiquitous phase, musical sounds are omnipresent and, so, hyperaudible, which in turn makes their semblance of vital activity, their lived abstraction, hyperapparent. Yet, like the constant droning of a ventilation system, these sounds and semblances become deafening, unhearable, as both a matter of volume and distraction. There's a whole world of sounds to *not* listen to. The din of musical ubiquity afforded by the phonograph, radio broadcasts, cassette players, Walkmans, satellite radio, MP3 players, and smartphones, and integrated even more fully and subtly into our ambient perpetual routines by hidden and invisible speakers, exterminates music, pushes it beyond its own end so that it no longer has any reason for being heard, contemplated, noticed, or even remembered. Baudrillard once described "music in which sounds have been clarified and expurgated . . . shorn of all noise and static" as *integral music* (2005, 27–28). But it is actually only in the earworm that music becomes fully integral, a complete coincidence between perception and thought. Completely "restored to its technical perfection," music felt as thought, felt in its most abstract, becomes pure technics. "Flawless and without imagination, merging into its own model" (28), earworms are music's fatal strategy of lived abstraction.

But is this still music? Even Baudrillard hesitated to completely judge "sounds [that] have been clarified and expurgated and . . . so to speak, restored to technical perfection" (2005, 28) as no longer music, for "technical perfection" entails the insertion of engineered noise into the signal to make it more musical. The earworm, however, has no frequency to tune, no wavelength to modulate, and, for that matter, no signal to corrupt. Where integral music disappears in its hyperfidelity, "in the technical perfection of its materiality . . . its own special effect" (Baudrillard 1994, 5), the earworm disappears in the thought of itself, in the technical perfection of its own mentality—its own nonsensuous perception. In other words, relieved of listening by the thought of listening itself, music, ironically, makes room for radical thought in the form of a hopeless but happy audition.

Three

THE WORM REFRAIN (OR, DOES NATURE GET EARWORMS?)

> A sight, an emotion, creates this wave in the mind,
> long before it makes words to fit it.
>
> —VIRGINIA WOOLF, letter to Vita Sackville-West, March 16, 1926

PREAMBLE . . .

Something about this chapter puts me in mind of other texts. It reminds me somehow of David Foster Wallace's (2011b) *The Pale King* or Renata Adler's (1976) *Speedboat.* Both are mosaic works, patches of thought held together more by the propinquity and mood of their parts than by narrative flow or line of reasoning. Perhaps this is because this chapter is simply a series of impressionistic responses to a film, combined with what you might call a hodgepodge of theory. Looking it over, I don't sense an argument. But what I do sense is a commotion, something exhibiting thought's stirring—a rhythm, maybe. This may sound noncommittal and frivolous, but I'll submit that from a pataphysical perspective, wherein a "universe comprised of exceptions implies an *equivalence* between imaginary solutions" (Hugill 2012, 9), any line of reasoning that I might conjure would be no more serious than a hodgepodge of theory is—and, for that matter, no less trivial. In other words, the former is just as much an imaginary solution as the latter. The difference is that while an argument is an imaginary solution to describe something that hangs together for good reason, a hodgepodge is an imaginary solution that describes something that hangs together *for no good reason*. Thus, a hodgepodge makes sense of something whose experiential dynamics resist articulating the objective links that arise between one thought and another, links whose conflux is regularly taken as justification for the concepts that emerge from thinking's doing.

Is a hodgepodge of theory a body of thought? Insofar as thought is just a less overt and therefore a less actual doing, a less actual body, it looks like it is. But to be less actual is not to be less real or less stylized; it is to be more virtual, more abstract. And to be more abstract is to be thought, which we tend to forget is "made of the same stuff things are" (James 1996a, 37)—activity. Indeed, thought may be defined precisely as an activity in which the subjective form of the experience ignores the dynamic pulse of its process.[1] The rhythmic and affective organization of thought is—at least outside the domain of poetry—rarely taken as a valid dimension of its event. Thus, the farrago that follows, a virtual body of fact and fiction, is still a something doing, but it's a something doing that hasn't yet forgotten itself as something being done. Unlike reason, in which ignorance of thinking's doing is taken as evidence of its objectivity, thought here is "present as yet only in the first stirrings of potential" (Massumi 2014, 32). As Virginia Woolf said of certain of her works—that they were written to a rhythm and not to a plot—in this I am making a commotion and not an argument.

To the extent that the film I discuss here—*Upstream Color*—is itself a narrativized hodgepodge of audiovisual atmospherics and partial plotlines executed at the level of form as well as content, a proper pataphysical reaction to the film's exceptional universe of humans, pigs, orchids, and worms would be a series of impressionistic responses that symbolically attribute these properties to their lineaments. Of course, this doesn't make for good sense, but then again, pataphysics isn't particularly interested in "good sense" so much as it is in the condition of sense, which, strictly speaking, is never the sense that is being said.[2] This is to say that a pataphysical reading of the film can only say the sense of what is not being said. Given this, the sense I might make of the film is not the sense of what I am saying about the film. The latter is for another text to say, a text that is not this one. In other words, the color of these words is not the color of the pschitt that happens upstream.

AMBLE ON . . .

Upstream Color (2013a) is American filmmaker Shane Carruth's weird and dolorous second feature-length film. His first film, *Primer* (2004), is also weird but differently so—less gloom, more time travel. But I'm going to stay with the former here, because *Upstream Color*'s preternatural weirdness symbolizes a curious way of thinking about being human—specifically, being one with a name, a job, reliable likes and dislikes—that raises questions regarding where exactly our lives are actually taking place and being lived.

X: ERRANCY

At the beginning of this film, we see a stranger ("Thief") harvesting worms and extracting from their bodies a toxin that he will use to mesmerize a woman ("Kris") in order to bilk her of her savings, and then we see, through an incredibly mannered cinematic syntax, how she and another man ("Jeff"), who later in the film we learn has suffered a similar experience as she, are drawn to one another in a way that has something to do with having the vermin that grew inside of them as a side effect of the mesmeric toxin transferred into pigs by a clairvoyant composer ("Sampler"), who uses a psychic gift to eavesdrop on the lives of other similarly fleeced persons ("Sampled") in order to find musical inspiration.

Of course, my description, despite its many detours, spiraling structure, and general errancy, is already a patchwork of ideas and doesn't quite traverse the relations that express the film's affective contortions or symbolic nuances. For example, the role that Henry David Thoreau's *Walden* plays in the narrative is completely omitted in this stroll, as is an account of the contrapuntal sensibility that organizes and drives so many of the film's scenes. But you'll notice that this account nevertheless pivots on a number of discontinuities that are not insignificant. Indeed, part of the film's charm and impact lies in how the elisions between its human protagonists, pigs, orchids, and worms are "performatively fused, without becoming confused" (Massumi 2014, 6), as well as how Kris's and Jeff's induction into a circuit of experience—a trans-individual life cycle—dramatizes issues of identity and otherness in a way that transforms their experience of a self into matters of continuity and discontinuity. In other words, a worm's or orchid's or human's or pig's experiences are shown in the film to differ from or synchronize with one another's according to how certain affective forms are taken up in a life cycle's unity of movement as differential poles "co-defining the same dynamic" (Massumi 2011, 30). The nonlinear cinematic rendering of this vital dynamic does not misrepresent the way "unfolding differentials phase in and out of integrating events" (31); it is, in fact, a stylized version of how human and nonhuman, living and nonliving terms, participate differentially in the same span of vital activity, without the distinction between any of their respective techniques or styles of existence being lost.

IIIa: EXPERIENCE

Because the film revolves around a bizarre conceit that implicates worms, pigs, and action at a distance into its reality, we might brand *Upstream Color* a work of magic realism. But the magic in the realism is less an occult phenomenon and more an effect of how the film's cinematic rhetoric seduces us to fill in its narratological gaps with esoteric purposes and enigmatic truths. In many ways, it's very similar in its obliquity, if not its preciousness, to Terrence Malick's impressionist works, such as *To the Wonder* (2012) and *The Tree of Life* (2011), which couple the flow of a Steadicam with rapid crosscuts to create the effect of a continuous quality of movement passing between scenes that are metaphorically, rather than logically, connected. *Upstream Color*, however—its formal inventions aside (for now)—is really just a simple tale about how we're affected, each of us, by events and forces that lie beyond the purview of our slender *Umwelt*. Besides the business of hypnosis and clairvoyance, ideas whose consistency grows over the narrative's ambulation, it's the image of experience extended beyond the individual that gives the film its fantastic overtones. While not exactly Haruki Murakami–odd or David Lynch–weird, the metaphorical connections it shows between the lives of pigs, humans, and orchids, via the transmission of a parasite, strain the consensus that experience is an individual affair, and, as such, the film's narrative defies the conventions that defy the reality of the unconventional.

The composition of experience articulated by *Upstream Color* is very odd. But it's not entirely dissimilar from the way William James understands experience as "a concatenated or continuous structure," one held "together from next to next by relations that are themselves part of experience" (1955, 199). The film, however, presents this concatenated composition from the less considered side of discontinuity. Although James argues that "the continuities and the discontinuities [of pure experience] are absolutely co-ordinate matters of immediate feeling" (1996a, 95), we are nevertheless more attuned to the continuous side of feeling in that this is where our sense of self is most effectively felt, or felt at its most effective. As Brian Massumi notes, "The monadic discontinuity between drops of experience is bridged over by a sense of interactivity that functionally passes over it" (2011, 66). Continuity, the pulse of experience that is most explicitly taken up as a self, passes over the gaps that are just as much a part of the pattern of becoming. "*Narrative*," writes Massumi, "is a powerful device by which the actual discontinuity between drops of experience is passed over" (66). By showing what happens when personal narrative is broken, *Upstream Color* brings out the discontinuous dimension of experience and shows us to be creatures who, despite knowing that what is taken to be relevant and meaningful to our individual person is inscrutable in its totality, nevertheless act as if the qualities of our self, such as thinking and feeling, are inherently ours, or at least ours alone. Much like commodity fetishism, which Karl Marx wryly formulated as "a very strange thing, abounding in metaphysical subtleties and theological niceties" (1991, 163), we assume the narrated "who" expressed by a snarl of signs, symbols, and feelings to be an objective property that belongs to "a life," rather than an effect of a broader something doing. In other words, the narrative of "a life" is like money, in the sense that we treat bare activity as if meaning inhered in its occasions, when in fact what we trade on is always an abstraction by which pulses of existence are compared, assembled, exchanged, and, ultimately, valued. Once existence becomes valued for its narrated forms—its "verbal meta-continuity" (Massumi 2011, 66)—and not for the living of it, "it changes into a thing which transcends sensuousness" (Marx 1991, 163). "Life" becomes a fetish object to which we give a name—"Kris," "Jeff," "Sampler," and so on. Vital brands.

Despite this diagnosis of narrative's fetishistic tendencies, I wouldn't describe *Upstream Color* as a critical film. Existence is not being reduced here to the process of exchange or fetishization, and the angle from which the story is told is not an analytic one. Instead, the film dramatizes the experience of the discontinuous and expresses what it might be like were you to find yourself one day unable to trust the assumptions and expectations that guide you from one moment to the next. It asks: What would the business of living feel like if your own story were disturbed in such a way that you had to compose a new set of conjectures and references, a new verbally achieved metacontinuity—and not from the passive synthesis of activity that you formerly took as your "self" but from the active assembly of *ambient information*, impersonal mannerisms, and anonymous desires? Strictly speaking, ambient information could belong to anyone, or, rather, to no one in particular. Impersonal mannerisms or anonymous desires are, by definition, not exclusive to human being. The film is in this sense a classic existential drama, with the exception that its concern extends beyond human existence to include decidedly *more-than-human* occasions of experience. In fact, it's through the distribution of a personal *Sehnsucht* (yearning) among humans, worms, pigs, and orchids that *Upstream Color* acquires its remarkable alien hue.

VI: ARTIFICE

Of course, Carruth could have contrived a less fantastic formula for cutting apart existential assumptions and personal narrative, but by making the source of this wound, as he says in an interview (Carruth 2013b), something "embedded in nature," something that would "continue on its own volition," he allows a sense of experiential incoherence to emerge in the film that avoids the conspiratorial or paranoid intimations of a control society. By bracketing out the din of culture—or what we could think of as the clamor of technics—Carruth creates a situation where we can imagine how the pulse of existence syncopates with the rhythm of things whose inclinations, tendencies, and affinities are not ours, not wholly human. This bracketing, however, does not show nature as something cleansed of artifice or as a domain purified of artfulness. Quite the opposite. Artifice is nature's way of doing more of what it does, and what it does is vary itself, expressively. Nature is thus not a mere set of mechanical activities blindly adapting their movements to predetermined conditions but a force of variation "animated by a tendency to surpass given forms" (Massumi 2014, 17). Nature is "overfull of artifice" (92) for the reason that the power of variation is a ludic operation—which is to say, a stylistics of becoming.

VII: REFRAIN

At this point, it may prove useful to conduct something like a rhythmanalysis of the parasite's life cycle. Understanding the latter as "a punctuated oneness in a manyness ongoing" (Massumi 2011, 31)—which is precisely what a rhythm is—affords us a way to think about worms, pigs, orchids, and people less as fixed elements and more as pulses of experience that "run into one another continuously and seem to interpenetrate" (James 1996b, 282).

In the roots of a certain blue orchid is a species of worm that, when ingested, makes the consumer highly susceptible to suggestion. A man referred to simply as "Thief" buys these orchids from a flower shop called "E+P Exotics," then harvests the worms and distills from their bodies a hypnotic toxin that he furtively (or forcefully, in the film) gives to individuals; when they are under his control, he then suggests that they bestow on him all of their financial assets. But Thief doesn't know that the toxin is a parasite that continues to grow inside his victims' bodies long after he's abandoned them and its hypnotic effects have worn off.

The next stage of the cycle begins when the new worm-human hybrid is drawn to a remote location by another man ("Sampler"), who imitates the practice of worm grunting or worm charming by broadcasting vibrations into the earth using a sound system, rather than the traditional method of driving a wooden stake (the stob) into the ground and rubbing it with a rooping iron. Lured to this sonic scene, the infected are brought into a mobile operating room, where Sampler transfers their parasite to a new host—a pig—that is then taken to a farm to rejoin a drift of other contaminated swine. Sampler, we learn later in the film, has a strange ability to access the psychic and emotional life of the individuals whose worm he has relocated. And he is also, ironically, a composer who writes music using sounds that he samples from the environment. So, Sampler samples sounds, but he also uses his empathic powers to sample impressions of each of the Sampled's postvermicular life.

Now, as is wont to happen, the pigs produce offspring. These piglets, however, although carrying copies of the parasite, are a source of distress for Sampler—for, unlike their parents, the piglets have no previous host to be sampled. (Or it may be that because the piglets' parents are progenitors of the piglets' parasites, the parents' experience is what Sampler samples through the piglets. This would trouble him because what he feels through the piglets' parasites is life on a pig farm, a life that is exactly the life he's trying to escape through his voyeuristic projections.)

Sampler commences the final phase of the life cycle when he disposes of the piglets by bagging and tossing them into a stream, where their decomposing bodies release spores into the water that are taken up by the root system of a tree on which white orchids grow—white orchids that progressively become blue and are eventually harvested by two women who work for E+P Exotics.

XI: REFRAIN (AGAIN)

I'm going to call the life cycle of *Upstream Color* "the worm refrain," for it is through the transit of blue-tinted vermin that an integral life cycle comes to multispecies expression. Like all refrains, this life cycle refers to a regular association of activities and elements that establish the laws, codes, or techniques by which a vital force expresses different modes of relation to itself. Yet, also like all refrains, the worm refrain is far from equilibrium, as the movement between its contributory forms "occurs not only, or not primarily, by filiative productions but also transversal communications" (Deleuze and Guattari 1987, 239). Hence, while the territory by which the refrain maintains its vermicular distinction as a discrete milieu may be consistent, the techniques by which worms, pigs, orchids, and humans exist are continually modulating each other's capacity to affect and be affected. Gilles Deleuze and Félix Guattari note that refrains are populated by zones of indiscernibility to effect a transcoding between, for example, the genetic material of different species. But because these zones of indiscernibility are composed not of distinct codes but of tendencies, motifs, or themes—adverbial qualities—what they transmit are propensities that alter the style of the analogous refrain. And as Henri Bergson notes, "The elements of a tendency are not like objects set beside each other and mutually exclusive, but rather like psychic states, each of which, although it be itself to begin with, yet partakes of others, and so virtually includes in itself the whole personality to which it belongs" (1998, 118). Put this way, we can understand that Thief's abiding tendency to take—to live appropriatively—means that he doesn't merely steal his victims' wills and wealth but modulates their existential investments, specifically those that support the speculative venture of a meaningful and effective self. By hijacking the mechanisms of volition and self-awareness using a mesmeric toxin, Thief interferes in the so-called futures of personhood.

II: NOISE

Basically, the film stages an occasion to contemplate how a sense of self is abstracted from vital activity that does not properly belong to any one entity. Although the worm refrain resembles the kind of figure of interdependence used in films such as Paul Thomas Anderson's 1999 film *Magnolia* to show a connectedness between otherwise-disconnected agents, it is more expressive of a transindividual *form* of life.[3] This is to say that the life cycle—as a refrain—expresses a "trans-situational movement [that] is in excess over [any particular] form" (Massumi 2014, 83). Curiously, the experience of this impersonal vital activity is, paradoxically, the experience of losing one's sense of self, for the self is an effect of experience taking account of itself in its continuous relations. To experience relations of discontinuity, then, is to experience a form of existential noise, and it's not by sheer coincidence that noise, as Michel Serres (2007) has pointed out, is a type of parasite, a vector of interference relative to a system that organizes itself around the offensive immanence of the medium through which its relations are composed and expressed. From this perspective, we can understand every agent in the worm refrain alternately as host, guest, and parasite. Every organism is another's parasite, another's noise. However, this model of noise is subdued in the film, for the story's focus on the angle of interference that affects Kris and Jeff downplays how the latter also function as parasites. So while the film concentrates on how Thief and the worms are occasions of noise that disturb the relational networks Kris and Jeff rely on to stabilize their respective senses of self—networks formed from their lines of work, their hobbies, their family roles, and so on—every entity belonging to the worm refrain is a parasite-host that both forces others and is forced to either expel or integrate the noise of a veritable outside, an outside that is in fact nothing but the meddling of the medium through which vital activities pass. But what is this medium, exactly?

In Serres's communicational model of noise, the medium is a context or an environment through which a message passes, but never passes unaffected—"the channel carries the flow, but it cannot disappear as a channel" (2007, 79). In other words, a medium is not a neutral dimension or an impassive conduit for the transmission of a signal but an extra something doing immanent to the conveyance of any message. As such, the medium has an affective capacity and thus continually impinges on the constitutive terms of any relational system. Serres qualifies this parasitic relationship as productive, for whether it empowers or diminishes the signal, it prompts the affected network of relations to reorganize itself—or, in terms used earlier, to express its power of variation. We see this modeled in the film by the way each of the Sampled, after Thief introduces the noise of a discontinuous experience into their system of self, is compelled to recompose their personal narratives based, as Carruth (2013b) says, "on information around them." In order for any of the Sampled to gain a clear signal of who they are, they cannot ignore the presence of the medium through which a self is composed and transmitted. But the medium is not wholly informational; it is affective and tendential. Although signs and codes play a part in the system of self, they are only aspects of what Massumi calls "the all-around lived medium, or experienced envelope of relation" (2011, 36). The worm refrain, which the film suggests has persisted alongside the human world for generations, in this respect stands in for the more radical outside of a "quasi-chaotic something-doing" (5) that sequences into objects, desires, habits, minds, people, societies, institutions, knowledge.

I: ?

This film may just be straight-ahead allegory. The connection among pig, person, worm, and orchid, strange as it is, symbolizes how we're always implicated in the rhythms and flows of something that lies just upstream from the bloated significance of our myopic concerns. For various reasons, which include biophysiological limitations, ideologically mannered blindnesses, and, of course, socioeconomic restrictions, our sensitivity to and reckoning of the "upstream" remains more or less obscure. But what makes *Upstream Color*'s allegorical posture less straightforward is how it explores the matter of action at a distance without attempting to explain its mechanics or to contrive a moral position from it. Everyone in the film participates in the same infralegible activities;

even the viewer, who has to learn how to watch the film as it evolves, is immanent to its occultations.

Carruth (2013b) puts it this way: "We already know that weird things happen . . . so let's just watch something happen, and let that be it." How it happens that the experiences of a pig and person are connected by a parasite is less important than the fact *that* it happens. Like shit. The elaboration rather than elucidation of the fact that much, or maybe even most, of our lives (like shit) is lived upstream undermines the moral or political imperative of allegory in a way that allows the film's symbolism, its logic of references, to become the object of contemplation. In a way, I think the film tries to do or to be what it symbolizes. Nicholas Rombes's (2013) review of the film in the *Los Angeles Review of Books* suggests that *Upstream Color*'s "elliptical editing and weirdly simultaneous temporal flow have as much to do with what this film is about as the plot." It makes a certain sense that a film about cycles and parasitism would perform the noise that it tries to depict—of course, it doesn't have to do this, but it does, it happens, and this is what makes *Upstream Color* itself so hypnotic. Shot largely with a shallow depth of field, assembled from a multitude of rapid crosscuts, and presented very often without any exposition, *Upstream Color* amasses a truly enigmatic significance from its formal organization, a significance that is "not logically discriminated, but is felt as a quality rather than recognized as a function" (Langer 1953, 32).

IIIb: FELT MEANING

Significance is not often treated as a felt quality, but this is how Susanne Langer treats meaning in art. For Langer, artworks have import more than they have meaning, because artworks give to perception a semblance of vital activity, and this semblance is directly perceived and known as an image or concept of subjective experience—what we call our "inner life." In the arrangement of a painting's brushstrokes or the harmonic progression of a musical work, for example, we perceive an abstraction of dynamic activity—like swelling, resting, rushing, hesitating, and so on—that we experience as a symbol of sentience, a symbol that we can't *not* imagine as the feeling of how feelings go. In this respect, the cinematic racket that *Upstream Color* presents is its *way* of feeling, and this way of feeling is something that we as viewers contemplate and by which we are affected. The dizzying manipulation of images and the exquisite sound design produce a semblance of shared intensities and parasitic operations whose significance is felt (by the viewer) as a quality of what it's like to live beside oneself, *downstream*, as it were, from the things that color who one is. (I'm thinking specifically here about a wonderful sequence in the film where sound takes the lead as we watch Sampler gather and transform a variety of noises into musical elements that slip in and out of the diegetic frame. This is cinematically interesting on its own, but it becomes even more interesting when Sampler's sampling activity is entangled in another series of diegetic resonances that are introduced by a string of crosscuts between Jeff's, Kris's, and Sampler's separate milieus. Sound in this sequence not only exemplifies but also performs how the something doing of pure experience is continually transitioning its character by the *relations* into which its stirring tendencies enter.)[4] To feel the significance of the color upstream is, then, to experience patterns of vital activity and discontinuous relations that are *not our self.*

The felt significance or vital import of discontinuity in *Upstream Color* is perhaps where the image of a human self comes most undone. But this is achieved not through a deconstructive maneuver that shuttles an integral other into the foreground of experience, for that would simply be to make the discontinuous continuous and to overlook the coordinate nature of immediate feeling. The artificial significance of discontinuous experience as articulated by *Upstream Color* is immediately felt as a semblance of a broader discontinuity that is only now beginning to become a factor of daily experience. Paradoxically, it is only with the establishment of global information and communication networks that we as a species are being made increasingly aware of just how much of our experience is composed of disjunctive relations. James spoke to exactly this dimension of experience more than a century ago:

> There is vastly more discontinuity in the sum total of experiences than we commonly suppose. The objective nucleus of every man's experience, his own body, is, it is true, a continuous percept; and equally continuous as a percept (though we may be inattentive to it) is the material environment of that body, changing by gradual transition when the body moves. But the distant parts of the physical world are at all times absent from us, and form conceptual objects

> merely, into the perceptual reality of which our life inserts itself at points discrete and relatively rare. Round their several objective nuclei, partly shared and common and partly discrete, of the real physical world, innumerable thinkers, pursuing their several lines of physically true cogitation, trace paths that intersect one another only at discontinuous perceptual points, and the rest of the time are quite incongruent; and around all the nuclei of shared "reality" . . . floats the vast cloud of experiences that are wholly subjective, that are nonsubstitutional, that find not even an eventual ending for themselves in the perceptual world—the mere day-dreams and joys and sufferings and wishes of the individual minds. These exist *with* one another, indeed, and with the objective nuclei, but out of them it is probable that to all eternity no interrelated system of any kind will ever be made. (1996a, 65)

It's curious that as we connect with more and more strangers (or "friends," depending on what social network you frequent), and as the data we extract from the world's goings-on swell to proportions previously unimaginable, our experience is of *more* rather than less discontinuity. Indeed, a mark of the posthuman may be its growing awareness of just how much of the world is discontinuous with ourselves. In other words, the posthuman condition may be characterized not by a growing and inflated sense of self but, paradoxically, by an expanding sense of what is not-self. Though this might seem to suggest a numinous stage in human evolution, I would propose that the sense of nonself emerging from the dilated envelope of disjunctive relations that our increasingly integral technological infrastructure is creating is not productive of an unaffected experience—a pure mystical experience—but of a hyperaffected one. To invoke a term used earlier in this chapter, it seems that things are incredibly noisy now. The proliferation of communication networks is a veritable outbreak of parasites, for the more connected we become, the more our milieu intrudes on us, and the more our milieu impinges on experience, the more discontinuous it is. Ironically, then, the greater the apparent transparency, the noisier the world.

POSTAMBLE

> Existence is a habit. In other words, being who we think we are is just second nature. But don't take this the wrong way. Habits aren't so bad; it's their reputation that's bad. Or perhaps more accurately, it's the habit of thinking that one's way of being is a matter of choice that gives habit its bad name. In this respect, habit is an affront to that precious thing called "will," for it undermines the option we believe we have to be able to not do something. It's because habit rarely asks permission to do what it does, and to be what it is that it does, that it comes off as "bad." But habits are neither good nor bad. They are just more or less consistent, more or less exceptional, depending on how the tendencies they express and the actions they turn into immediately available effects allow one to focus on other matters. This is to say that habits are a type of currency. By extension, existence, too, is neither good nor bad but a currency whose cost fluctuates according to the relative value of voluntary or involuntary activity. In this economy of activity "the self" becomes a commodity of existential proportions and its worth a measure of consistency. Thus, the inconsistent self is expressive of an insolvent existence. However, like any currency, its worth is an abstraction of a much broader set of discontinuous relations that exceed its form such that its continuity—its value—is perpetually fluctuating according to the narratives that explain, justify, rationalize, excuse, give cause, and make these discontinuities of existence, of habit, understandable.
> —'NONYMOUS

To end, I want to consider how the loss of personal narrative is so difficult for Jeff, Kris, and the rest of the Sampled. Clearly, all of these individuals have been traumatized; however, not one of them ever experiences the event that breaks their story.[5] For each of the Sampled, something has just gone awry with how the things that have occurred to them are retained and ordered, and it's all that any of them can do to make sense of their situation while being pummeled by forces that they can feel but cannot qualify. This kind of sensitivity to ambient existence is how James describes the basic transindividual field of experience: "What we conceptually identify ourselves with and say we are thinking of at any time is the centre; but our *full* self is the whole field, with all those indefinitely radiating subconscious possibilities of increase that we can only feel without conceiving, and can hardly begin to analyze" (1996b, 132).

In certain mystic traditions, sensitivity to these subconscious possibilities would constitute a union with the divine, of being disabused of the fantasy of a self that is the necessary condition for liberation, and, paradoxically, an increase in being. Yet for this to be the case, certain circumstances that could support the erasure of self would have to be in place. For example, things such as solitude and quiet are necessary conditions for the veritable extinction of a life's distribution. In other words, the dissolution of the self must be accompanied by techniques and institutions to give form and momentum to a nonself that, paradoxically, no one can ever be. However, to the extent that one continues to exist within a circuit of affective and symbolic exchange that perpetuates the idea of a self and the reasons for it to be circulated and traded on the market of existence—as each of the Sampled is—the loss of the self's consistency is definitely *not* liberating. To lose confidence not in the system but in the *reasons* that produce and justify one's story—which, frankly, are reasons that are probably never entirely justified in the first place—is terrifying. You can't be at ease with not being who you thought you were if you're still in the habit of trying to be you. What's so difficult, then, for Kris and Jeff is not that they've completely lost their system of self but that they are still in the habit of trying to be who they thought they were.

The parasite, which the film teaches us to see not as one thing but as a whole ecology or network of noisy agents, hasn't in fact destroyed any of the Sampled's systems of self. Instead, it has forced them each to compose a new complexion. The problem for the Sampled isn't a lack of forces, feelings, or ideas for them to invest in. Clearly there's a surplus of distractions in the world with which they could bond. (Although maybe this abundance is actually something that hinders attachment.) The problem is that none of them can *willfully* cleave a self from the vital activity that flows through them, for the composition of a self is something that is passively contracted, just as a habit is.

As James argues, the "empirical aggregate of things objectively known" as me by a succession of moments "different from that of the last moment, but *appropriative* of the latter"—what is called "I"—is formed by habits, and "habit depends on sensations not attended to" (1984, 191, 131). Walter Benjamin (1968a) also talks about habit as an inclination contracted in a state of distraction, a state of *nonconscious* perception. And Deleuze, too, argues that habits are acquired passively by the prereflexive "contemplation" of a "soul" (a faculty of both organic and inorganic matter) that contracts repeated events into regular tendencies: "A soul must be attributed to the heart, to the muscles, nerves and cells, but a contemplative soul whose entire function is to contract a habit. . . . What organism is not made of elements and cases of repetition, of contemplated and contracted water, nitrogen, carbon, chlorides and sulphates, thereby intertwining all the habits of which it is composed?" (1994, 73, 75).

The soul of habits is not, however, a metaphysical entity but a synthetic power that, through repetition, transforms a *capacity* to act into a *tendency*. "Every organism . . . is the sum of its retentions, contractions and expectations" such that "we speak of our 'self' only in virtue of these thousands of little witnesses which contemplate within us" (Deleuze 1994, 73, 75). It would seem, then, that the self lies irretrievably downstream from the activities that condition it, so that, logically speaking, it could never affect itself to effect itself. The corollary of this is that any self that aims to affect and modulate its conditions will always be too late, for the desire to act is already a tendency or blossoming of habit. As noted in *Upstream Color*'s tagline: "You can force your story's shape, but the color will always bloom upstream."

Thus, until the Sampled have been infested with a new complex of habits so as to be virtually swarming with a set of inclinations that dispose each of them to be who they are, they can only sympathize with who they are not. In the meantime, which is "the moving soil occupied by the passing present" (Deleuze 1994, 79), all each of them can do is be a parasite, be the noise that we already are and have been all along.

Notes

INTRODUCTION: EARWORM

1 See Bailes (2006, 2007); Beaman and Williams (2010); Farrugia et al. (2015); and Liikkanen (2011).

2 Although once extremely popular and highly influential, Langer's work has largely fallen out of favor. In one respect, this is owing to changes that took place within Anglo-American philosophy during the second half of the twentieth century that saw in the so-called linguistic turn a move away from the kind of speculative semio-bio-philosophy that Langer practiced and a move toward addressing the internal epistemological problems of philosophy. In another respect, the empirical studies on which she based so much of her philosophical anthropology of mind have changed in the decades following her death, which, although it doesn't entirely undermine her truly remarkable contribution to the field, does soften the farsightedness of her project. And in yet another respect, the neglect of this exceptionally lucid and original thinker is perhaps due to a rejection of what is taken as the overly formalist convictions of her aesthetic theory and the philosophical commitment she makes to the symbolic transformation of experience as a peerless human faculty. While it's true that, for her, art's import lies in its formal relations and that organic processes arise from a dynamic matrix of spatiotemporal processes—she calls these "acts"—that follow a form of impulse, acceleration, climax, and cadence, her formalism never excludes the role that the social and cultural play in philosophy's mission to interpret the conditions of interpretation. In fact, as Langer sees it, the abstraction of form is basic to all organic processes and can be understood to scale up from the simple cyclic act-event to symbolic processes that find expression in ritual behavior and myth and, finally, in the forms of art and the ideas of science. Her formalism is, then, not a reductive gambit but a heuristic that finds continuity between material forces and conceptual powers as well as variation in self-maintaining and self-reproducing systems.

CHAPTER 1. FELT AS THOUGHT

An earlier version of "Felt as Thought" was published in *Sound, Music, Affect: Theorizing Sonic Experience*, edited by Marie Thompson and Ian Biddle (London: Bloomsbury, 2013), 45–63.

1 "Ambient" is Langer's translation for Jakob von Uexküll's *Umwelt*—a monadic surround or vital territory defined by the way an organism's activities filter out deleterious or irrelevant influences.

2 Try concentrating on the more arcane points of David Foster Wallace's argument against Richard Taylor's proof of fatalism after having missed a meal. See Wallace's *Fate, Time, and Language: An Essay on Free Will* (2011a), in which Taylor's essay, along with the most significant responses to its conclusions, is reprinted.

3 If the feeling-tone of hunger was a mere nuisance to the sheer expression of ideas, the flow of thinking, consider how unimaginative a newly lacerated fingertip is.

4 Background music may be, however, the most abstract of all music in that its realization entails emptying any given work of all content or fixed meaning in order to make its occurrence (what ideally amounts to a palpation of the acoustic environment) a cipher through which the vital potential of *any* aspect of experience may pass into aesthetic or quasi-aesthetic relevance.

5 The conflation of feeling, which is a biological activity, with an *idea* of feeling, which is an abstraction of those biological activities, has been addressed by John Shepherd and Peter Wicke (1997) as an issue arising from the way musical practices use sound to generate elements of signification from somatic processes and affective states. In their semiological model, Shepherd and Wicke argue that sound treated musically functions as a *medium* whose structural characteristics—the qualities of dimension and/or extension—are implicated in processes of meaning production. Sound in music functions as a "technology of articulation" in that its being heard as musical, and *not* as noise or speech, is its being heard as a medium whose experiential moment "cannot help but call forth a response that is affective" (118). And because this response is "affective to the degree and in a manner related to the characteristics of the sounds of the medium" (118), it is incredibly difficult to differentiate the mental experience of a musical sound from "the *same* experiential moment constituted through the calling forth of socially and culturally mediated subjective states of awareness as elements of signification" (121).

6 This use of the term "becomes" is important, for it denotes how the assimilation to music's illusion is an act of abstraction—a virtual event—that describes a process wherein the relation *between* heterogenous terms is the object of perception. In this respect the principle of assimilation anticipates certain of Deleuze and Guattari's (1987) thoughts about music and the refrain.

7 "Technique of existence" is an expression that Massumi uses to describe a way of doing something that "event-fully effects a fusional mutual inclusion of a heterogeneity of factors in a signature species of semblance" (2011, 143). Anything that exists can be said to possess a technique of existence insofar as a technique of existence is a necessary condition for existence. However, Massumi treats the arts as exemplary techniques of existence, for their execution brings about an abstraction (semblance) that makes the qualitative-relational order of their occasion emphatic.

8 Think of *0'00"*, Cage's 1962 follow-up to *4'33"*, which raises the conceptual ante of the latter with a score consisting of this one sentence: "In a situation provided with maximum amplification (no feedback), perform a disciplined action."

CHAPTER 2. EARWORMS, DAYDREAMS, AND THE FATE OF USELESS THINKING

"Earworms, Daydreams, and the Fate of Useless Thinking in Cognitive Capitalism" has been expanded from a version published as "Earworms, Daydreams and Cognitive Capitalism," in *Theory, Culture and Society* 35, no. 1 (2018): 141–62.

1 Strictly speaking, SSPS exists only as a US patent (#5159703), filed by Lowery on December 28, 1989, granted on October 27, 1992, that describes how spoken messages may be placed in an acoustic or vibratory field without their being consciously heard. The system that he delineates is simple and relies on taking an input signal from a microphone or other source and passing this signal through an oscillator that modulates it to another frequency in the upper audio spectrum, where its presence is effectively undetectable. Interestingly, the system includes our human hearing apparatus in that our ear's responsiveness plays a role in how these modulated frequencies are demodulated. In the patent claim, Lowery asserts that "the amplitude of the demodulated output is not high enough to be detected by the conscious mind but is sufficient in amplitude to be detected by the sub-conscious mind" (1992, 3). Not surprisingly, Lowery's system, which distinguishes its technique from the (at the time) more common practice of masking lower-volume messages with louder foreground sounds, takes an unnuanced view of subliminal stimuli and their relationship to behavior. For a recent study that opposes the equation of subliminal information processing with the unconscious and involuntary behavior, see Bargh and Morsella (2008).

2 I borrow the expression "technologies of lived abstraction" from Brian Massumi and Erin Manning's book series with MIT Press, not so much to mobilize its concept that philosophy and creative production share a common experimental ground as to hijack its valences and overtones that point to life's technical and virtual premises.

3 See Bailes (2007); Beaty et al. (2013); and Liikkanen (2008, 2011).

4 I'm speaking here of a trend in psychology to reconceptualize psychic states such as mind-wandering and daydreaming as vital to mental health and socioemotional competence. This trend derives from the emerging paradigm of what is being called resting-state research, a model of understanding brain activity when it's not directed toward external tasks. See Gusnard et al. (2001); Gusnard and Raichle (2001); and, more recently, Baird et al. (2012); Immordino-Yang, Christodoulou, and Singh (2012); Mason et al. (2007); and Raichle and Snyder (2007). I take up the issue of resting-state research later on.

5 The term "inutilious" is taken flagrantly from the venerable science of imaginary solutions (pataphysics), for what could be more pataphysical than putting daydreams to work?

6 Walter Benjamin's argument for an innate mimetic faculty installed at the level of the nervous system suggests that we would indeed develop at least a *functional* relationship to an earworm's mechanical repetitions (1978). However, as Mark Hansen argues, insofar as our contemporary milieu operates at speeds and in rhythms that surpass cognitive representation, and given that our mimetic faculty conducts itself at the molecular level of experience that "bypasses our normal psychological means of processing external stimuli" (2000, 252) to find expression as "embodied habitual response" rather than operational thinking, it could be argued that the earworm is *already* expressive of just such a "functional" relationship. So much for the revolution.

7 Those familiar with Marcel Proust's *À la recherche du temps perdu* may be inclined to compare the earworm's irruption in thought to the involuntary memory triggered by the taste of a madeleine. However, while there's clearly a resemblance between the way an earworm hijacks one's thinking and Swann's being taken hostage by the memory of Sunday mornings at Combray, because the earworm doesn't seem to drag much, if anything, of its past into its event, it lacks the affective intensity that's crucial to Proust's experience. However, Benjamin's reading of Proust's *mémoir involontaire* through Freud suggests that memory, in fact, relies on the initial experience not having entered consciousness. According to this model, then, the experience of an earworm is like the taste of a madeleine on the condition that we don't consciously hear the song from whence the earworm came. This is hardly an uncommon condition; in fact, the music industry and sonic branding companies bank on its frequency. For how Benjamin complicates the distinction between voluntary and involuntary memory, see his essay "On Some Motifs in Baudelaire" (1968b).

8 PUNCH, BROTHERS, PUNCH
Conductor, when you receive a fare
Punch in the presence of the passenjare!
A blue trip slip for an eight-cent fare
A buff trip slip for a six-cent fare,

A pink trip slip for a three-cent fare
Punch in the presence of the passenjare!
Punch, brothers! Punch with care!
Punch in the presence of the passenjare!

9 It's a long-standing debate just how much genetics determine the development and evolution of animal values. Because human values have received so much attention and have come to be regarded as intimately entwined with the species' use of technology, nonhuman animal values tend to be construed—when or if they are at all—largely in terms of their biotic relations. Although it doesn't directly impact the argument I make in this chapter, the technogenesis of human values and human thinking doesn't entirely account for the difference between human and nonhuman animals.

10 I want to be clear that I am sensitive to the fact that, as Derrida (2008) argues, there is no such thing as "animal," but only "giraffe," "wasp," "worm" . . ."virus" (?), etcetera. (And of course within each of those categories there are species of giraffe, wasp, worm, and then individuals, and so on.) Homo sapiens are animals, too, and their appellation "human" is as much a construct as "animal" is. That said, I don't think the term "animal" is necessarily a diminishing category, as some might suggest it is, and in this regard I use it respectfully as a way to acknowledge a difference in techniques of existence rather than a difference in status of being. For a sustained and thought-provoking mediation on this issue of writing (about) animals, see David Brooks's *Animal Dreaming* (2021).

11 Massumi (2014) has recently written on the relationship between humans and nonhuman animals in a way that does not rely on a technogenetic premise to determine their difference. For him, animals and humans mark degrees of expressive complexity that describe variations of an impersonal transspecies power to surpass the given. The major distinction between human and animals is not a technical matter so much as a matter of technique, which is to say, a matter of *how* the given—the limiting conditions of any milieu—is surpassed. Artifice, or what we might call creativity, is immanent to the power to surpass the given that humans share with all nonhumans. Technology is in this sense not a defining element of human being but a mode of artifice, a species-specific technique for intensifying life's power to vary itself. Although it doesn't directly impact the argument that I advance in this chapter, the power of artifice and technique is the focus of another study in which I relate the practice of ventriloquy to Massumi's extended reading of Gregory Bateson's theory of animal play. (See chapter 1 of *Event* on the flip side, especially the Scholium on What It's Like to Have a Mind, EV11–EV18.)

12 The idea of a general aesthetic equivalence is the thrust of Peter Szendy's (2012) work on the political economy of musical hits, which sees the circulation and repetition of pop tunes as exemplifying advanced capitalism's reliance on a "pure structure of exchange." Although Szendy doesn't articulate

it as a technical issue—the "hit parade" is a technological extension of an originary musical technics—his characterizing the repetition of hits as effecting an existential blockage that gives access "to what is most singular and hidden within oneself" (81) points to an essence that is entirely technical, for what is most singular and hidden within oneself is an aptitude for systematically extracting a qualitative form from the quasi-chaos of the world's vague goings-on for use in another occasion of something doing. In other words, we are essentially abstraction machines.

13 This description of a distraction span is actually how Crary portrays our experience of a decidedly nonmetrical duration. I'm intentionally taking it out of context to bolster my point that distraction is less intimate with continuity than it is expressive of a particular technicity whose efficacy obscures, as William James puts it, the way "disjunctive and conjunctive relations present themselves as being fully co-ordinate parts of experience" (1996a, 42–43).

14 Although it's beyond the scope of this chapter to elaborate, I think it's plausible that animals have technologies of existence whose abstractions are lived at the degree of their felt importance, which is to say, lived in the affective resonance or interference that one situation has with another. I take this up on the flip side by asking, among other things, whether animals get earworms and how sound's becoming-felt-as-the-thought-of-what-feeling-the-world-feels-like may be less a specifically human exploit and more of an animal achievement.

15 Think of *Tafelmusik* (table music), for example, which describes the music played at banquets to set the mood.

16 Most of the experimental psychology literature treats exposure, familiarity, and emotional association, along with repetition itself and the latter's neurobiological responses, as requisite factors in the contraction of an earworm (Beaman and Williams 2010; Beaty et al. 2013; Liikkanen 2011; Williamson et al. 2011). Clearly, repetition has something to do with the onset of earworms, but despite the seeming plainness of it, repetition is a rather enigmatic thing, for it is at one and the same time a force of preservation and extinction, the refrain of a self-subverting stability. For Margulis (2013), the compulsive character of earworms is linked to the way our brains encode phenomena in sequences or "chunks" that cannot but be experienced in their entirety. Moreover, highly repetitive sequences acquire a psychic robustness because of the way musical sounds enlist the neural circuitry responsible for motor activity and habit formation. It's in this sense that the earworms become, as Margulis writes, "a literal hook, compelling a person to execute the sequence imaginatively" (74). Although Margulis's theory is compelling, psychoanalyst Theodor Reik's 1953 study *The Haunting Melody* offers a more intriguing take on the intrusive nature of earworms that aligns their emergence and persistence with the principles of repression and parapraxis—musical slips that evidence an internal conflict.

17 Dominic Pettman (2015) has a similar view on the way our present media environment encodes into its operation a protocol for dispersing attention into asynchronous microexperiences. Pettman calls this media protocol "hypermodulation" and contends that, rather than standardizing our thoughts and behavior, it configures the spectacle in such a way that our energies and attention can never resolve into a collective form of awareness that could usher in radical sentiment.

18 Of course, functionality is a notoriously difficult concept to mobilize. As Gilles Deleuze and Félix Guattari contend, the principle of natural drift permits functionality to range over such a vast array of activities that it's impossible to understand whether those activities are pragmatic or aesthetic. For them, functionality is better understood as a dimension of desiring circuits. See "Molecular Unconscious" in Deleuze and Guattari (1983, 283–95).

19 Felix Ravaisson speaks of "an obscure intelligence that through habit comes to replace reflection" and establish an order of existence in which "the real and the ideal, being and thought, are fused together" (2008, 55).

20 See also Steve Goodman's (2010) "The Earworm" for more on the ways in which jingle makers and sonic branding companies are attempting to bind affects to earworms.

21 The "MBT" stands for "Musical Brain Trainer." See http://www.earwormslearning.com.

22 See, for instance, the work of Tiziana Terranova (2000), Michael Hardt and Antonio Negri (2004), Maurizio Lazzarato (1996), and Yann Moulier-Boutang (2011). Each of these works proposes that capitalism has entered an "affective," "immaterial," and/or "cognitive" phase of development.

23 Just to make it clear, earworms do not have a sensory correlate. Melodies and tunes have actual correlative acoustic impressions; however, properly speaking, the melodies and tunes to which earworms correspond are abstractions. In other words, earworms are nonsensuous perceptions of nonsensuous perceptions.

24 Anahid Kassabian's 2001 study on ubiquitous listening considers how genre differences between background and foreground music break down under the virtual omnipresence of music made possible by the proliferation of playback technologies that not only make it possible to project music in all places and at all times but also condition a mode of listening that does not require active or focused attention. Although background and foreground music are, strictly speaking, industry categories, their discursive implosion is nevertheless a counterpart to the experiential ambivalence that begins to develop whenever it takes an effort, even if minor, to discern whether the music one is experiencing is actually being heard (in the background) or being virtually listened to (in one's head).

CHAPTER 3. THE WORM REFRAIN (OR, DOES NATURE GET EARWORMS?)

1 In some respects, the history of human reasoning may be seen as the intensification of this forgetting of thought's processual nature.

2 Gilles Deleuze's *The Logic of Sense* (1990), which entails a serial exposition of sense's structural nature, shows that good sense is a conceit requiring the continuous displacement of that which has no sense. He illustrates this with Lewis Carroll's *Hunting of the Snark*, which tells the story of a search for a creature that exists insofar as it is never found, because when it is found, the Snark is a Boojum, you see.

3 A notable difference between *Magnolia*'s and *Upstream Color*'s depictions of interrelation is that while the former presents the interrelatedness of its events from a supplementary dimension that it makes explicit with a prologue and voice-over, the latter only implies this dimension.

4 Danijela Kulezic-Wilson (2014) suggests that "images, sound, music, and editing . . . are the principal elements that create the atmosphere, convey the sense of the protagonists' brokenness, and reveal the connection between the characters." For her, the film's intensification of the "sensuous qualities of the audio-visual material" appeals to the same logic of form that musical works do, a logic in which perceptible patterns of relation intensify "a mode of perception that encourages absorption of the subtext," or what she calls "the metaphorical meaning of the film." This is not far from Langer's position; however, the subtext for Langer wouldn't be so much the metaphorical meaning of the film but the idea of a feeling whose understanding involves something that is "more like *having a new experience* than like entertaining a new proposition" (1942, 263). In this respect, the patterns of relation established by the principal elements of music, sound, and editing produce a semblance of experience in which the patchwork of the world's hangings-together are lived abstractly.

5 Arguably, no one *directly* experiences a traumatic event, insofar as what makes an event traumatic is its resistance to being integrated into the kind of affective or cognitive order that passes for experience. However, from a radical empiricist perspective, trauma is not so much outside of experience as much as it is a form of discontinuity.

Works Cited

Adler, Renata. 1976. *Speedboat*. New York: Random House.

Adorno, Theodor W. 1993. "The Essay as Form." In *Notes to Literature*, edited by Rolf Tiedemann, translated by Shierry Weber Nicholson, 1:3–23. New York: Columbia University Press.

Anderson, Paul Thomas, dir. 1999. *Magnolia*. New York: New Line Cinema.

Bailes, Freya. 2006. "The Use of Experience Sampling Methods to Monitor Musical Imagery in Everyday Life." *Musicae Scientiae* 10 (2): 173–90.

Bailes, Freya. 2007. "The Prevalence and Nature of Imagined Music in the Everyday Lives of Music Students." *Psychology of Music* 35 (4): 555–70.

Baird, Benjamin, Jonathan Smallwood, Michael Mrazek, Jilia Kam, Michael Franklin, and Jonathan Schooler. 2012. "Inspired by Distraction: Mind Wandering Facilitates Creative Incubation." *Psychological Science* 23 (10): 1117–22.

Bargh, John, and Ezequiel Morsella. 2008. "The Unconscious Mind." *Perspectives on Psychological Science: A Journal of the Association for Psychological Science* 3 (1): 73–79.

Baudrillard, Jean. 1994. *The Illusion of the End*. Translated by Chris Turner. Cambridge, UK: Polity.

Baudrillard, Jean. 1995. "Radical Thought." *Parallax* 1 (1): 53–62.

Baudrillard, Jean. 1996. *The Perfect Crime*. Translated by Chris Turner. New York: Verso.

Baudrillard, Jean. 2001. *Impossible Exchange*. Translated by Chris Turner. New York: Verso.

Baudrillard, Jean. 2005. *The Intelligence of Evil: Or the Lucidity Pact*. Translated by Chris Turner. Oxford: Berg.

Baudrillard, Jean. 2008. *Fatal Strategies*. Translated by Philippe Beitchman and W. G. J. Niesluchowski. Cambridge, MA: Semiotext(e).

Beaman, C. Phillip, and Timothy Williams. 2010. "Earworms (Stuck Song Syndrome): Towards a Natural History of Intrusive Thoughts." *British Journal of Psychology* 101 (4): 637–53.

Beaty, Roger, Chris Burgin, Emily Nusbaum, Thomas Kwapli, Donald Hodges, and Paul Silvia. 2013. "Music to the Inner Ears: Exploring Individual Differences in Musical Imagery." *Consciousness and Cognition* 22 (4): 1163–73.

Benjamin, Walter. 1968a. "Art in the Age of Mechanical Reproduction." In *Illuminations: Essays and Reflections*, edited by Hannah Arendt, translated by Harry Zohn, 217–52. New York: Schocken Books.

Benjamin, Walter. 1968b. "On Some Motifs in Baudelaire." In *Illuminations: Essays and Reflections*, edited by Hannah Arendt, translated by Harry Zohn, 155–200. New York: Schocken Books.

Benjamin, Walter. 1978. "On the Mimetic Faculty." In *Reflections: Essays, Aphorisms, Autobiographical Writings*, edited by Peter Demetz, translated by Edmund Jephcott, 333–36. New York: Schocken Books.

Bergson, Henri. 1998. *Creative Evolution*. Translated by Arthur Miller. Mineola, NY: Dover.

Brooks, David. 2007. "The Outsourced Brain." *New York Times*, October 26. https://www.nytimes.com/2007/10/26/opinion/26brooks.html.

Brooks, David. 2021. *Animal Dreams*. Sydney: Sydney University Press.

Buckner, Randy L., Jessica R. Andrews-Hanna, and Daniel L. Schacter. 2008. "The Brain's Default Network: Anatomy, Function, and Relevance to Disease." *Annals of the New York Academy of Sciences* 1124 (1): 1–38.

Callard, Felicity, and Daniel Margulies. 2010. "The Industrious Subject: Cognitive Neuroscience's Revaluation of 'Rest.'" In *Cognitive Architecture: From Bio-Politics to Noo-Politics: Architecture and Mind in the Age of Communication and Information*, edited by Deborah Hauptmann and Warren Neidich, 325–45. Rotterdam: 010 Publishers.

Carroll, Lewis. 1876. "The Hunting of the Snark." The Poetry Foundation. Accessed 26 May 2021. https://www.poetryfoundation.org/poems/43909/the-hunting-of-the-snark.

Carruth, Shane, dir. 2004. *Primer*. Dallas: ERBP.

Carruth, Shane, dir. 2013a. *Upstream Color*. Dallas: ERBP.

Carruth, Shane. 2013b. "How Shane Carruth's *Upstream Color* Explains Your Dysfunctional Relationships." Interview by Charlie Jane Anders. *Gizmodo*, April 2. https://io9.gizmodo.com/how-shane-carruths-upstream-color-explains-your-dysfun-465799671.

Cassirer, Ernst. 1957. *The Philosophy of Symbolic Forms*. Vol. 3: *The Phenomenology of Knowledge*. Translated by Ralph Manheim. New Haven, CT: Yale University Press.

Crary, Jonathan. 2013. *24/7: Late Capitalism and the Ends of Sleep*. London: Verso.

Deleuze, Gilles. 1990. *The Logic of Sense*. Translated by Mark Lester. New York: Columbia University Press.

Deleuze, Gilles. 1994. *Difference and Repetition*. Translated by Paul Patton. New York: Columbia University Press.

Deleuze, Gilles, and Félix Guattari. 1983. *Anti-Oedipus: Capitalism and Schizo-*

phrenia. Translated by Robert Hurley, Mark Seem, and Helen R. Lane. Minneapolis: University of Minnesota Press.

Deleuze, Gilles, and Félix Guattari. 1987. *A Thousand Plateaus: Capitalism and Schizophrenia*. Translated by Brian Massumi. Minneapolis: University of Minnesota Press.

Derrida, Jacques. 2008. *The Animal That Therefore I Am*. Edited by Marie-Louise Mallet. Translated by David Wills. New York: Fordham University Press.

Farrugia, Nicholas, Kelly Jakubowski, Rhodri Cusack, and Lauren Stewart. 2015. "Tunes Stuck in Your Brain: The Frequency and Affective Evaluation of Involuntary Musical Imagery Correlate with Cortical Structure." *Consciousness and Cognition* 35:66–77.

Flusser, Vilém. 2013. *Post-history*. Translated by Rodrigo Maltez Novaes. Minneapolis: Univocal Publishing.

Fransson, Peter. 2006. "How Default Is the Default Mode of Brain Function? Further Evidence from Intrinsic BOLD Signal Fluctuations." *Neuropsychologia* 44 (14): 2836–45.

Goodman, Steve. 2010. "The Earworm." In *Sonic Warfare: Sound, Affect, and the Ecology of Fear*, 141–48. Cambridge, MA: MIT Press.

Greicius, Michael, Ben Krasnow, Allan Reiss, and Vinod Menon. 2003. "Functional Connectivity in the Resting Brain: A Network Analysis of the Default Mode Hypothesis." *Proceedings of the National Academy of Sciences of the United States of America* 100 (1): 253–58.

Gusnard, Debra, and Marcus Raichle. 2001. "Searching for a Baseline: Functional Imaging and the Resting Human Brain." *Nature Reviews: Neuroscience* 2 (10): 685–94. https://doi.org/10.1038/35094500.

Gusnard, Debra, Erbil Akbudak, Gordon Shulman, and Marcus Raichle. 2001. "Medial Prefrontal Cortex and Self-Referential Mental Activity: Relation to a Default Mode of Brain Function." *Proceedings of the National Academy of Sciences of the United States of America* 98 (7): 4259–64.

Hansen, Mark B. N. 2000. *Embodying Technesis: Technology beyond Writing*. Ann Arbor: University of Michigan Press.

Hardt, Michael, and Antonio Negri. 2004. *Multitude: War and Democracy in the Age of Empire*. New York: Penguin.

Hugill, Andrew. 2012. *'Pataphysics: A Useless Guide*. Cambridge, MA: MIT Press.

Immordino-Yang, Mary, Joanna Christodoulou, and Vanessa Singh. 2012. "Rest Is Not Idleness: Implications of the Brain's Default Mode for Human Development and Education." *Perspectives on Psychological Science* 7 (4): 352–64.

James, William. 1955. *Pragmatism and The Meaning of Truth*. Cleveland, OH: Meridian Books.

James, William. 1984. *Psychology: Briefer Course*. Cambridge, MA: Harvard University Press.

James, William. 1996a. *Essays in Radical Empiricism*. Lincoln: University of Nebraska Press.

James, William. 1996b. *A Pluralistic Universe*. Lincoln: University of Nebraska Press.

Kant, Immanuel. 1987. *Critique of Judgment*. Translated by Werner Pluhar. Indianapolis: Hackett.

Kassabian, Anahid. 2001. "Ubiquitous Listening and Networked Subjectivity." *Echo* 3 (2). http://www.echo.ucla.edu/volume3-issue2/kassabian/index.html.

Kulezic-Wilson, Danijela. 2014. "The Musical Flow of Shane Carruth's Upstream Color." *Sounding Out!* (blog), July 24. https://soundstudiesblog.com/2014/07/24/the-musical-flow-of-shane-carruths-upstream-color/.

Langer, Susanne K. 1930. *The Practice of Philosophy*. New York: Holt.

Langer, Susanne K. 1942. *Philosophy in a New Key: A Study in the Symbolism of Reason, Rite, and Art*. 3rd ed. Cambridge, MA: Harvard University Press.

Langer, Susanne K. 1953. *Feeling and Form*. New York: Charles Scribner's Sons.

Langer, Susanne K. 1962. *Philosophical Sketches: A Study of the Human Mind in Relation to Feeling, Explored through Art, Language, and Symbol*. Baltimore: Johns Hopkins Press.

Langer, Susanne K. 1967. *Mind: An Essay on Human Feeling*. Vol. 1. Baltimore: Johns Hopkins University Press.

Langer, Susanne K. 1972. *Mind: An Essay on Human Feeling*. Vol. 2. Baltimore: Johns Hopkins University Press.

Lazzarato, Maurizio. 1996. "Immaterial Labor." In *Radical Thought in Italy: A Potential Politics*, edited by Paolo Virno and Michael Hardt, 133–50. Minneapolis: University of Minnesota Press.

Liikkanen, Lassi. 2008. "Music in Everymind: Commonality of Involuntary Musical Imagery." In *Proceedings of the 10th International Conference of Music Perception and Cognition*, edited by Ken'ichi Miyazaki, 408–12. Sapporo: ICMPC.

Liikkanen, Lassi. 2011. "Musical Activities Predispose to Involuntary Musical Imagery." *Psychology of Music* 40 (2): 236–56.

Lowery, Oliver M. 1992. "Silent Subliminal Presentation System." US Patent 5159703A, filed December 28, 1989, and issued October 27, 1992.

Lucier, Alvin. 1988. *Sferics*. New York: Lovely Music. Vinyl record.

Malick, Terrence, dir. 2012. *To the Wonder*. San Antonio, TX: Brothers K Productions.

Malick, Terrence, dir. 2011. *The Tree of Life*. Rigby, ID: Cottonwood Pictures.

Malinowski, Bronisław. 1972. "Phatic Communion." In *Communication in Face-to-Face Communication*, edited by John Laver and Sandy Hutcheson, 146–52. Harmondsworth, UK: Penguin.

Margulis, Elizabeth. 2013. *On Repeat: How Music Plays the Mind*. New York: Oxford University Press.

Marx, Karl. 1991. *Capital.* Vol. 1, *A Critique of Political Economy*. Translated by Ben Fowkes. New York: Penguin Classics.

Mason, Malia, Michael Norton, John Van Horn, Daniel Wegner, Scott Grafton, and C. Neil Macrae. 2007. "Wandering Minds: The Default Network and Stimulus-Independent Thought." *Science* 315 (5810): 393–95.

Massumi, Brian. 2002. *Parables for the Virtual: Movement, Affect, Sensation*. Durham, NC: Duke University Press.

Massumi, Brian. 2011. *Semblance and Event: Activist Philosophy and the Occurrent Arts*. Cambridge, MA: MIT Press.

Massumi, Brian. 2014. *What Animals Teach Us about Politics*. Durham, NC: Duke University Press.

Massumi, Brian. 2015. *Ontopower: War, Powers, and the State of Perception*. Durham, NC: Duke University Press.

Moulier-Boutang, Yann. 2011. *Cognitive Capitalism*. Translated by Ed Emory. Cambridge, UK: Polity.

Otter, Ken, Alexandra McKenna, Stephanie LaZerte, and Scott Ramsey. 2020. "Continent-Wide Shifts in Song Dialects of White-Throated Sparrows." *Current Biology* 30 (16): 1–5.

Peirce, Charles Sanders. 1955. *Philosophical Writings of Peirce*. New York: Dover.

Pettman, Dominic. 2015. *Infinite Distraction*. Cambridge, UK: Polity.

Poe, Edgar Allan. 1845. "The Imp of the Perverse." *Graham's Magazine*, July, 1–3.

Priest, Eldritch. 2013. "Felt as Thought (or, Musical Abstraction and the Semblance of Affect)." In *Sound, Music, Affect: Theorizing Sonic Experience*, edited by Marie Thompson and Ian Biddle, 45–63. London: Bloomsbury.

Priest, Eldritch. 2018. "Earworms, Daydreams and Cognitive Capitalism." *Theory, Culture and Society* 35 (1): 141–62

Proust, Marcel. 2002. *À la recherche du temps perdu*. Paris: Gallimard. First published 1913–27 by Grasset (Paris).

Raichle, Marcus, and Abraham Snyder. 2007. "A Default Mode of Brain Function: A Brief History of an Evolving Idea." *Neuroimage* 37 (4): 1083–90.

Ravaisson, Felix. 2008. *Of Habit*. Translated by Clare Carlisle and Mark Sinclair. New York: Continuum.

Reik, Theodor. 1953. *The Haunting Melody: Psychoanalytic Experiences in Life and Music*. New York: Farrar, Straus and Young.

Rombes, Nicholas. 2013. "The White Worm: Shane Carruth's 'Upstream Color.'" *Los Angeles Review of Books*, June 10. http://lareviewofbooks.org/article/the-white-worm-shane-carruths-upstream-color/.

Sacks, Oliver. 2007. *Musicophilia*. New York: Alfred A. Knopf.

Schafer, R. Murray. 1969. *The New Soundscape: A Handbook for the Modern Music Teacher*. Scarborough, ON: Berandol Music.

Serres, Michel. 2007. *The Parasite*. Translated by Lawrence R. Schehr. Minneapolis: University of Minnesota Press.

Shepherd, John, and Peter Wicke. 1997. *Music and Cultural Theory*. Cambridge, UK: Polity.

Stern, Daniel. 1985. *The Interpersonal World of the Infant*. New York: Basic Books.

Stiegler, Bernard. 1998a. *Technics and Time*. Vol. 1, *The Fault of Epimetheus*. Translated by Richard Beardsworth and George Collins. Stanford, CA: Stanford University Press.

Stiegler, Bernard. 1998b. "The Time of Cinema." Translated by George Collins. *Tekhnema* 4:62–113.

Stiegler, Bernard. 2010a. *For a New Critique of Political Economy*. Translated by Daniel Ross. Cambridge, UK: Polity.

Stiegler, Bernard. 2010b. "Memory." In *Critical Terms for Media Studies*, edited by W. J. T. Mitchell and Mark B. N. Hansen, 64–87. Chicago: University of Chicago Press.

Stiegler, Bernard. 2011. *Technics and Time*. Vol. 3, *Cinematic Time and the Question of Malaise*. Translated by Stephen Barker. Stanford, CA: Stanford University Press.

Szendy, Peter. 2012. *Hits: Philosophy in the Jukebox*. Translated by Will Bishop. New York: Fordham University Press.

Terranova, Tiziana. 2000. "Free Labor: Producing Culture for the Digital Economy." *Social Text* 18 (2 [63]): 33–58.

Thompson, Clive. 2007. "Your Outboard Brain Knows All." *Wired*, September 25. https://www.wired.com/2007/09/st-thompson-3/.

Thompson, Clive. 2013. *Smarter Than You Think: How Technology Is Changing Our Minds for the Better*. New York: Penguin.

Twain, Mark. 1876. "A Literary Nightmare." *Atlantic Monthly*, February, 167–70.

Virno, Paolo. 2004. *A Grammar of the Multitude: For an Analysis of Contemporary Forms of Life*. Translated by Isabella Bertoletti, James Casciato, and Andrea Casson. Cambridge, MA: Semiotext(e).

Wallace, David Foster. 2011a. *Fate, Time, and Language: An Essay on Free Will*. New York: Columbia University Press

Wallace, David Foster. 2011b. *The Pale King*. New York: Little, Brown.

Williamson, Victoria, Sagar Jilka, Joshua Fry, Sebastian Finkle, Daniel Müllensiefen, and Lauren Stewart. 2011. "How Do 'Earworms' Start? Classifying the Everyday Circumstances of Involuntary Musical Imagery." *Psychology of Music* 40 (3): 259–84.

Index

abstraction, 14–19; and advancement, 18–19; and the arts, 9, 16–17, 63; and the body, 10; and feeling, 4, 8–10, 13–14, 31, 47; and language, 15–16; lived, 2, 6, 15, 23, 31, 39, 49–52, 57, 71n2; maximized, 26–27, 51; and music, 5–6, 10, 14, 21–27, 38–41, 49, 63, 70n4, 70n6, 75n23; and perception, 8, 15; and potentiality, 5, 8; and self, 61; and thought, 54; and value, 57, 66. *See also* symbolism
Adorno, Theodor: on the essay form, 6
Anderson, Paul Thomas: *Magnolia*, 61, 76n3
architecture: and the capacity for enchantment, 23
artifice: as creativity, 73n11; and nature, 58–59. *See also Upstream Color* (Carruth)
attention: appropriation of, 29; automated hyperattention, 2; as compulsory, 36–38; continuous, 6, 36–39; as currency, 31; outsourcing of, 34–36; scattered/dispersed, 42, 75n17; self-focused, 48; wandering, 37, 48, 72n4. *See also* distraction
audio technologies: and earworms, 3, 31, 51; and repetition, 3, 40, 75n24; and sound's materiality, 30. *See also* music; Muzak
autonomy: of musical objects, 41

background music, 26–27, 41, 51, 70n4, 74n15, 75n24. *See also* music
Baudrillard, Jean, 6; on the freedom of value-relieved things to circulate, 32–33; on integral music, 51–52; on systems, 50–51
Beethoven, Ludwig van: as not abstract enough, 16–17
Benjamin, Walter: on the age of mechanical reproduction, 34–35; on habit, 67–68; on memory, 72nn6–7
Bergson, Henri: on the elements of a tendency, 60
birds: and catchy tunes, 4–5
body, the: and duration, 29; as event matrix, 15; and music, 9–10, 24, 39; and perception, 9–10; and the senses, 39; and waiting, 10
Brahms, Johannes: as not abstract enough, 16–17
brain: and earworm, 2, 6, 29; resting, 47–49, 72n4. *See also* mind
branding: of life, 57; sonic, 44, 72n7
Brooks, David: on our "external cognitive servants," 33

Cage, John, 16–17; *0'00"*, 71n8; *4'33"*, 5, 24–27, 71n8
Callard, Felicity: on neuroscientists' rhetoric of productivity, 48
capitalism: and cognition, 29, 44–49; commodity fetishism, 57–58; and displacement, 37–38; and distraction, 32; and repetition, 73n12. *See also* entertainment; value

Carruth, Shane: on letting/watching weird things happen, 63; *Primer*, 55; *Upstream Color*, 6, 54–68, 76nn3–5
Cassirer, Ernst: as influence for Langer, 7; on symbolic forms, 22. *See also* symbolism
catchiness: and bird sex, 4–5; of earworms, 3, 33; functionalization of, 44–45; of pop hits, 44–45
clairvoyance, 55–56, 59. *See also Upstream Color* (Carruth)
compulsion: and attention, 36–38; and earworms, 74n16; and repetition, 42
conceptualism: as the height of abstraction, 26–27. *See also* abstraction
continuity. *See* discontinuity
Crary, Jonathan: on attention and duration, 36–38, 42, 74n13

daydreaming, 35, 47–49, 65; and earworms, 28, 49; and mood, 26; and music, 26; as performance, 47–49; as positive, 31–32, 48–49, 72n4; as proxy to living life, 7; sound as, 5; swallowing, 24–27
death, 50–52
Deleuze, Gilles: on functionality, 75n18; on good sense, 76n2; on "larval selves," 44; on refrains and indiscernibility, 60; on the self, 68
discontinuity, 38–39, 43, 56–61, 64–65, 76n5
distraction, 28, 37; as continuity, 38; as cost, 31; distracted listening, 26; distraction span, 38, 74n13; and earworms, 38; infinite, 3; and productivity, 32, 48. *See also* attention

earworms: and audio technologies, 2–3, 31, 51; and capitalism, 29, 44, 49; and daydreams, 28, 49; and distraction, 38; etymology of, 1; as intrusive, 1–3, 74n16; and madness, 51; and musical training, 2; as nonsensuous, and 75n23; as parasite, 6, 29; as pathology, 2; as recursive, 32; and rhythm, 38; and social assemblage, 2, 6; as stuck in your head, 1, 3, 28, 33, 47; and utility, 32; and virtuosity, 46–47, 49
Earworms MBT (Musical Brain Trainer), 45, 75n21
Eno, Brian, 16–17
entertainment, 42–44, 49–50
enthusiasm: and death, 50
event, 50–51

feedback loop, 43–44. *See also* entertainment
feeling: and abstraction, 4, 8–10, 13–14, 31, 47; and action, 10–13; and continuity, 57; exogenous and autogenous, 11–12; feeling the possibility of, 10; feeling-tone, 12–13, 18, 26, 70n3; felt significance, 17, 22, 63–64; and hearing/listening, 1, 5–7; vs. the *idea* of feeling, 70n5; immediacy of, 57; and meaning, 63–65; and mood, 12–13; and music, 19; and reality, 21; and rhythm, 11; semblance of, 7–10; and temporality, 11; and thought, 3–27, 38, 41–42, 47, 51–52; virtual, 21. *See also* sensation
flowers, 5–6, 54–56, 58–60, 62. *See also Upstream Color* (Carruth)
Flusser, Vilém, 6; on entertainment and sensation, 42–44, 51
Freud, Sigmund, 8, 12, 43

Guattari, Félix: on functionality, 75n18; on refrains and indiscernibility, 60

habit: as currency, 66; earworms as, 47; listening as, 31, 41; and music, 74n16; and reflection, 75n19; and repetition, 44; and will, 66–68
hallucinations, 28–29
headphones: and intimacy, 40
hearing. *See* listening
hodgepodge, 53–54

imagination: and affect, 7, 18; and concept, 20; and feeling, 13; and mind, 18; and music, 10, 19–21

immediacy: of feeling, 57; of sensation, 42–43
instruments, 30–31. *See also* music

James, William, 15; on experience, 57, 64–67, 74n13; on living abstractly, 18; on the self and habits, 67

Kandinsky, Wassily: the figural in the abstract work of, 17
Kant, Immanuel: and the earworm, 1–2
Kasparov, Garry: and computer-collaboration, 35
Kassabian, Anahid: on background vs. foreground music, 75n24
Kulezic-Wilson, Danijela: on *Upstream Color*, 76n4. *See also Upstream Color* (Carruth)

Langer, Susanne, 69n2; on action, 10–13; on art's semblances, 5, 7–9, 14, 19–20, 27, 31, 63; on "felt as thought," 3–5; on intellection, 18; on the life-abstract, 18; on music, 7, 9, 21–23, 26–27; on perception, 8; *Philosophy in a New Key*, 5; on the principal of assimilation, 23, 26; on sentience, 4; and Whitehead, 7, 10–11
language: and abstraction, 15–16; acquisition (and bad music), 45; and the experience of abstraction, 15–16; vs. music, 16
limit: of expression, 26; of silence, 25; of techniques of existence, 24–25
listening: distracted (listening nonlisteningly), 26, 40–41, 51; and feeling, 1, 5–7; as habit, 31; to light, 30; as never not productive, 29, 41; nonconscious, 30; as speculative content (in Cage's *4'33"*), 25; ubiquitous, 75n24
loss: overcoming, 6, 62, 66–67. *See also Upstream Color* (Carruth)
Lowery, Oliver M.: silent subliminal presentation system (SSPS), 30, 71n1
Lucier, Alvin: *Sferics*, 30

Mahler, Gustav, 25
Malick, Terrence, 56
Malinowski, Bronisław: on phatic speech, 47
Margulies, Daniel: on neuroscientists' rhetoric of productivity, 48
Margulis, Elizabeth: on audio technologies and repetition, 3, 40, 74n16
Marx, Karl, 47; on commodity fetishism, 57–58
Massumi, Brian: on art/music, 14–17, 24–25, 39, 41, 71n7; on bodies and enablement, 12; on concept, 20; on experience and continuity, 57; on humans vs. nonhuman animals, 73n11; on the lived medium, 62; on nonsensuous similarity, 20; on the senses as prostheses of the body, 39; on techniques of existence, 24–25, 39–41, 44, 51, 71n7, 73n11; on thought, 15, 31, 54
medium: and affect, 62; as the passage, 61–62; sound treated musically as, 70n5
memory: and earworms, 1–2, 29, 46–47; and human reasoning, 76n1; industrial, 36; lack of (in the self-entertained), 42–43; and the nervous system, 72n6; offloading of (mnemonic exteriorization), 31–39; politics of, 35; and repetition, 45; as (cognitive) talent, 46–47; and thinking, 35–36; and the unconscious, 72n7. *See also* offloading (mnemonic exteriorization)
mental health: and "useless thinking," 31–32, 48–49, 72n4. *See also* daydreaming; thinking
mind, 41; and compulsion, 36–37; and earworms, 47; exteriorization of, 6, 29; as imagination (broadly construed), 18; and labor, 45–46; wandering, 37, 48, 72n4. *See also* brain; daydreaming
mood: and distracted listening, 41; and music, 5, 7, 26, 41, 74n15; and phatic utterances, 47; and reverie, 26; as that which holds together, 53; and the unfelt, 12–13

music, 14–27; and abstraction, 5–6, 10, 14, 21–27, 38–41, 49, 63, 70n4, 70n6, 75n23; background, 26–27, 41, 51, 70n4, 74n15, 75n24; and the body, 9–10, 24, 39; and daydreaming, 26; as exterminated by ubiquity, 51; and feeling, 19; and imagination, 10, 19–21; integral, 51–52; and language-acquisition, 45; vs. language, 16; and mind, 5, 7, 26, 41, 74n15; and myth, 21–23, 26; and noise, 64; pop hits, 44–45; and symbolism, 7, 14, 19–22, 30–31; as technique of existence, 39–41, 71n7; as unheard, 20, 23; and the virtual, 7. *See also* audio technologies; instruments; musical training; Muzak
musical training: and earworms, 2. *See also* earworms; music
Muzak, 7. *See also* music

narrative: as bridging experiential discontinuity, 57–58, 66–68. *See also Upstream Color* (Carruth)
nature: and artifice, 58–59. *See also Upstream Color* (Carruth)
noise: into music, 64; parasite as, 60–61, 65, 68; and transparency, 65
novelty: earworm as, 51; and obsolescence, 37–38; as preference, 4; and semblance, 19–20

offloading (mnemonic exteriorization), 31–39, 44; and creativity, 35. *See also* memory
onto-power, 6, 47
orchids. *See* flowers; *Upstream Color* (Carruth)

parasite: and communication, 65; earworm as, 6, 29; and growth, 25; as noise, 60–61, 65, 68; and rhythm, 59; in *Upstream Color*, 6, 56, 59–63, 67–68. *See also Upstream Color* (Carruth)
pataphysics, 53–54, 72n5
Peirce, Charles Sanders, 18
perception, 8–10, 15–16: and abstraction, 8, 15; and the body, 9–10; and potentiality, 14; shaping of, 36; and thought, 51
Pettman, Dominic: on microexperiences and attention-dispersal, 75
phonograph, 30, 36, 51
pigs, 5–6, 54–56, 58–60, 62. *See also Upstream Color* (Carruth)
Plato: on the effect of musical sound, 7
playback technologies, 40–41, 75n24. *See also* repetition
Poe, Edgar Allan: and the earworm (in "The Imp of the Perverse"), 1, 33
potentiality: and abstraction, 5, 8; and expression, 18; and feeling, 12; and perception, 14; and virtuosity, 47. *See also* abstraction
puns: and earworms, 1

Ravaisson, Felix: on a reflection-replacing intelligence, 75n19
Reik, Theodor: on the intrusiveness of earworms, 74
repetition: and audio technologies, 3, 40, 75n24; and capitalism, 73n12; and compulsion, 42; and contemplation, 43; and earworms, 1–3, 6, 28, 74n16; endless, 43; of "felt as thought," 4; and habit, 44; as irksome, 2, 32; and memory, 45; and pop hits, 73n12; as useful, 32
rhythm, 59; and concept, 20; and earworms, 38; evolution of, 4; and feeling, 11; more-than-human processes of, 6, 58; and parasite, 59; and thought, 54
ringing in the ears, 1, 33
Rombes, Nicholas: on *Upstream Color*, 63. *See also Upstream Color* (Carruth)

Sacks, Oliver: on the long history of being haunted by earworms, 33
Satie, Erik, 16–17
Schafer, R. Murray: on "schizophonia," 40. *See also* schizophonia
Schiller, Friedrich, 14
schizophonia, 40–41

semblance: and abstraction, 14; of art/ music, 5, 7–9, 14, 16, 19–24, 26–27, 31, 63; of continuity, 38; of feeling, 7–10; of fixity, 40; vs. sensation, 26–27
sensation: vs. consciousness, 42, 49–50; and entertainment, 42–44, 51; vs. semblance, 26–27. *See also* feeling
Serres, Michel: on noise as parasite, 61–62
Shakespeare, William: on our glassy essence, 11
Shepherd, John: on sound as music, 70n5
silence: and artworks, 16; limit of, 25. *See also* Cage, John
speculation: and the arts, 8–9
speech: phatic utterances, 47; and the social, 46–47
speed: and feeling, 13; and things in themselves, 15
Stern, Daniel: on music and "vitality affects," 15
Stiegler, Bernard, 6; on the offloading of thinking, 33–36
subjectivity, 63; production of, 46; representation of, 49
symbolism: confusion of the symbol and the symbolized, 21–23, 26; and the human, 8–10, 26; and music, 7, 14, 19–22, 30–31. *See also* abstraction
Szendy, Peter, 49, 73n12

techniques of existence, 5–6, 24–27, 39–41, 44, 50–51, 71n7, 73n11
temporality: and the earworm, 2; and feeling, 11; fractalized present, 43; and humanity, 34; and novelty, 37; passing present, 68; temporal objects, 36
thinking, 10, 37, 54; as commotion, 1; and feeling, 3–27, 38, 41–42, 47, 51–52; and flows/breaks, 3; as a form of labor, 5–6, 45–47; and language, 15; as life lived abstractly, 15, 23; and memory, 35–36; vs. reason, 54; and perception, 51; and rhythm, 54; sonorous, 30; useless, 29, 31–32, 48–49. *See also* daydreaming; mind
Thompson, Clive: on offloading data as freeing, 35, 37
truth, 20–21
Twain, Mark: as possession by a jingle, 33, 72n8

Upstream Color (Carruth), 6, 54–68, 76nn3–5

value: and abstraction, 57, 66; and circulation, 32–33; of existence, 57–58; of involuntary nervous activities, 3, 29; and virtuosity, 46. *See also* capitalism
variation, 58–59, 62
Virno, Paolo, 6; on capitalism's erasure of the distinction between labor and nonlabor, 48; on the role of sentience and know-how in the production of surplus-value, 45
virtuosity, 46–49

Whitehead, Alfred North: and Langer, 7, 10–11
Wicke, Peter: on sound as music, 70n5
Wittgenstein, Ludwig, 8
Woolf, Virginia: on waves before words, 53; on writing to a rhythm (rather than a plot), 54
worms, 5–6, 54–56, 58–62, 73n10; wormlikeness, 42–44, 49–50. *See also* earworms; *Upstream Color* (Carruth)

EVENT+EARWORM

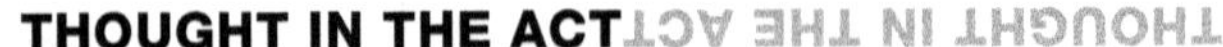

A series edited by Brian Massumi and Erin Manning

ELDRITCH PRIEST

EVENT + EARWORM

MUSIC, DAYDREAMS, AND OTHER IMAGINARY REFRAINS

Duke University Press · *Durham and London* · 2022

Printed in the United States of America on acid-free paper ∞
Project editor: Lisa Lawley
Designed by Matthew Tauch
Typeset in Garamond Premier Pro by Copperline Book Services

Library of Congress Cataloging-in-Publication Data
Names: Priest, Eldritch, author.
Title: Earworm and event : music, daydreams, and other imaginary refrains / Eldritch Priest.
Other titles: Thought in the act.
Description: Durham : Duke University Press, 2022. | Series: Thought in the act | Includes bibliographical references and index.
Identifiers: LCCN 2021022847 (print)
LCCN 2021022848 (ebook)
ISBN 9781478015369 (hardcover)
ISBN 9781478017981 (paperback)
ISBN 9781478022596 (ebook)
Subjects: LCSH: Music—Philosophy and aesthetics. | Music—Psychological aspects. | Upstream color (Motion picture) | BISAC: MUSIC / Essays | ART / Criticism & Theory
Classification: LCC ML3800 .P84 2022 (print) | LCC ML3800 (ebook) | DDC 780.1—dc23
LC record available at https://lccn.loc.gov/2021022847
LC ebook record available at https://lccn.loc.gov/2021022848

Cover art: Eric Blum, *Pattern N° 076-3*, 2012. Archival pigment print. 30 × 30 in. Courtesy of the artist and RULE Gallery.

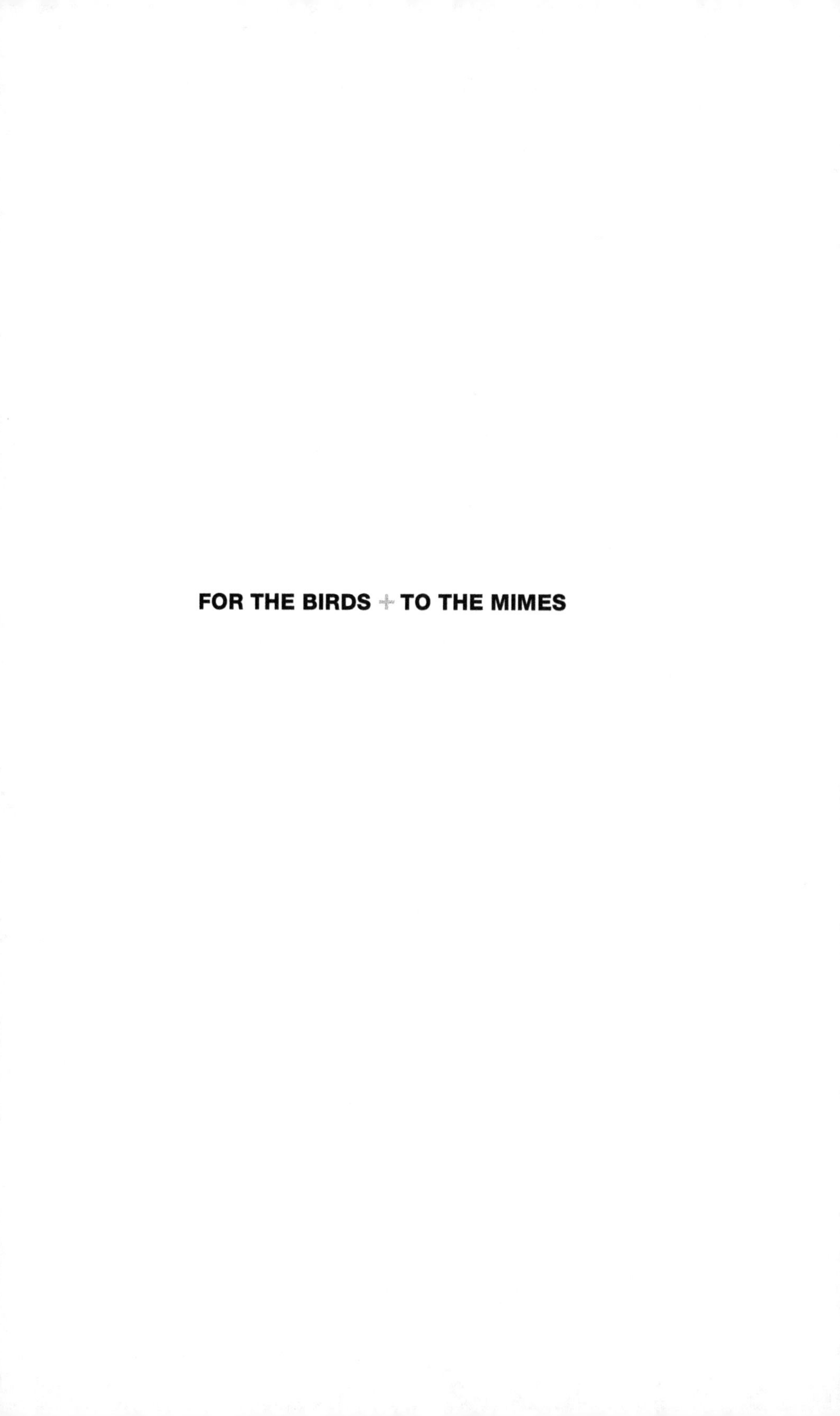

FOR THE BIRDS + TO THE MIMES

Contents

ACKNOWLEDGMENTS ix

INTRODUCTION · Event 1

ONE · What It's Like to Think Like What It's Like to Think Like What It's Like 8

TWO · Beating a Dead Beetle 23

THREE · Impractical Enthusiasm 29

FOUR · Ex Post Facto ex Ante (or, It's All in the Setup. . . .) 39

FIVE · Do Earworms Have Daydreams? 44

NOTES 65 · WORKS CITED 79 · INDEX 87

Acknowledgments

I worked on this book for the better part of a decade, hemming and hawing about its need to be written and wondering, if were to be written, whether I'd be the one to do it. That you have the book in your hands and that my name appears on it is because I was privileged to share its content, in a variety of guises, with friends and colleagues along the way who both encouraged the project and enriched my thinking about what I think it means to think with earworms, daydreams, and other imaginary refrains. A sincere thank-you goes, then, to Sanem Güvenç, Saygin Salgirli, T'ai Smith, Margret Grebowicz, Deborah Kapchan, Carla Nappi, the anonymous readers of the manuscript, and especially Claudette Lauzon, all of whom took the time to be the kind of intellectual companions we dream of having when sailing uncertain waters. Thanks go as well to Jonathan Adjeman for his incisive copyediting, and to Josh Rutner for the incredible indexes. I would also like to thank Brian Massumi and Erin Manning for inviting me to publish this work in their wonderful series, and Ken Wissoker, as well as Ryan Kendall, along with the design team at Duke University Press, for supporting and helping me bring this project to light. The other members of The Occulture—David Cecchetto, Marc Couroux, Ted Hiebert, Rebekah Sheldon—and everyone who attended Tuning Speculation over the years should be thanked as well, for it is with them that I was able to conjure the context that sustained the experimental thrust of this project. I want to express my gratitude to Jack Rachman, Maureen Whittal, and Kyle Burns for helping me learn to think differently about thinking. And thanks to Rocket for keeping me on my toes, and for my favorite French coat.

This work was supported in part by funding from the Social Sciences and Humanities Research Council and Simon Fraser University.

Introduction

EVENT

Unbidden, uninvited, and always smack in the middle of things. Starting again and again without ending, without concluding, which is to say, without clearly beginning or commencing, I hear a song, though it's less a song than scraps of a song that are not really *heard* so much as they are *thought*, like an idea, or, better, like a daydream that winds in and out of the spins and stalls of that abstract commotion called "thinking." What I'm describing is what it's like to have a song stuck in my head, to have an earworm. It's not so unusual for me. I almost always have one of these parasites spinning around, competing for my attention. Sometimes they loop for days, but mostly they linger only as long it takes until they're replaced by another catchy louse that I pick up from the background music overheard in a coffee shop, from a spoken phrase that reminds me of a passage of a familiar tune, or from my daughter absentmindedly singing along to her own hangers-on. Often they change for no reason that I can put my finger on. It seems, then, that earworms are nothing if not opportunistic.

Yet even if opportunistic, they are not predictable. Certain factors appear to favor their occurrence—formal and situational factors such as recency and tempo are thought to play a role, as is one's level of musical training and/or interest as well as cortical thickness in brain regions relevant to auditory processing.[1] I've also suggested that our musical technics and audio technologies establish conditions that exploit our powers of abstraction and thereby set the stage for the proliferation of earworms.[2] All of this just makes earworms seem more like the weather than a proper thought. But maybe there's something to be said about the earworm's weather-esqueness that's more interesting and important than its etiology or even its phenomenology. Maybe the way an earworm trends is worth considering because its chaotic unfolding says something about how thought might behave when it's taking place not under but to the side of conscious awareness. Perhaps, then, like a weather pattern, an earworm's event is something to track rather than define. And because its event moves across all manner of psychic terrain—an earworm carries on whether you are reckoning, daydreaming, strategizing, or problem-solving—it might be more illuminating to contemplate the ways in which it entangles itself with other events. To do this, however, requires an approach that takes seriously an event's sensitive dependence on initial conditions. In other words, the kind of thinking about the kind of thinking that I want to do is a thinking that takes its cue from the fact that even though it starts somewhere, it can't already know how it will go.

In some ways, this is to say that the earworm is my starting point for a series of thought experiments. But the thought experiments that I have in mind are not like the thought experiments familiar to analytical philosophers that help guide (or, as Daniel Dennett [2014] suggests, deflect) thinking through a set of hypotheses using subjunctive expressions to articulate a conclusion whose status is necessarily counterfactual. Instead, my thought experiments resemble those that Steven Shaviro attributes to science fiction, experiments that are not so much interested in the truth conditions of this or that issue as they are in imagining "*what it would be like* if they were true" (2016, 9). For Shaviro, science fiction "*embodies* . . . issues in characters and narratives" that make its aims "pragmatic and exploratory." But where science fiction's methods are "emotional and situational" (9), mine are paralogical and expressive. This means that the fabulations I concoct about earworms follow a dreamlike logic that draws out certain lyrical and rhythmic aspects of repetition and obsession. Simply put, my experiments, while also embodied and interested in *what it is like*, are driven less by "speculative extrapolation" (9) than by oneiric transformation.

In this side of the book, through a series of thought experiments, or what I'll simply call "reveries," I explore the earworm's event by asking questions that, when considered oneirically, can be understood to address what might be called "the earworm unconscious." For the most part, my method seeks productive and/or imaginative distortions between multiple focal points rather than bootless explications of a unified phenomenon. This means that instead of supposing that the earworm's dream-life matters because it discloses something otherwise unsayable about it, I take the life oneiric to be a transversal technique for assigning significance to the world polyphonically. Hence, I play fast and loose with concepts and writing styles drawn contrapuntally and without pretense to mastery from a variety of sources including animal studies, process philosophy, stand-up comedy, philosophy of language, stream of consciousness, and neuroscience to perplex certain of the metaphysical distractions of recent sound studies as well as to lighten up the unduly sober remit of the cognitive sciences that overlook just how funny earworms are.[3]

Although I'm not entirely opposed to metaphysical distractions, nor is my take on the earworm entirely free from its own such diversions, one of the primary aims of this work, especially on this side of the book, is a writerly aim. That is, what motivates this study is an abiding interest in the way thinking takes place *in the act of writing*. For me, writing is not about transcribing the ideas that I have already thought. It's not first and foremost a medium for the *conveyance* of ideas but rather, as Eric Hayot suggests, "a medium for research and discovery," such that writing should not simply "involve saying things you already understand and know, but instead let you think new things" (2014, 1). And this is precisely what I endeavor to do here, with the earworm as my dreaming companion—to think thoughts that come unbidden, uninvited, and always smack in the middle of things, starting again and again without ending, without concluding, without clearly beginning or commencing. In this regard, I make writing in circles a form of thought that, like an earworm, like a dreaming earworm, is best experienced in medias res. But this approach also means that my thoughts have a way of getting away from me. These vermicular refrains go where they want to go, which is to say that my writing often wanders into territories where symbols and metaphors begin to function factually and literally. In other words, the ideas created by this writing do more than explain or elucidate—they modulate thinking to bring it into a new key, a key where it makes perfect sense that mimes are truthful liars, that melodies are heard backward, and that language is a virus. The key to this key, then, is not simply understanding what's written but spiraling along with it.

In the first reverie, "What It's Like to Think Like What It's Like to Think Like What It's Like," I ask if animals can get earworms. I ask this not because I think it matters whether they do or not but because the question opens a line of thought that treats thinking about thinking as a necessarily creative and poetic affair. By ventriloquizing J. M. Coetzee's alter ego, Elizabeth Costello, and hijacking Susanne Langer's theory of symbols, I suggest that it's possible to think our way into the being of another to the extent that what is thought is what Brian Massumi calls "the being of analogy" (2011, 123). For Massumi, the being of analogy describes a nonsensuous similarity that, through Langer, I read as a symbol whose "factor of significance is not logically discriminated, but is felt as a quality rather than recognized as a function" (Langer 1953, 32). Such a symbol is presentational rather than discursive and appeals to another semantic order in which the meaning of a symbol is understood through the relationships of its elements to a total structure. This kind of symbol lends itself to articulations that, as Langer argues, are expressive of the patterns of sentience, or, as she says, the inner life. But because the sense these symbols make can't be separated from the forms that express it, they are often not experienced as symbols but as the thing symbolized. In other words, a symbol of the inner life has a way of being (mis)taken as the being of inner life. And creatively mistaking the being of analogy is exactly what I exploit in order to develop the thought that we might be able to think what it's like to think that animals might get earworms.

Having set the ground rules for how we might ask if animals can get earworms, the second chapter, "Beating a Dead Beetle," tackles the question head-on. However, in proper oneiric form it pivots into a discussion on the seeming impossibility of answering such a question, only to find itself confronted not with a worm but with a beetle in a box. Drawing on Ludwig Wittgenstein's famous thought experiment, which challenges the position that the inner life can have a private presentation, I suggest that asking whether animals can get earworms is a way of playing a game with language. As Wittgenstein (who goes simply by "W" in the chapter) notes, speaking about interior experience is like telling others that you have a beetle in a box without ever being able to show this bug to anyone. This, W insists, does not negate private experiences but makes anything we might say about them, even to ourselves, reliant on a shared way of using language. W calls this sharing of language use a game and suggests that its rules of play are not only highly contextual but radically pragmatic. Language use is so pragmatic, in fact, that by turning inward upon itself, it effectively takes leave of the means by which it is able to convey meaning. From W's perspective, this leaves the kind of talking that philosophy gets up to particularly hamstrung. However, from my perspective, this doesn't leave philosophy hamstrung so much as it shows it to be a very peculiar language game, a game whose rules encourage a type of play that requires that its rules be continually made and remade *for the sheer sake of doing so*. Thus, where W might say that philosophy uses language in a way that puts language out of play, I suggest that it not only keeps it in play but ups the ante. Taken this way, the question of whether animals get earworms should be understood as a move in a language game that doesn't play for truth but rather for the fun of making language dizzy, which, by the way, makes language say new things.

What a dizzied language can say is the thrust of the next two reveries. "Impractical Enthusiasm" is the title of the third chapter, which is concerned primarily with transposing the question about animals and earworms into a refrain that turns Langer's "act concept" into a literary strategy. In her philosophy of mind, Langer developed the notion of the act to conceptualize a "formal unit, or modulus, of living processes" (1967, 288). This unit, which encompasses events as disparate as a shiver down the spine, a sudden sense of disappointment, a sneeze, or a random thought, is characterized by a distinctive phase structure marked by incipience, acceleration, consummation, and cadence (288–89). For Langer, these acts arise from "a situation [which] is a constellation of other acts in progress" (281) to concatenate with one another and produce a matrix of interdependent hierarchies that give vital processes their characteristic forms and functions. The act as I take it up in this chapter is similarly conceived but also deployed as a conceit that directs, motivates, and elicits the conceptual moves that mark the text as a dynamically charged field. As such, the earworm's repetitive act becomes a trope of enthusiasm that finds expression in the gyrations and revolutions of a cockroach, a hedgehog, a mouse, a cat, and a gorilla. Mimes, too, make an appearance as event-artists just before I end with a telling of the further adventures of Gregor Samsa, who learns that his metamorphosis into a bug was only one part of a spiraling series of further transformations.

The fourth reverie, "Ex Post Facto ex Ante," is something of a send-up of Wittgenstein's offhanded remark that a philosophical work could be written consisting entirely of jokes (quoted in Malcolm 2001, 27–28). Although not all of this chapter is made of jokes (nor is it entirely philosophical), it borrows the rhythms and gestures of jokes to put into play thought's propensity to split itself into multiple series. Thus, rather than advancing an argument, there is expression, the expression of a non/sense that, in Deleuzean terms, "resonates across all of [thought's] disjuncts" (Deleuze 1990, 176). After an opening wisecrack that demonstrates an initial ramification of sense, the chapter rapidly wends its way through a daydream, talk of rumors, the psychoanalysis of fire, a musing on frisson, the abstraction of waves, the logic of having a song stuck in your head, and the perfidy of melody to conclude that everything is in the setup. And, in a way, this daydream is itself a setup for the next reverie, which has been more imagined than written.

The fifth chapter, "Do Earworms Have Daydreams?" takes the experiments of the previous reveries further by presenting itself explicitly as a reverie on reveries. Borrowing this conceit from Gaston Bachelard, I think about—and think by—daydreaming in order to say something about both its recently acquired reputation as a cognitive resource for the labor of the self and its emerging pathological profile as a new form of obsession. I do this for two reasons: One, the new daydream imaginary very literally puts reverie to work composing and maintaining a sense of self, and I want to suggest instead that daydreaming has a more fundamental role in bringing the imagination of material to lyrical expression. Two, as Bachelard argues, the imagery of dreams "can only be studied through the image, by dreaming images as they gather in reverie" (1969, 53). In other words, reveries are not explained but expressed, and their expression takes the form of more imagery. Thus, in multiplying the imagery of daydreams, I simulate the drifts and divagations of a wandering mind in a way that mimics its compulsive condition, a condition also known as "maladaptive daydreaming."[4] I suggest that maladaptive daydreaming, although not yet officially recognized as a mental disorder, is poised to replace ADHD (attention deficit hyperactivity disorder) as our new favorite inner affliction, for the more continuous distraction becomes, the more seductive daydreaming is. The kind of reverie on reverie that I have in mind, then, dreams of music that is unplayingly played, of the way distraction resembles attention, of the way some thoughts don't take account of their own appearance, of whether I would want my ideas if someone else had them, and of the possibility that an excessive use of metaphor might risk turning language into a virus that can be cured only by singing. In this way, I want to valorize thought in the act of taking its expressive share, a share that risks capture by an apparatus of distraction that in multiplying the images of an intensive surreality starts every image over and over again, each time without ever really getting anywhere, which is to say, without clearly ending, and so without clearly beginning or commencing.

One

WHAT IT'S LIKE TO THINK LIKE WHAT IT'S LIKE TO THINK LIKE WHAT IT'S LIKE

In the flip side of this book, I suggest that the earworm is a technical affair. To be more specific, I say that it's a vector for a fatal tendency immanent to musical techniques of abstraction.[1] For the most part, I cast this as a very human affliction and argue that the proliferation of audio technology spreads a certain type of technical mentality to traditionally idle fields of experience—such as daydreaming—where sonic events are felt as thought more than they are heard. In this picture, the abstractive techniques of music appear as primarily a human accomplishment engineered through a species intimacy with "organized inorganic beings"—aka technical objects (Stiegler 1998, 17). I'm still largely convinced by this but only to the extent that this species intimacy marks an intensification of a power that humans share with other living beings to abstract value—actionable, conceptual, aesthetic, social, symbolic, and so on—from their existential situation. This means that what is proper to human music, and what makes the earworm its fatal condition, is not the act of abstracting value from sound but the techniques used for prolonging, extending, varying, comparing, distributing, and, importantly, contemplating the events that such abstractions express.

Yet if the earworm is a tendency immanent to a shared power of abstraction, then is it possible that nonhuman animals might experience something like an earworm? As a technical affair, meaning an effect of human technicity, it would seem that the answer is no. But if an earworm is just the effect of how a certain technology of existence (which is what music is) isolates and intensifies its own techniques of abstraction, then, theoretically, any technology of existence can produce "a mode of mired becoming, spinning its wheels" (Massumi 2014, 109n51). For instance, you can view a video on YouTube that shows about a dozen turkeys circling a dead cat.[2] The official word is that these birds were simply curious about the carcass. But it was also suggested that these birds were lured into this circumambulation because of an instinct to stick together by following the tail most directly in front of them (Potenza and Becker). "Sticking together" might be considered a technology of existence and abstraction that in this case finds its fatal condition as an enacted obsession. We can surely call this behavior a form of mired becoming, but what is it for a turkey to experience this? To borrow a phrase from Thomas Nagel (1974), is there something that it would be like? Having an earworm is definitely like something—like hearing a song in parts again and again, like remembering something partway without trying to remember it, like thinking about thinking about thinking. If there's something that it's like to be a circling turkey, I assume, then, that it might be like having an earworm.

But I can only imagine what it's like, which is okay because "what it's like" is a matter of expression, and expression is an eminently creative affair.

⁂

The celebrated Australian writer Elizabeth Costello, delivering a pair of talks for Appleton College's Annual Gates Lectures, makes exactly this point by suggesting that we can and do think our way into death when we think about what it's like to be a corpse. She says: "For instants at a time . . . I know what it is like to be a corpse. The knowledge repels me. It fills me with terror; I shy away from it, refuse to entertain it. . . . What I know is what a corpse cannot know: that it is extinct, that it knows nothing and will never know anything any more. For an instant, before my whole structure of knowledge collapses in panic, I am alive inside that contradiction, dead and alive at the same time" (Coetzee 2001, 32).

Costello argues by analogy that if we can think our way into our own death, then we can surely think our way into the life of another by imagining what it is like. As she sees it, "what it is like" is not a rhetorical device (nor even a very good argument against philosophical reductionism) but the naming of a capacity to "share at times the being of another" (33). In her example, this capacity at its limit extends to sharing in the nonbeing of her own self, but it also extends in a less incongruous way to her sharing the being of a fictional character, as she did in her novel *The House on Eccles Street*, which tells James Joyce's *Ulysses* from the perspective of Leopold Bloom's wife, Marion. "Marion Bloom," she writes, "was a figment of James Joyce's imagination. If I can think my way into the existence of a being who has never existed, then I can think my way into the existence of a bat or a chimpanzee or an oyster, any being with whom I share the substrate of life" (35). Costello could think her way into Marion Bloom's fictional being because the status of fictionality doesn't prevent there being something it is like to be her. For Costello, the difference between what it's like to be a fictional Marion and what it's like to be a real bat is trivial, in much the way that the difference between what it's like for her to be a corpse or for a corpse to be a corpse is trivial. But the something that it's like to be a bat, a corpse, or Marion is not really a *thing*. It's a doing, and a doing isn't something to be presented but a consistency to be expressed. This means that in *The House on Eccles Street* Costello doesn't think her way into an already-determined state of what it's like to be Marion Bloom but linguistically extracts and expresses in her own discursive way a sense of vitality that "after the fact . . . will be fully and finally recognized and authorized as the 'what' it had been about in that situation" (Massumi 2014, 88). The difference may seem subtle, but it points to the way in which what it's like to be Marion (or a bat, or a corpse) isn't about accessing an established existential territory so much as inventing another. Using novelistic techniques to describe how the passing of a day in early twentieth-century Dublin is incarnated in and as "Marion," Costello writes herself into "an existential territory where nothing ever sets foot, being purely lived abstraction" (86). What it's like to be Marion is a pure expression—a semblance of being her. But, again, the difference between being her and what it's like is trivial, for if what it's like to be Marion can be "expressed without [her] actually appearing," then the semblance of what it's like is simply "the form in which what does not appear *effectively* expresses itself" (Massumi 2011, 23; my emphasis). In this sense, the semblance that Costello thinks herself into is not the being but the extra-being of another—what it's like purely in its manner of expression.

As a writer, Costello's conceptual cues for this sympathetic thinking lie in poetry. During the second of her lectures, she draws on Ted Hughes's "The Jaguar" and "Second Glance at a Jaguar," suggesting that "in these poems we know the jaguar not from the way he seems but from the way he moves," and continuing, "The body is as the body moves, or as the currents of life move within it. The poems ask us to imagine our way into that way of moving, to inhabit that body" (Coetzee 2001, 51). For Costello, Hughes's poetry does more than report on an encounter—it "shows us how to bring the living body into being within ourselves" (53). Of course, she's not being literal. But she's not speaking figuratively either. The jaguar's *living body* is an abstraction whose livingness is the expressed sense of how its body moves. Its livingness, in other words, is not a thing but the event—the extra-being—of transformation that its bodily movements incarnate. The implication is that the livingness passing through the jaguar can be expressed otherwise. Where this livingness is effectively expressed and felt by the jaguar in the tonus of its organic rhythms and a gestural repertoire that articulates its movements with those of its vital domain, for Costello it is expressed in Hughes's poem as the poem's *import*. Through the differential participation of verbs, comparisons, scansion, and striking imagery, "Second Glance at a Jaguar" expresses a livingness that is directly perceived not as an interpretation or meaning but as a pattern of sentience, of what it's like. This formulation of sympathy resembles Susanne Langer's notion of semblance.

SCHOLIUM ON WHAT IT'S LIKE TO HAVE A MIND

Whenever Langer's name is invoked (if it ever is), it's often with respect to her theory of symbolism and philosophy of art. And not without good reason. *Philosophy in a New Key* (1942) and *Feeling and Form* (1953) are impressive works. They show an erudite and original thinker carrying out an assault on logocentrism in a way that not only presages the concerns that would preoccupy poststructuralist thinkers during the second half of the twentieth century but also anticipates certain feminist interests in the importance of experience, the polyvocality of meaning, and the centrality of feeling in thought and life. But Langer's philosophy has always been a philosophy of mind. It's not always recognized as one, first because she doesn't really engage with the prevailing philosophies of mind of her day, choosing instead to follow the then current scientific literature in order to develop her own idiosyncratic theories, and, second, because she treats mind as a form of feeling. This somewhat-counterintuitive image of mind as feeling is peculiar, not just because it departs from the familiar images of mind as a faculty responsible for abstract thinking but also because it makes of mind a mode of doing. As Langer writes, "To feel is to do something, not to have something" (1967, 20). And if "whatever is felt in any way, as sensory stimulus or inward tension, pain, emotion or intent, is the mark of mentality" (4), as Langer argues, then mind is an activity continuous with, yet distinct from, the vital processes that underwrite its expression. The framing of feeling as a doing that marks mentality as a process rather than a product makes mind not a thing but an event. This draws directly from her teacher Alfred North Whitehead's metaphysics; however, unlike Whitehead, who assigns to feeling a role that admits mentality (or a mentalistic sentiment like creativity) into any and all processes (1978, 219–35), Langer insists that feeling is strictly an intraorganic affair: only "vital activities of great complexity and high intensity, usually (perhaps always) involving nervous tissue, are felt" (1967, 21). Feeling, in other words, is done only by organisms, which by extension means that mind is done only by living things.

Put another way, although Langer sees that all matter does something, only those doings whose rhythms interact in such a way as to give rise to other rhythmic doings can develop a relationship to their own vital processes that can be felt (as inward tension, pain, etc.). Thus, only to the extent that organic doings feel the various patterns of their own activities can they be said to have a mental aspect. Moreover, for Langer, only the feeling of vital activities that are felt purely for their expression, for their sheer appearance, can be felt as mind. Thus, not all doings that are felt do the same thing, and only some doings do "mind." So how, then, is mind done? Which is to say: How is mind felt?

Langer's position, which never really changes over the course of her decades-long career, is that mind is done by a process of symbolization, a process that she also identifies as abstraction. While abstraction is a wholly natural process, one that extends from microorganisms to great apes, it is only when abstraction leads to an "attitude toward objects *in absentia*" (1942, 31) that it begins to be felt as mind. Abstractions that don't promote such an attitude still constitute a form of mentality, but this mentality does not a mind make.

Insects, earthworms, and simians all have a form of mentality rather than mind. This is not, however, because their feelings lack complexity, so much as that the attitudes they develop toward what William James famously called the "blooming, buzzing confusion" (1950, 488) of the world only ever enter into their given perceptual context and existential situation as a stream of ongoing signals for immediate action. Langer writes, "If we would speculate on what an animal sees or fails to see in its environment" (or, I would add, what it feels abstractly) "we must start from what it is doing; for it sees [feels] whatever will implement or frustrate its acts" (1972, 77). As such, animal mentality—the ways of feeling patterns of impingements pass into signals and indications to act—is largely oriented by practical demands.[3] Thus, what animals feel, what they "think," is not forms or concepts but values that extend their creaturely behavior into a vital milieu.[4]

But the "minded" creature, the human being, develops a rather different attitude toward the welter of impingements and goings-on that compose what become its *forms* of feeling. Its attitude to the perplexity of feelings from which it formulates or abstracts a world of ideas develops out of what Langer sees as an unprecedented *need* to symbolize, a need to transform the valences of experience into devices for making an abstraction. Unlike animals, which only need the flow of experience to yield actionable values, humans seem to require that it yield expressive ones, too. That is, for humans, something of the blooming, buzzing confusion needs to make an appearance apart from its sheer carrying on. Chaos needs a little symbolizing. The feeling called "mind" refers, then, to an activity whereby experience is felt abstractly as it is transformed into something that stands for something else. Mind, therefore, distinguishes itself *formally* from simple (animal) mentality by the way humans treat sense data as abstractions that *represent* experience and thereby satisfy the distinctive human need for symbolic expression.

However, there is another aspect to this symbolic transformation that is obscured by the formalization of experience. Given that mind, like all forms of feeling, is wrought by the vital rhythms and motivations that underwrite organic existence, it is also distinguished *practically* (and ironically) by its impractical enthusiasms. As Langer puts it, "Only a part—howbeit a very important part—of our behavior is practical. Only some of our expressions are *signs* [by which Langer means signals], indicative or mnemonic, and belong to the heightened animal wisdom called common sense; and only a small and relatively unimportant part are immediate *signs of feeling.* The remainder serve simply to express ideas that the organism yearns to express, i.e. to act upon, without practical purpose, without any view to satisfying other needs than the need of completing in overt action the brain's symbolic process" (1942, 43).

If it's right, as Langer argues, that the mind is "an organ in the service of primary [human] needs" (38–39)—including this need to symbolize—and is distinguished from creaturely mentality by the production of acts that are expressive rather than exclusively practical or even communicative, then the satisfaction of *this* need has to be found in an order of activity that is somehow set off from or *exceeds* the imperatives of biological existence. That is, while the need for expression is determined (as all organismic processes are) by physiological processes, its fulfillment is affirmed by activities that yield something other than practical effects. Said another way, the symbolic transformation of experience satisfies the need for activities that are marked precisely, if not entirely, by their impractical enthusiasms.

But what exactly marks an enthusiasm as impractical? In Langer's model, nothing is impractical—even expression—so long as it satisfies a biogenetic need. And that is exactly what abstraction does for humans—satisfy a need. This need, however, manifests in a particular way. As Langer writes, "It is only natural that a typically human function [the symbolic transformation of experience] should require a typically human form of overt activity." And this activity "is just what we find in *the sheer expression of ideas*" (1942, 43). (The phrase "overt activity" is confusing here, because what Langer means by "overt" isn't an outwardly observable behavior but simply the explicit activity of ideating. Although this activity is, practically speaking, covert, since it is felt rather than unfelt by the organism, it is, strictly speaking, an overt activity.)

So, the chatter in our head, or the daydreams we have, or the intractable scrap of melody we notice only after we've been virtually auditioning it for hours, days, or weeks on end is practical to the extent that it satisfies an organic craving to abstract, to symbolize. But given that what is practical is a matter of degree, as Gilles Deleuze and Félix Guattari (1983, 3) illustrate in their analysis of Rube Goldberg and stone-sucking machines, we could argue that our inner babble, earworms, reveries, and so on, which exemplify the sheer expression of ideas, are *functionally* impractical enthusiasms. These, however, are not the only activities that are functionally impractical. To this list of private passions we can add, as Langer does, the more public enthusiasms of myth, ritual, and art. For Langer, these activities are marked as impractical enthusiasms to the extent that their very occasion, before they even *mean* anything, coincides with their expression, which is to say (somewhat tautologically) that what is impractical is expressive, and what is expressive is impractical.

But what does it mean for an activity to be impractical? In short, it means to be "empirically senseless" (Langer 1942, 51). However, more broadly it means being symbolic. Over the course of her career, Langer offers a number of ways to consider what a symbol might be and directly writes in *Feeling and Form* that a symbol is "any device whereby we are enabled to make an abstraction" (1953, xi). But a clearer way of understanding a symbol's impractical enthusiasm can be found in Langer's discussion of Sigmund Freud's take on ritual activities. Freud, she writes, "recognized that ritual acts are not genuine instrumental acts, but are motivated primarily *a tergo*, and carry with them, consequently, a feeling not of purpose, but of compulsion" (1942, 50). Ritual acts are not carried out for utilitarian ends but rather extend from "a sheer inward need" and "are best interpreted as *expressive* behavior" (50, 51). Thus, from Freud's insight, she concludes that "human behavior is not only a food-getting strategy" (51) but also a performance that entails the production of feelings that feel their own abstraction from the push and pull of life's practical relays. This means that "every *move* is [for human beings] at the same time a *gesture*" (51)—in other words, an expressive form. In Langer's estimation, a gesture is expressive before it is communicative, an impractical enthusiasm felt abstractly before it is felt functionally. An act becomes symbolic, then, to the extent that it is felt as a "quality without practical significance," a quality that, incidentally, "makes the forms of things . . . present themselves *in abstracto*" (1953, 51). In a sense, symbolization is a process of self-abstraction.

This process of self-abstraction is also described by the British anthropologist and early cyberneticist Gregory Bateson, who, unlike Langer, understood it not as the feeling of expressive forms but as the direct perception of difference. In his theory of play and fantasy, Bateson (1972, 183–98) suggests that an act that draws value from its own performance stages a paradox, and this paradox establishes the conditions by which map and territory—symbol and symbolized—can be discriminated. Bateson's example is the famous case of play-fighting monkeys, whose actions did not denote what the actions for which they stand would have denoted. The simians' play fight abstracts from their movements a stylistic disparity between play and actual combat such that one and the same gesture—a "bite"—comes to be logically distinguished from another: a "nip." Yet, at the same time, this disparity is, to use Langer's words, "felt as a quality rather than recognized as a function" (1953, 32).

The paradox of play—play is something that is not what it would be—marks, for Bateson, an evolutionary leap in communication. But the lived abstraction that is play also marks a step in the evolution of a human need. The execution of a fight that is not a fight has a value that first satisfies an expressive need. That is, before play fighting serves as an instructional model of how to wage war, play's abstraction is felt as a vitalizing force. But if play does this and it satisfies an animal need, then Bateson's theory would seem to undermine Langer's thesis regarding symbolic transformation as an exclusively human need. To the extent that the paradox of play creates a semiotic situation, it would seem that animals do have some inkling of mind, for play's paradox shows in its peculiar form of abstraction an impractical enthusiasm—sheer symbolific activity.

That abstraction matters to animals isn't so outrageous. Langer readily admits that animals respond to and orient their actions around elements drawn from their immediately lived situation. Indeed, she writes, "The interpretation of signs is the basis of animal intelligence" (1942, 59). But, for her, "directly felt inward and outward acts, springing from impulse and ambient pressions and opportunities, are sufficient for all animal needs" (1972, 138). However, the fact that animals play—that at times their actions do not denote what those actions for which they stand would denote—suggests there's something about play that satisfies what should also probably be called an expressive need.

This is something that Brian Massumi takes up in his recent work on animal instinct and sympathy. Building on Bateson's insights and making a refrain of the idea of the ludic gesture, Massumi creates a conceptual territory that gives animal mentality its expressive due and restores an instinctive edge to the human mind. For Massumi, a ludic gesture is, very simply, a form of abstraction. More precisely, it's a behavioral form that "performs an abstraction on its action" to yield an expressive excess (2014, 5). The *manner* in which an activity is carried out, Massumi says, is what gives certain animal behaviors their "-esqueness," their pure expressive value (10). The ludic gesture is, in other words, a feeling. But its feeling is an abstraction that makes it a thinking-feeling absolutely one with doing.

In this respect, the ludic gesture has the same function as Langer's symbolic transformation, for both concepts point to a process by which an "excess is felt as a palpable enthusiasm" (9). For Langer, this enthusiasm finds its way into distinctly human acts such as ritual and art but also, more mundanely, the endless chatter in our head. But from Massumi's point of view, this abstraction needn't be construed as symbolic activity per se. An animal, he says, "performs something extra to the functions of its behaviors" through the -esqueness of its act—a flourish of the tail, a flash in the eye, a bounce in the step all satisfy an expressive need (59). The status of the transformation as "symbolic" is, for the animal, not as important as the doing of this something extra.

⁂

Now, it's quite possible that I am reading something extra into this idea of expressive need that Langer didn't intend. And perhaps I'm even saying something heretical by virtue of the way my extrapolation converts her concept of symbolic transformation into an abstract force of impractical enthusiasm. But given that I'm human, and humans have a need to transform experience into forms that are purely expressive, or interpretively creative, my heresy is not only condoned by Langer's notion of symbolic transformation but conceptually pre-endorsed. Furthermore, humans, like all animals, like to play. In fact, "when we humans say 'this is play,' we are assuming our animality" (Massumi 2014, 8). And when we assume our animality, we are composing ourselves around "the -esqueness of the analog animal" (59). Becoming-animal is, then, a way of reading something extra into vital activities *with vital activities themselves*. And this is also how animals experience their becoming-human.

If that's not reason enough to take up the conceptual overspill of expressive need into a creative interpretation, then consider this: the symbolic transformation of experience that makes a bite a nip is an animal capacity. Yet, if it's an animal capacity, then, equally, "when animals play, they are preparatorily enacting human capacities" (8). Thus, "play dramatizes the reciprocal participation of the human and the animal, from both sides" (8), to effect an effective paradox that makes it possible to ask: Do animals have wistful fancies? Do they have a need to express the extra-being that belongs to their form-of-life signature style? Do they have impractical enthusiasms? If so, is the manner in which they surpass their form-of-life signature felt as thought or as style?

....

In *Feeling and Form* (1953), Langer advances a theory of virtuality based on her insight, developed in *Philosophy in a New Key*, that "*great art is not a direct sensuous pleasure*" (1942, 205). Although there is no artwork without some kind of sensuous support, for her art is a symbolic affair in the sense that what's made and what's perceived, via the differential involvement of abstracted forms, whether painted, sounded, sculpted, built, filmed, or written, is a *semblance of life*, a nonsensuous perception of what it feels like to feel the world. Langer calls the semblance produced by artworks a symbol of feeling and argues that its function "is to give forms [the sheer appearance of things] a new embodiment in purely qualitative, unreal instances" (1953, 50). This gives art's semblances their characteristic otherness and, paradoxically, their transparency as "strange guests" whose direct perception brings the "elusive and yet familiar pattern of sentience"—what it's like—within ourselves (50, 52). As isomorphic to patterns of sentience, the art symbol's significance—what Langer terms its "vital import" (32)—subsists, then, in the analogous correspondence of relational structures.[5] However, an art symbol's import is not merely a factor of significance "felt as a quality rather than recognized as a function" (32). Import is what Massumi calls "a being of analogy *occurring* in the in-between event of the two component events' coming abstractly together" (2011, 123). This means that in the poems Elizabeth Costello analyzes, Hughes's artistic technique brings the jaguar's expressions of livingness together with those of language to co-compose another event whose expression is felt abstractly, which is to say, felt as thought. For Langer, this co-composition of abstraction expresses a logical similarity that is experienced directly and qualitatively as nonsensuous. In other words, a semblance of life is the expressed being of analogy, or, rather, the abstractly lived extra-being of a nonsensuous similarity.

Although she doesn't put it this way, what Costello is doing when she thinks herself into the being of another is contemplating a symbol of feeling in the way that Deleuze (1994, 70–79) says a flower contemplates the sun's rays, a muscle contemplates oxygenated blood, or a trickle of water contemplates a runnel. That is, Costello contracts aesthetic qualities into a semblance of what it feels like to be alive. For insofar as directly perceived aesthetic qualities "enter into the form [of feeling] and in this way are as much one with it as the relations they, and only they, have" (Langer 1953, 52), a symbol of feeling makes felt abstractly what it's like to be alive in the world as Marion, as a bat, or, strange as it seems, as a corpse.

It's also what it's like to be Elizabeth Costello. But of course, Costello is a fiction. Invited to deliver the Tanner Lectures on Human Values at Princeton University in 1997, the novelist J. M. Coetzee tells a story about an Australian novelist named Elizabeth Costello who, when invited to deliver a guest lecture at a fictional Massachusetts college, speaks not on literature but on animal rights. In this metafictional story, Coetzee has Costello argue against the human practice of ratiocination as a trait that justifies its judgment of animals as a diminished form of life and contest the apparent inaccessibility of the so-called inner life of the nonhuman. During the lecture Coetzee-Costello advances a number of criticisms concerning the way scientists conduct their experiments regarding animal thought and suggests that they reach imbecilic conclusions because they ask questions that are not only anthropocentric but simply boring. Citing Wolfgang Köhler's (1925) classic study on apes, and the case of Sultan in particular, in which an ape is subjected to the maddening task of retrieving bananas under constantly changing conditions of privation, Coetzee-Costello avers, "At every turn Sultan is driven to think the less interesting thought. From the purity of speculation (Why do men behave like this?) he is relentlessly propelled towards lower, practical, instrumental reason (How does one use this to get that?) and thus towards acceptance of himself as primarily an organism with an appetite that needs to be satisfied" (Coetzee 2001, 29).

Coetzee-Costello's criticism shows that such experiments not only are misguided but enforce a particular view of what thinking is and how it might be done. Even if nonhuman animals don't actually speculate or contemplate in the ways that we do (or think that we do), were we to ask more interesting questions, we might develop a less prescribed sense of what counts as thinking—and thus what it is like, otherwise.

This last part is particularly important because what Coetzee demonstrates *by doing*—by creating a semblance of a life that we can contemplate just as Costello contemplated the semblance of a jaguar's life—is that we very much can think our way into the being of another if we expand not our definition of being but our definition of what thinking is (or is like). For Coetzee-Costello, poetry's symbolic form is clearly just such an expanded form of thinking. And this is Langer's argument, too, although, for her, poetry is just one of many forms, which include myth, ritual, and the other arts, for articulating thought nondiscursively. As she writes, "The limits of thought are not so much set from outside, by the fullness or poverty of experiences that meet the mind, as from within, by the power of conception, the wealth of formulative notions with which the mind meets experiences" (1942, 8).

Basically, by this she says that thought is much more than what can be *said* of it. Our conceptual powers extend not to the limits of some transcendental schema but as far as the expressive medium will allow their articulation. Put another way, there is no thought apart from its expression, and expression comes in many forms. Language is only one medium of thought, whose primary mode of expression is discursive. Myth, ritual, and art are media with modes of expression that are distinctively *not* discursive. So, then, it's not that what can't be said can't be thought but rather that what isn't symbolized—or, as Langer might say, what isn't transformed into concepts—isn't experienced. Moreover, and more subtly, what is felt as thought is not always felt in one and the same way. Felt discursively, thought appears more like reasoning, whereas, felt nondiscursively, it appears more like feeling. The difference lies not in *what* is expressed but in *how* a medium is used to articulate and express what is felt as thought. Probably for historical and political reasons, discursive expression has come to define what it means to think. It feels different to symbolize discursively, if only because we've grown accustomed to believing that "if *x*, then *y*" is less embodied in precisely the inverse way that we've become accustomed to believing the to-ing and fro-ing of a melody is more embodied. Both modes of expression are felt, and both are felt as thought. But only a nondiscursive mode of expression can, "without conscious comparison and judgment but rather by direct recognition" (Langer 1953, 82), express the sense and thus the feeling of what livingness is like.

So, having said all this, for the rest of this study I'm not going to theorize what this expanded sense of thinking is in order to ask if nonhuman animals experience anything like an earworm, but, like Coetzee thinking his way into a semblance of Costello, I'm going to quasi-nondiscursively *think* my way into it.

SCHOLIUM ON METHOD

And I'm going to do this by creating semblances of what I think this thinking is like, so that like Costello, like Coetzee, we can think our way into an earworm's event. But there's one specific challenge to doing this with words. Not because words can't produce a semblance—indeed, literature and poetry are emphatically a way of using words to create "a semblance of events that is *experience-like*" (Langer 1953, 265)—but because this book, in being published by Duke University Press, encourages a way of treating these words as though their use were governed by rules, so the seeming directness of the propositional forms in the texts that follow might make them be read *discursively* when they ought to be read *presentationally*. Here I am referring to Langer's central and career-defining distinction between two symbolic modes that possess separate logics and expressive powers, and I'm invoking the distinction here to emphasize that although my text at times appears to be unambiguously discursive, it's not. Despite, and in a way against, the obviousness of the verbal statement that, as Langer says, "hides the characteristic forms of verbal figment" (234), my words, sentences, and so on are motivated by a *manner of use*, by a commanding form that they produce rather than the successive unfolding of relatively independent semiotic units. Like a novel, then, whose material is often indistinguishable from ordinary speech, yet whose "product is not discourse, but the illusion of life directly lived" (297), each semblance of what I think this thinking an earworm's event is like has an import above the suggested significances that are elements in their written expression. So the import isn't something that I can tell you about; it's not a matter of fact but a matter of expression, much as a joke is something to be told rather than explained.

I'll say now that the manner in which I use language from here on in/out is poached directly from David Markson's work, especially from his novel *Wittgenstein's Mistress* (1988), which is largely an accumulation of deadpan statements regarding trivial facts about artists, composers, writers, and thinkers throughout Western history. What makes *Wittgenstein's Mistress* significant for this text (and what beguiles it) is the way in which the novel's narrator's solipsistic stream of consciousness is marked by continual moments of thought revision. Rather than stating facts once as though they were all that is the case, the narrator revisits and revises her thoughts again and again in a way that's characteristic of an earworm's way of starting and stopping, starting again, intruding into other feelings and ideas. For me, this stream of thought revision isn't just a stylistic conceit but is instead a technique of existence for writing semblances of "certain dynamic patterns of human [and maybe nonhuman] experience" (Langer 1943, 226) that, whether a snippet of song or a statement of fact, are stuck in your head.[6] That said, although I don't think that I've entirely captured Markson's style, I believe that I've adapted something of its spirit to the "fundamental feeling [or event] to be explored and expressed" (Langer 1953, 389) in the semblances that follow.

....

Two

BEATING A DEAD BEETLE

> Mental processes just are strange.
>
> —LUDWIG WITTGENSTEIN, *Philosophical Investigations*, 2009

> A serious and good philosophical work could be written that would consist entirely of jokes.
>
> —LUDWIG WITTGENSTEIN, in Norman Malcolm, *Ludwig Wittgenstein: A Memoir*, 2001

I've always wondered if animals get earworms. I suppose it's possible, but it seems unlikely. Then again, we're animals, and we get earworms. This doesn't mean that your cat knows what it's like to have a song stuck in its head. But supposing it did—how would you even know? I only know that *you* have an earworm because you tell me that you do. At the very least, I can infer that you have an earworm by your behavior, by the way you absentmindedly hum parts of a song to yourself or distractedly sing the repeating ditty out loud. (Although if you're *humming* or actually *singing* a tune, then, strictly speaking, though it may be stuck, it's no longer just in your head.) But can your cat tell you that it has an earworm? And if it can't (and I don't actually think it can), then can it show you? And if what it shows you is a form of behavior, then might this, like your humming, effectively dementalize the event and thus turn the earworm into a beetle, a beetle that is not in a box but "in your head"?

I may be beating a horse as dead as the metaphor just invoked, but the business with the beetle bears rehearsing, if only because it homes in on how baffling thinking about thinking is, and thinking about a beetle in a box reminds me that philosophy is first and foremost a funhouse of thought. To set the scene: I only know what it means for you to have a song stuck in your head when the term "earworm" is used in the context of other behaviors in which overt acts—the act of absentmindedly humming a song, for instance, or saying, "I have a song stuck in my head"—*mean* covert ones. This, of course, is to restate Ludwig Wittgenstein's interrogation of language in his *Philosophical Investigations*, in which he famously asked, "If I say of myself that it is only from my own case that I know what the word 'pain' means—must I not say that of other people too" (2009, §293)? In posing this question, W supposedly wants to show that a private language is impossible, and that if it were possible, it would be meaningless. To clarify this, he developed a thought experiment in which we could imagine a group of people, each having a box in which they say is contained a beetle. However, this "beetle" may turn out to be a different thing for each person—but as W notes, what the beetle "is" doesn't actually matter because the *meaning* of the word "beetle" has nothing to do with the thing it denotes. What matters is how everyone uses the word "beetle" to designate what's in their box. Hence W's claim: "A Nothing would render the same service as a Something about which nothing could be said" (§109). Thus, when I say I have an "earworm," I may as well have a "beetle"—that is, if a beetle is what it means to have a song stuck in my head.

Now, the box in W's experiment is obviously the mind, and clearly his aim wasn't to dispel the reality of private or inner experiences. He wasn't saying that if you stub your toe it won't hurt. All the beetle in the box is meant to show is that the sense we make of concepts like "hurt" has less to do with what hurt actually is and more to do with how we learn to deploy the term "hurt" in the ordinary circumstances of a toe being stubbed. *Talking* about a beetle in a box, then, is a way in which we *linguistically* take part in the circumstances of our living with other beetle boxers and indicates more about our capacity to successfully participate in those coleopteric circumstances than about what the beetle is or isn't. So, to speak about a song stuck in your head isn't to address the reality of a supposedly inner entity or an event but to get involved in a form of listening in which songs that are not actually being performed or broadcast over and over again are nevertheless being heard—being thought.

But what's really interesting about the beetle in the box is that it shows that what things *are* is irrelevant to how they *mean*. As W writes, "If we construe the grammar of the expression of sensation on the model of 'object and name,' the object drops out of consideration as irrelevant" (§293). A song stuck in your head may not be a sensation the way a stubbed toe may be, but, like the pain, it's irrelevant to how you or I know what it means. And furthermore, like "the verbal expression of pain [that] replaces crying"—I stubbed my toe!—your telling me "I have an earworm" doesn't describe your state of mind but expresses it (§244). An earworm, therefore, doesn't have that song that's stuck in your head as its meaning but has it in its use as an expression.

The bit about the beetle also reveals something about the limits of language. In showing how language works, how meaning reflects social use rather than pointing to an ideal or even singular referent, W ultimately showed how it doesn't work, which is not to say how it fails, but how it takes time off. "Philosophical problems," he writes, "arise when language goes on holiday" (2009, §38). Take the words "mind," "feeling," and "thought." Ordinarily, they're employed as useful tools of expression that are straightforwardly intelligible in the context of a way of living. Our capacity to know how others feel, what they're thinking about, or what they mean when they say they have a song stuck in their head is unquestioned. But when these terms are entertained as something that names objects, states of affairs, persons, actions, qualities, or concepts, "particularly when a philosopher tries to fathom the relation between name and what is named by staring at an object in front of him and repeating a name, or even the word 'this,' innumerable times," they stop working (§38). Words, in other words, take a vacation.

Yet just as "giving orders, asking questions, telling stories, having a chat, are as much a part of our natural history as walking, eating, drinking, playing," so is philosophizing (§25). To question the nature of existence, the status of values, and the way in which we know what we think we know *is* a way of using language. But it's an odd way. Finding problems in the things we say or write about is a way of using language.

The problem, though, is that it's a use that generates the very problems that philosophy identifies in the things we say or write about. It's a bit like putting language in a fly bottle that way, or like an obsessive-compulsive disorder, in that using language philosophically means using it repeatedly to check on itself, to be blinkered by the uncertainty that its own activity breeds but that it also needs in order for its manner of use to exist.[1] For this reason, philosophy is like any other language. It's bound by a fluctuating set of rules that make its use more like playing a game than applying a collection of definitional axioms and transformation rules. But philosophy's game is unlike other games, because the problems that drive it are self-produced—or, to put it more nicely and less pathologically, autopoetic. To do philosophy is to take language into a veritable funhouse, where familiar forms of use are distorted into concerns such as the unity of heaps, the justification of induction, or the status of free will.

In some ways, philosophy is its own enemy and would be best done by being undone—by, as W notes, simply observing "the bumps that the understanding has got by running up against the limits of language" and leaving everything as it is (§119, §124). So all the setups, all the requests to imagine "this" or suppose "that," make the beetle in a box less a philosophical argument than a therapeutic intervention into the obsessive-compulsive nature of philosophy's language game. The beetle, in other words, leads the fly from the bottle.

Okay—*now* that beetle is good and dead. (Or was it a horse?) Trying to explain things, to theorize, is a mug's game. But sniffing out truffles of nonsense and leaving everything as it is is a language game! A queer game but a game nonetheless. But what does any of this have to do with your cat? Who cares if it has an earworm? And how does a beetle in a box tell us anything about earworms?

It's beginning to look like the fly isn't going anywhere, like the beetle is still twitching. (Or is it a horse?)

If we really want to know whether animals get earworms, there are a couple of things that we're going to have to do—or not do—or maybe both. First, we're going to have to *not* do philosophy. As noted in the minor exordium you just read, philosophy is kind of bad at language games. It's not entirely hopeless, of course. It plays its own game well enough—that is, if you consider self-defeat a kind of winning. Philosophy is awful at language games only to the extent that it interferes with the way language is played by humans as they live their lives *apart* from philosophy. Unless we want spend our time tracking gibberish while leaving everything as it is, then, forget philosophy.

But, second, now that I think about it a little more, we're going to have to do philosophy. Although it's dreadful at most language games, philosophy is actually extremely skilled at making Nothing render the same service as a Something. Philosophy may be lousy at using words in a way that matters to how human beings ordinarily live their lives, but it's extremely good at using them in ways that exploit their playability. W's notion of language as a set of interlocking games performed by members of a language-using community implies a register of play that shouldn't be denied to philosophy just because the way it uses language leads to a special kind of dizziness. Indeed, there are many types of game play, and not all entail making sense—particularly those that are "based on the pursuit of vertigo and which consist of an attempt to momentarily destroy the stability of perception and inflict a kind of voluptuous panic upon an otherwise lucid mind" (Caillois 2001, 23). Roger Caillois gave these games the name *ilinx* and suggests that their pursuit expresses a desire to yield "to a kind of spasm, seizure, or shock which destroys reality with sovereign brusqueness" (23). By plucking words from their ordinary circumstances and spinning them around and around—"repeating a name, or even the word 'this,' innumerable times" (Wittgenstein 2009, §38)—for the pleasure of drawing the oddest conclusions from them, philosophy is making itself dizzy. In this respect, philosophy's self-mystification is less a disabling constraint than an expression of its own ludic intemperance. To use language philosophically is, then, like playing a game whose goal is not to *mean* anything, not to be sure or to get things right—and definitely not to tell the truth or even "to pass from a piece of disguised nonsense to something that is patent nonsense" (Wittgenstein 1958, §464)—but simply to *suspend* the circumstances in which words acquire their ordinary sense.[2] Said another way, these philosophical language games do not play the game that those language games for which they stand would play.

(If you want another take on philosophy's ludic intemperance, read the endnote to this sentence.)[3]

So, in keeping with W's resolution that philosophy may in no way interfere with the actual use of language and must leave everything as it is, yet accepting that philosophy is (maybe) a kind of hyperludic language game played for the purpose of producing epistemic vertigo (or at least to suspend the sobriety of ordinary language games), let me ask again, but this time without meaning it: Do animals get earworms?

I don't think so, but I think they do get refrains.

Three

IMPRACTICAL ENTHUSIASM

ACT I

A novelist, a philosopher, and a musician walk into a bar. Sensing their ingress is the setup for a joke, the novelist immediately goes on a tangent about her distaste for metafiction, stemming from a deeply unsatisfying Twitter conversation she composed last year between Friedrich Nietzsche and Kim Kardashian. The philosopher is much keener to indulge the gag, given that for her a joke is as meaningful or meaningless as any other proposition. The musician, however, is already laughing his head off.

Do animals get earworms? Yes. But they do so only by radicalizing what they mostly are: A refrain. A rat. Or better still—a bug. Or as the Germans say: *Ungeziefer.* "We call a refrain any aggregate of matters of expression that draws a territory and develops into territorial motifs" (Deleuze and Guattari 1987, 323). Animals are a viable habit of chaos, a workable tic, or a layout of behaviors and affects that hang together by contracting variations into a theme—mostly. A bug's refrain is its motif. For instance, there's the kind of bug that David Foster Wallace, in his essay "Consider the Lobster" (2007) likens to the pure late-date American tourist—an insect on a dead thing. And then there's the bug that Harry Caul in Francis Ford Coppola's *The Conversation* (1974) believes is hidden in his apartment—"The bugger got bugged, huh?" is a line from the film. But a bug is also a flaw that lives in computers. People, too. Live in people, that is, a bug.

Parasite, trespasser, defect.

But what about obsession? An excessive enthusiasm that makes a virtual theme of its intrusive motif is the most radical kind of bug. Why? Because it's all refrain, sheer vital enthusiasm in the shape of a going that goes compellingly nowhere. Or, just the same, a spirited going that stays intensely where it is, so that one feels what it feels like to be alive apart from any circumstance of life's being actually lived. Perched on something dead; a buggered bugger; a glitch; and a vital fixation.

So what should I make of this cockroach that I've been watching walk in circles on the concrete floor of a laundromat in Florence? Like my clothing in the dryer, it's been circling around itself for the past thirty minutes; however, unlike my clothing, the center of this circle has been drifting slowly to my left, and the bug has paused once or twice. It doesn't look injured. One, two, three, four, five—six legs. Maybe it's mad. (I would be if I lived in a laundromat.) Maybe it's composing a new refrain. Maybe it's tracing an expressive line of flight that leads away from its pestiferous activities toward, who knows, more geometric affairs and imperatives. Or maybe it's just art. I suppose it could be any or even all of these: its rotations are clearly a motif of some kind, yet its matters of expression have all the marks of insanity. And, indubitably, this aimless peripatesis gives some kind of aesthetic yield. But, then again, maybe it's all just an act—not a fake-out, I mean, but an event. Yet even so, a fake-out is itself still an act, still an event; so, fake or not, an act is still an act.

But what's an act, really? What's the difference between a bare activity and an act?[1]

In one sense, an act is just a spatiotemporal occurrence. But that's a boring way to describe it. A spatiotemporal occurrence may as well be, as Ludwig Wittgenstein (2001, 5) says, everything that is the case. In another sense, an act is a formal affair, one having to do with everything that is the case that shows phases of incipience, acceleration, consummation, and cadence (Langer 1967, 288). Said another way, an act is everything that is the case, with a phase structure. Said another way, again, an act is an absolute value for everything that is the case that *will have been* the case—an act is the shape of change, so to speak.

Now that's a much less boring act. This act brings us to an interesting place where we can talk about the shape of acts as something having both vital and nonvital profiles. This means, "It is action that living and non-living mechanisms may have in common" (Langer 1967, 304). This also means that we can think about enthusiasm as a form of appearance and as a directly perceived quality of acts in their form of coming to pass.

So, again, what can we make of that cockroach's gyrations? Well, it's obvious that this bug has an act—although it also looks as if it has no act at all, since each step is at the same time both the impulse of a new phase and the consummation of a previous one.[2] But no one said that acts are discrete. In fact, they are completely *concrete*. Being grown together, that is. Like an infection. Like a rhythm.

ACT II

Like an act's virulence, I mean.

Acts are particularly contagious things, especially for bodies that live on a diet of "flows and stows . . . speed, arrest, terrific excitement, calm, subtle activation, and dreamy lapses" (Langer 1953, 27).

But that's presuming a lot about bodies.

Aren't bodies what they are rather than not what they are because they exhibit a capacity to grow out of acts?

"Bodies" being exactly what acts are called that keep themselves going.

That there's a body at all is the case when acts are drawn into other acts in rising phases.[3]

In falling ones, too.

"Involvement" is a good word. So is "concatenation."

A body is an involved concatenation of acts. A matrix, even. Another good word.

Although if acts are first, then bodies are really the exact reflection of the former, being the counterpart of the functional matrix of activities, being also the syntactic way of this sentence, too (Langer 1953, 329).

"By reason of the involvement of its act[s] with each other" I understand now what I meant when I said that acts are contagious (Langer 1971, 317).

An act always involves other acts. It always "presses for expansion and engulfs whatever substance will serve to implement it" (Langer 1967, 374).

Which means that it will meet either entrainment or repression by other acts (374).

Which means, also, that it will exercise such on others.

Will give as good as it gets, in other words.

That's not quite right, about contagion. Even though I suggested it.

But why shouldn't thought include poor suggestions and dead ends?

How much of our thinking actually comes to anything? And I don't mean the 99 percent of ideas that we hold true that are "unterminated perceptually" (James 1996, 69).

I mean the 100 percent of inklings or velleities or guesses or gists or daydreams that have absolutely no truck with truth and so have no reason to substitute for knowing in the completed sense (69).

Thinking that is simply expressing its own coming to pass is a thinking that doesn't recognize itself as thought. It doesn't recognize itself as anything but the pulse of ongoing involvement.

Which is not to say it doesn't value its involvement, since every act's motivation is prepared by progressively changing conditions of the integral whole (Langer 1967, 322).

I don't think the cockroach has caught an act, then. I think it's better said that it's caught *in* the act of its own involvement of refusing to become what it can become.

Well, maybe it's not better said that way, because it seems like I'm saying that it's doing something wrong.

Which, as far as I can tell, it's not.

The problem with idioms, I suppose.

Also the idiom of problems being a way of saying this differently.

Antimetabole being what this other way of saying this differently is a case of.

Perhaps I should have said that the bug is "stuck in the act."

Doubtless that would have been clearer. But then I wouldn't have had the occasion to write "antimetabole," which is yet another good word. A great word, maybe.

Now that I've written "antimetabole" twice, I should go on with what I was going on about.

Actually, it's three times I've written "antimetabole."

Make that four.

Language really can get away from you sometimes.

Can get you stuck in the act, to get back to what I was saying about the cockroach.

Which is also to get back to what I was saying earlier about enthusiasm.

Although I was thinking of enthusiasm as a bug then.

Now I'm thinking of the bug as an act in suspense.

That's a good way to think about it.

Or at least thinking of the bug that an act whose action finds its practical force and normal function in suspense is (Massumi 2014, 4).

But does it make any sense to think about an act apart from its performance?

I suppose I should have thought of that before writing it down.

As I said, language can get away from you sometimes.

Thinking, too, apparently.

I like the idea that thinking can get away from the one doing it. Like a daydream. Like an earworm. Like an insect on a dead thing.

Charles Sanders Peirce likened anonymous thinking to a "Strange Intruder."[4]

What he meant is that thought has both ego and nonego profiles.

Thought can still be thought, be done, even if no one in particular is doing it.

Like listening apart from what's heard, or breathing apart from what's inhaled.

But what about an act apart from its performance? What's a doing without its doer, its actually being done?

As far as I can tell, it's thought.

I mean that thought is the case of a doing without its actually being done.

Or the way the extra-being of what's being done does.

This doesn't make sense. But it still has a value, if only because colorless green ideas sleep furiously.[5]

Which is to say, "Fuck all."

Actually, to say, "Fuck all" is to say, "Fuck all," whereas to say, "Colorless green ideas sleep furiously" is to *mean* "Fuck all."

It's amazing that one can mean nothing and still make sense.

But maybe it's not that amazing. A false proposition makes just as much sense as a true one.

The equation 1 + 1 = 3, for example, makes as much sense as the case that all babies are illogical and that nobody is despised who can manage a crocodile; therefore, illogical persons are despised.

Perhaps what matters isn't the *truth* but the *sense* of things.

Because truth-value is fixed to the formal relations that sense makes sayable, "we always have as much truth as we deserve in accordance with the sense of what we say" (Deleuze 1994, 154).

We never run a truth deficit. Truth is cheap, in other words.

Sense, however, is costly.

It seems we never have enough sense and are always trying to make it.

Well, not make it, but extract it from the problems that differential elements in their reciprocal relations pose.

I hope that last sentence meant something because it came close to impressing me for a moment.[6]

The cost of sense is linked to its expression and concerns the way in which things matter. Expressive value is what sense is worth, therefore.

I can only guess that this is why a mime gets away with what he does.

Makes a living from showing that sense is extracted and expressed from things as what effectively occurs, is what I mean.

Trapped-in-a box. Tug-of-war. Sense stripped bare by its pantomime, even.

Being extracted and expressed makes me think of sense as something like oil. Except nothing died to make sense. Although I may have come close to dying a few sentences ago.

I wonder if there's any sense to the idea of "peak sense."

Like oil, peak sense isn't a marker of depletion but the point of maximum production, just to be clear.

Would maximum sense make for a truer world? It couldn't because "sense does not ground truth without also allowing the possibility of error" (Deleuze 1994, 153).

A better question: Would peak sense entail more or fewer mimes?

There's clearly a correlation between the number of mimes that exist at any given time and what we can say is true or false.

Mimes make sense; true and false are not crocodiles. Therefore, nonsense is not a crocodile, and I'd rather be caught in the act than trapped in a box.

Hedgehogs, even.

What should we make of a hedgehog walking in clockwise circles?[7] Even though it's not in Florence, in a laundromat, on a concrete floor, but rather on a paved road, at dusk, somewhere in America, it's clearly caught the same enthusiasm that caught the cockroach.

Or at least it's expressing the sense of it.

Like a mime.

A pure enthusiasm.

Like a bug.

A refrain.

A feeling of the conditions of life without a life being actually lived.

But how on earth did this enthusiasm pass from cockroach to hedgehog?

As far as I can tell, it's pure fiction. Just like this.

ACT III

One morning, when Gregor Samsa woke from troubled dreams, he did not find himself transformed in his bed into a horrible pest (Kafka 1995). That happened long ago. Instead, he found himself walking in clockwise circles on the concrete floor of a laundromat, somewhere in Florence. His memory was not great these days. Since becoming vermin, he'd been less and less able to separate his perception of things from his actions.

For Gregor, the world had lost that impassive edge that had allowed him to plot his life along an ordered series of mutually limited and distinct images. He could no longer plan for the future or take stock of all he'd learned in life. He tended now to make his way, melody-like, from impulse to impulse, much as an improvising musician finds her way from one phrase to the next.

And although he still had a sense of absurdity, if not humor, he couldn't express it as he used to. He could no longer tell jokes or explain why he was late for work. Everything was motivated always, it seemed to him, in favor of action.

Sounds, movements, shapes, and rhythmic changes like swinging, revolving, and flowing had become for Gregor extensions of directly felt inward and outward acts, springing from impulse and ambient pressions and opportunities (Langer 1972, 138).

That he couldn't remember how he arrived in this moist and linty world of dirty socks and sweaty underwear was therefore not particularly surprising, nor entirely worrying. But the enthusiasm he felt at every turn did make him wonder, "Why am I walking in circles?"—which immediately led him to ask, "What is a circle?"[8]

As quickly as Gregor forgot this question, he woke from whirling dreams to find that he had transformed into a mouse. A less horrible vermin, indeed.

+⁺+

With no brown carapace, no slightly domed belly, and no spindly legs to wave about helplessly before him, Gregor was pleased with his pointed snout, small rounded ears, scaly tail, and light gray fur. He was also pleased to learn that he was as enthusiastic as ever.[9]

Cued to the melodic character of his perception, he felt he could venture from home on the thread of a tune. And while he wasn't certain what exactly a tune was—or a thread, for that matter—he was glad for the refrain.

He did notice, however, that his excursions were rather brief and in fact quite dizzying. Every step he took prepared the way for the next, and each always brought him back to where he had already been. This wasn't really a problem for Gregor, given that his sheer enthusiasm seemed to conduct him away from the humbler reaches of practical reason, where it would matter that he get somewhere, and toward the purity of speculation through which somewhere passes (Coetzee 2001, 29).

But, of course, his spiral migration and impractical enthusiasm wouldn't appear as a form of speculation, for who would recognize his winding murine drift as thought, especially if speculation, like most forms of thinking, resolves itself as a subtraction from the commotion of acts that compose experience? But he was *full* of thought. Brimming with a whiskered wonder. Perhaps, were he a cat, his conjectures would be more evident.[10]

Cats, Gregor surmised, have a way of casting their enthusiasm beyond the envelope of their skin, of making what's felt as thought something that belongs to the feltness of experience and not just its recognition.

And as if to prove a point, Gregor found in the pristine speculation that his rodential enthusiasm had in effect already become the very thing that he was thinking, the catness he was thinking-doing.

It was as though life spinning idle were the refrain of change as such, and thought the vector through which the enthusiasm of metamorphosis comes to virtual expression.

For Gregor, this meant that to know what it's *like* to be a cat is an aesthetic matter. To know what it's like to be a cat or to know what it's like for a cat to be a cat was for him a trivial distinction, insofar as "what it's like" only concerns the -esqueness or the extra-being of the feline as it's taken up in creative ways. Style—in other words, the singular *how* of a cat's generic way of carrying on, "the manner in which the animal continuously performs something extra to the functions of its behaviors" (Massumi 2014, 59)—doesn't represent a model of being (*l'être du chat*) but expresses being and spreads *this* particular variation on its sense across every utterance, gesture, and thought that indicates, manifests, or signifies it.[11]

In Gregor's case, a specifically imaginary uptake of extra-feline enthusiasm appeared to find expression in an extra-rodential enthusiasm, which as far as he could tell was equally the imaginary uptake of a "specifically written uptake" (59) of extra-roachity. In this regard, Gregor concluded that there is no limit to the extent to which he could think himself into the extra-being of another's enthusiasm.

And with this thought, Gregor's tale of metamorphosis became a tale of trans-morphosis, for if Gregor's thinking himself into the extra-being of a cat, a mouse, a cockroach, or a gorilla, even, is a matter of expression, and writing takes expression to the limit, then perhaps by taking up his species overspill into creative language the writer of these very words could think his own way into a writerly produced enthusiasm or extra-noetic refrain that would take on the appearance of a daydream, because a daydream, maybe even more than this sentence, runs on the force of its own contemplation of what it could become without actually becoming those things, making its minor doing felt as a thought going intensely nowhere more exciting than the idea that from a bug's spins and stalls could be woven a yarn about act forms and sense making that makes as much sense as it needs to make in order to accomplish the written uptake of the writer's extra-being, which would take on the appearance of a daydream whose discursive drift, maybe even more than this chapter, is driven by the sheer enthusiasm of contemplating what it could express without actually meaning those things, so as to make its digressions felt as thought becoming intensely nothing more significant than the demonstration that from a buggered motif could be composed a line of thinking, of which mimes and fictions make as much sense as needed to express the writer's extra-being as a semblance of a thought in the making of an occasion of experience that, by any other name, is thought in the act of its own contemplation of refusing to know in advance what it can do to give its form of doing the appearance of not doing anything more involved than spinning yarns about bugs and mimes and animals that give expression to a little something extra whose value is worth as much as a completely unnecessary if not entirely unfunny joke.

Four

EX POST FACTO EX ANTE (OR, IT'S ALL IN THE SETUP. . . .)

Okay, how about this: "Two cannibals were eating a clown. One of them turns to the other and asks, 'Does this taste funny to you?'"

It's all in the setup, I say to myself.

Now what's that? Ah, coffee's ready. I'm glad of the intrusion because, you see, I have trouble exiting my daydreams. Of course, we all like to fantasize about what life actually isn't, but there's something about the counterfactual matrix of people, places, and events that I really like. I mean, I *really* like it. I've been told that this fondness for gathering wool, for collecting stray thoughts plucked from the psychic fleece of my shaggy mind, is a condition. My daydreams are maladaptive.[1] Because I can't help but lose myself in thoughts like a friend suggesting, as he poured me a cup, that coffee could be the foundation for an ontology, an idea that took hold in the Harvard philosophy department around the time William James was "meaning" Memorial Hall and having conjunctive experiences of sameness and fulfilled intention but that ultimately was abandoned as a serious metaphysical pursuit when the Brazilian government between 1931 and 1934 attempted to valorize its coffee monopoly by immolating approximately 26.6 million bags of the stuff, only to be rekindled one afternoon by a friend suggesting, as he poured me a cup . . .

Lost, kind of like that . . . Now, okay . . . Where was I? Ah yes, my coffee.

But no, before that. Right—I was thinking about a joke and how its setup requires you to hear it as such only after the fact. Like rumors. Like the furnace-heated air swirling around my ankles sounds as it spills onto the kitchen floor from a dust-coated vent in the wall: a thousand little whispers. A pure language of noise whose semblance of truth is grasped only when it's mistaken as such.

But now that I'm on about this sibilous din of plosives and continuants, it strikes me that whispers and rumors pulse and surge in exactly the way that facts don't. Rumors—they're more like flames: seemingly nothing, flickering in and out of existence, yet they burn nevertheless. No wonder Gaston Bachelard thought that fire could be psychoanalyzed (or, more precisely, that "our convictions about fire" could be).[2] Like every other hormone of the imagination, fire is poetry first and foremost, a sheer myth-complex whose sparks are seeds, whose movement is dance. Fire is a chemical reaction only when we're at our most *un*lyrical. So it's no surprise that these reveries of fire and therapy are chilling me, so much so that I'm actually (or figuratively?) getting a shiver down my spine.

Some call this shivering feeling "frisson." Some also call frisson by the more lurid expression "skin orgasm." I don't. It hasn't really stuck (the term, that is). Maybe that's because "skin orgasm" is just too on the nose. Or maybe we're not prepared to grant that orgasms might happen outside of capital sex. Can you imagine an orgasm running up your spine? Better just to use the more alien "frisson," I suppose. Its pleasant tingling feeling or emotional thrill doesn't make us think what an orgasm makes us think—which, ideally, is nothing. But this idea of thinking nothing is now maybe a little ironic, given that so-called thinking off has become a new form of sex, and because a skin orgasm is itself thought incarnate—a veritable thinking of the skin.[3]

And this would make frisson a thought that moves: it edges down my spine, spreads across my arms, climbs up my neck, and pushes through my scalp. Sometimes it even pulses. Like an orgasm. Frisson has a rhythm, in other words. Like a song stuck in my head. I mean the expression "song stuck in my head." *It* has a rhythm. But I suppose the thought does, too. The stuck song, that is. Actually, I suspect that thinking in general has a rhythm, then. Virginia Woolf thought so. "I am writing to a rhythm and not to a plot," she wrote (1981, 204). But she must have thought this as well. I've also tried to think a rhythm: "Now we are safe . . . Now you trail away . . . Now you lag . . . Now they have all gone . . . Now the cock crows like a spurt of hard, red water in the white tide . . . Now we must drop our toys . . . Now they suck their pens . . . They wag their tails; they flick their tails; they move through the air in flocks, now this way, now that way, moving all together, now dividing, now coming together . . . Now the terror is beginning . . . Now I cannot sink . . . Now grass and trees . . . Now the tide sinks . . . Now my body thaws . . . Now we are off . . . Now I hang suspended without attachments. We are nowhere."

These are bits I filched from Woolf's *The Waves* for *Ludic Dreaming*.[4] The former is amazingly festooned with all types of nows that Woolf makes exotic. The latter's nows, my nows, however, are not at all exotic. They're completely ordinary. In fact, they're what you might call infra-ordinary. My nows are endotic nows, the kind that Georges Perec would find infra-ordinary or exceptionally unexceptional.[5] Either way, it still seems that where there is rhythm there are no wrong words, bucket.

But that rhythm makes sense of things, that it is an "answer to chaos," as I've heard it said, isn't especially insightful—especially because my nows are merely an abstraction of Woolf's.[6] Which is to say, an abstraction of the rhythm of *The Waves*. Which is curious, because *The Waves* is itself an abstraction of the rhythm of the waves. Which is even more curious, since the waves—the spumey and spindrifty kind—are abstractions of tidal and atmospheric variations.

Rhythm, it seems, is an abstraction all the way down.

And strangely concrete, too, for the reason that its variability composes the consistency of a world in continuous change. It's also utterly synthetic. Artificial. It's why we hear "tick tock" and not "tick tick." Rhythm is why a sequence of follicular erections along my back is a shiver and not a pinch.

But then there's that song stuck in my head. It doesn't tick tock, and it doesn't shiver either. It doesn't even really begin or end. Its comings are as unnoticed as its goings, which is to say that it doesn't really have a rhythm. It also doesn't really do anything.

But what should it do? Isn't all thought essentially a nothing doing, a kind of doing that doesn't really matter?

> Thoughts are ephemeral, they evaporate in the moment they occur, unless they are given action and material form. Wishes and intentions, the same. Meaningless, unless they impel you to one choice or another, some deed or course of action, however insignificant. Thoughts that lead to action can be dangerous. Thoughts that do not, mean less than nothing. (Leckie 2013, chap. 16)

This is a thought that Ann Leckie had. Or, more accurately, it's a thought that the synthetically intelligent troop carrier *Justice of Toren*'s sole surviving ancillary, One Esk Nineteen, had in Leckie's sci-fi novel *Ancillary Justice*.[7] As a single segment of *Justice of Toren*'s ancillary, which is a unit of twenty human bodies that each possess *Justice of Toren*'s entire consciousness, One Esk Nineteen (also named Breq) thinks that a thought is nothing unless an effect can be deduced from its being had—however insignificant.

A song stuck in my head must be even less than nothing, then, because its being had again and again suggests that its being had the first time amounted to nothing. That is, unless the mere fact that a thought about a song follows a previous thought about the same song can be thought to have quasi-caused the condition of being stuck. But if this is so, then it's only so ex post facto—after the fact. And this would mean that being stuck is not actually a fact but an event, a variability that a series of listening-like thoughts makes felt as the sense of being stuck. In other words: like a law or a rule, being stuck doesn't happen so much as it gets expressed. Which is probably why it's so difficult to shake the feeling that thought without deed or course of action is still causally efficacious.

For instance, that my thoughts of daydreams and rumors led to thoughts of flames and psychoanalysis, which in turn gave rise to the idea of a chilling fire, shivers down my back, and songs stuck in my head, obviously substantiates a causal sequence. But there's nothing about this sequence to suggest that it develops according to any rule or law—strict or nonstrict. Yet the mere exhibition of causal efficacy is often enough to express the semblance of a law. And as we know, a semblance of law or truth is good enough if, as William James says, you can ride it "into satisfactory relations with other parts of . . . experience" (2000, 30).

Honestly, who wouldn't be seduced by the truth-value of "if not *q*, then not *p*"? This is a counterfactual truth, but it's a truth nevertheless. Which is why life understood backward, as Søren Kierkegaard said (2008, 179), is *always* true. Which means that, lived forward, life is *never* true. Which is not to say that it's false but that it's exempt from having to be either true or false. Or obliged to deal with facts, for that matter, since facts are a matter of understanding. Sounds great, yes? A life of absolute becoming that is less a form of facts than a chemistry of concepts and sensations is a marvelous idea.[8] But it's really difficult to actually live such a life because, like it or not, we're symbol-mongering creatures who without at least the air of truth will choke on life's sheer happenstance.

Understanding, therefore, breathes life into life not by making it true but by sparing it from being lived accidentally.

But, then again, who has ever lived who has not understood? Understanding *is* a kind of living. It's a mode of life, one lived *ex post facto ex ante*—after the fact in anticipation.[9] What else could it be? Call this mode of life "knowing," or, better yet, call it "make-believe." Either way, what's lived as understanding is an abstraction. Like a melody. Which is kind of a lie, or, as Bachelard says, a "temporal perfidy": "While it promised us development, it keeps us firmly within a state. It takes us back to its beginning and in doing so, gives us the impression that we ought to have predicted where it was going" (2000, 123).

But it's only *kind of* a lie. A lie is born from truth, is cradled in a fact from which it strays. A melody, however, doesn't have a source at all but invents one as it happens, determining, as it transpires, the form of which it is the expression. Melody's perfidy is in this respect the semblance of a lie.

I suppose this means, then, that knowing what one is doing, if it's like a melody, is kind of a way of lying to one's self—for what is knowing but a semblance of certainty, a condition of preempted happenstance whereby statements of fact give the impression that what one thinks is expressive of the sense it makes? If I knew what I was doing when I wrote this, for instance, what I was thinking about as I plotted one idea after the other, I should have led you to believe that this is what I meant to mean all along. Yet here I am, at the end of it, no longer in a state, and I'm pretty sure I haven't fooled anyone (especially me), which is the best I can do since it's all in the setup:

Two clowns were eating a cannibal. One turns to the other and says, "I think we're telling this joke wrong."[10]

Five

DO EARWORMS HAVE DAYDREAMS?

It has been suggested that a lack of sleep leads to an increase in mind-wandering.[1] But it has also been suggested that mind-wandering leads to a lack of sleep.[2] These studies, of course, are correlational rather than causal, but if they did reveal a causality, it would probably be a circular one, virtuous or vicious depending on one's perspective. Regardless of which comes first, in both cases the connection is suggestive of how certain of life's apparently stable weaves—being asleep and being awake—seem to be coming undone. Insomnia, for instance, holds us at the border of sleep, where the extinction of being and its dimensioned world of things and concerns gets dragged along the asymptotic course of a night that never completely falls. And the wandering mind, tarrying with our sense of intentionality, projects a flicker of agency usually found only on the dream side of sleep.

From the perspective of sleep studies and the emerging sleep industry with its proliferation of devices and smartphone apps designed to induce, track, manage, and optimize our nocturnal ways of being, insomnia appears rife with theoretical and practical problems. Metaphysically speaking, insomnia is an oddity, in that it's a state of being determined and affirmed precisely by what it can't be. Pragmatically, however, its ontological status is a lesser concern than the fact that its growing frequency impinges not only on a person's psychic well-being but on the general economic and social health of industrialized cultures. In a more critical vein, insomnia can be construed as an alternative form of life arising from the reconfiguration of labor as an activity no longer quarantined to diurnal rhythms. But in spite of insomnia's several conceptual prospects and the practical need for an intervention into its growing frequency, daydreaming, although not entirely unrelated to insomnia, is potentially more important to consider. Unlike insomnia, which already has a chronic profile, daydreaming is just beginning to develop one, which is something quite different from simply not being able to get some shut-eye. This means, I think, that what it means to think is changing.

In this chapter I want to indulge in a reverie on daydreaming. That is, I want to think about—and think by—daydreaming in a way that puts its cognitive refrain to play so that I can say something about its present status that is not objectively but expressively the case. In this I take my cue from Gaston Bachelard, who insists, "It is a non-sense to claim to study imagination objectively." Just as the image of a dancing flame that brings life to shadows "can only be studied through the image, by dreaming images as they gather in reverie" (Bachelard 1969, 53), daydreaming, I suggest, can't be studied without doing it. For instance, while an exothermic redox chemical reaction perfectly explains what a flame is as a physical event, it explains nothing about a flame as something that elicits stories from people when they gather around it, or about the sense of safety that its brightness brings on a dark and stormy night, or about the way its flickering intensity lends itself to metaphors of dancing, sexuality, and vital activity in general. These descriptions say little about the act of combustion, but they are no less expressive of what a flame is. As such, these images, these poetic re/presentations, show how the understanding of a flame isn't exhausted by a disinterested breakdown of its chemical transformations. They also show how the lyrical impulse integral to their advent isn't an encumbrance to understanding but, as Bachelard puts it, indicates how "one really receives the image only if one *admires* it" (53; my emphasis). A reverie on daydreaming is, then, a way of admiring its image—or, rather, its images—by mimicking its refrain. Others can ask after the brain states that correlate with daydreams or the psychological laws that govern (or not) its flow, but I'm going to dwell in the duality of its wanderings that make it both a dissociative and an absorptive affair and to linger over how its drifts and divagations are becoming compulsive and contagious.

The kind of reverie I have in mind, however, is not the kind associated with absentmindedness but the active sort that Bachelard calls "poetic reverie." For Bachelard, daydreams are those spontaneous and involuntary moments when, to quote Samuel Beckett, the mind is no longer "on the alert against itself" (1995, 157). A daydream, in other words, is where the mind goes to get lost; reverie, however, is where the mind finds itself. Unlike a daydreamer who loses her mind over and over again, "the dreamer of reveries . . . is able to formulate a *cogito* at the center of his dreaming-I" (Bachelard 1969, 129). In other words, reverie is not "a mind vacuum" (64) but "an oneiric activity in which a glimmer of consciousness subsists" (150). It is where the poetizing I intervenes and begins the hard, creative work of valorizing being and multiplying its images, of expressing reality by freeing it/me from "immediate images and *chang*[*ing*] them" (Bachelard 1988a, 129) into an *unreality*. Thus, waking consciousness is never entirely without its oneiric fringe, and because of this it is always partly dreaming about itself. Just as one can sing a song about a song, valuing and varying its images and refrains with new refrains and new images, so, too, can a dreamer of reveries dream about daydreaming and raise the refrain's digression to the status of being. That said, I have no intention of observing Bachelard's distinction between daydreaming and reverie with any sort of strictness. To quote Steven Connor (2008), who says something similar about thinking and objects, I will "mix my usages promiscuously, as the demands of my argument, or of alliteration, dictate."[3]

ABOUT THAT SONG ABOUT A SONG . . .

Imagine a work of music that makes daydreaming a part of its realization. All music does this, I think. But not all music does it in a way that affirms distraction and digression as an expressive element. When music is presented as an object for aesthetic contemplation, for example, daydreaming is often treated as something to be banished from its performance and reception. But in practice this is rarely achieved. In practice, all musical events are, to some degree, infused with thoughts that happen to the side, to the side where execution and hearing shade into memory and desire. However, for daydreaming to directly and intentionally belong to the musical event, for it to resonate with a set of structural relations and become a part of the work's lived abstraction—which is to say, for daydreaming to participate in what Susanne Langer (1953) calls its semblance of lived time—it would have to meet certain conditions. What would these be? Well, it's difficult to say in advance, because there's no set of rules or discrete sequences of action that will ensure that the tendency for a mind to wander contributes to the way the music's parts hang together. In fact, it seems impossible that what is by definition a digression could do anything other than cleave a perceptual whole into disparate parts. But "cleave" has two senses, and there are strategies and tactics that one could speculate might make a phrenic detour cleave to the musical semblance. For the most part, these performative devices will trade in paradox, but there's nothing saying paradox can't be played.

So how might this music go? It might go many ways, but one way it would almost certainly go is slowly. Nothing gets the mind going like waiting for the next thing to happen. But it also would probably be long, because if it's true that we spend at least half our waking time daydreaming (Killingsworth and Gilbert 2010), then we'd want to at least double the time we wait for the next thing to happen. That way we'd be sure to lose attention exactly as often as we focus it. Let's say this music would last for about two hours. But being long isn't itself sufficient. People routinely sit through three-hour operas and ninety-minute symphonies like Gustav Mahler's *Symphony No. 3* (1896). Max Richter's *Sleep* (2015) is long. It's eight hours, and people seem to enjoy it. But the dreaming that it provokes is the kind one has while slumbering soundly. (Richter wrote the piece as a lullaby and intended it to be listened to while asleep.) Maybe this work would be little more than a single melody, a winding and aimless thread with only the occasional suggestion of harmony or counterpoint to thicken the weave. This melody wouldn't be entirely without character, however; it'd probably be modal and notated in a way that would belie its complexity to ensure that its integrity remains obscure and that nothing but expressive difference returns. Not the difference of repetition but a difference that differs from itself. A schizogenic or expressive difference that makes variations rather than themes of an anfractuous lyricism. Importantly, in performing this languorous air, the musicians would have to be encouraged not to simply play what's written but asked (confusingly? ironically? inexplicably?) to "unplay" it. How they might go about unplaying a work would be awkward, but it might involve asking performers to commit to their idiosyncrasies and play away from what's given. The melody that's (un)played would, then, not sound like what the melody for which it stands would sound like. Weird.

Divaricating instructions like these would, in effect, pull the work in two directions at once. The performers would be at odds and in agreement with themselves and each other as they collectively use the same material to exercise their will to differ. The stylistic logics of "playing toward" and "playing away," conforming to or deviating from this arche-melody, would, then, infuse every gesture and every attempt to playfully unplay the music with an ambivalence that makes it difficult to discern which logic is in play at any given moment. Like animal play, wherein the senses of combat and game "twist together in reciprocal presupposition" (Massumi 2014, 22), these musical logics would become "performatively fused, without becoming confused" (6). But where animal play invents and trifles with the difference between a nip and a bite to give creatures the "capacity to mobilize the possible" (8), the play of this work would contrive an event that gives the performers the capacity to mobilize the unachievable. In unplaying the melody, the "played upon area of activity" of pitches and rhythms is not only presented "in the mode of possibility" (5, 6), as actual combat is presented to its stylized analogue, but suggested in the mode of *impossibility*. What can't be done—an unperformance—would be, paradoxically, directly embodied in action, so the undoing of the melody would be a type of "*enactive cartography*," a cartography that doesn't simply conform "to the given contours of the dynamic form it draws"—the melody—but "prolongs the gestural lines with which it draws the lived map of the given form" (23).

In other words, unplaying this music would mean improvising on the given form to create the territory *as it maps it*. Committing to one's idiosyncrasies would be key to executing such a cartography, but not just because it activates those "stylistic extras and excesses that introduce the never-seen-before" (23). Because idiosyncrasies concern capacities, and capacities are equally determined by inability, one cannot but commit to one's incapacities as well. Thus, a lack of sight-reading skills, or dodgy intonation, or an inability to interpret complexly notated passages would also be assimilated to the performance and its capacities, as would one's powers of concentration—*or lack thereof*. For a music that would make daydreaming a part of its play, the capacity for the mind to wander from the task at hand—to lose focus from its present commission—

would be a musical asset. Even more than performative tics or stylistic mannerisms, the decoupling of attention from outward perception inevitably arising as one's interest in the material wanes would activate the paradox of doing the undoing of the music.

Yet daydreaming as music would manifest very differently for those (un)playing the melody than it would for those listening to it. For the performers, their daydreaming would have an indirect sonic effect that effectively expressed the contours of digression. Even if that contour is technically silent, it would still inform the situation with an imaginary departure that puts the esoteric plasticity of the melodic ideal virtually onstage. Each articulation of the melody would, in other words, carry "a double charge of reality," for the undoing being done would be "infused with what *would* be doing" (Massumi 2014, 8–9; my emphasis). The listener's reverie, although it wouldn't actively impinge on the melodic play, would carry out its own crypto-oneiric performance. Listening to this slow-moving, possibly impossible melody would involve not only hearing the actual passage of tones but also, strangely, hearing what isn't actually played as well. That is, part of what might be included in listening to a musical brown study would be, in a sense, hallucinated—or, more positively, imagined. This means that the distraction spans of the listeners' and the performers' respective reveries, along with their spans of attention, would form a counterpoint of immanent a/sides.[4]

***Portrait d'un philosophe*: Gaston Bachelard (1961)**
Directed by Hubert Knapp
Interviewer: Jean-Claude Bringuier
INA.fr, December 1, 1961, https://www.ina.fr/video/CAF89004641
[01:19 – 02:00. Transcribed and translated from the French.]

JEAN-CLAUDE BRINGUIER: When we arrived, you were listening to the radio. How interested are you in the news?

GASTON BACHELARD: It seems essential to me. My daughter bought me a transistor radio, and I take in all the newsflashes from 7 A.M. to 9 P.M. Every hour.

JEAN-CLAUDE: Why?

GASTON BACHELARD: Because for three minutes, I feel like the world is spinning around me, that the world is bringing in news of the universe. It's perfect.

In his book *The Poetics of Reverie*, Bachelard celebrates the emergence of an era of the free imagination and the advent of a new poetisphere. "From everywhere," he writes, "images invade the air, go from one world to another, and call both ears and eyes to enlarged dreams" (1969, 25). How could a philosopher of the imagination see in the swarm of electromechanical imagery anything but an outbreak of dreams? Given his position that images are sparks that set fire to the real as it's given, melting down first impressions to forge second, imaginary, ones, it follows that a luxuriance of images would, for Bachelard, indeed yield a plurality of occasions to dream. However, as much as he sees the imagination as a force by which *all* humans live a more real reality, it's only for those practiced in the art of reverie that images might, as he says, "spring from a simple brochure" (25)—or, to be more current, a pop-up ad. Maybe this is all that he meant when he announced the arrival of a new poetisphere: those who have a knack for dreaming the dynamism of substance will indeed find themselves "animated by new imagery" (25). But if he meant that a surfeit of imagery would be cause to make dreamer-poets of us all, things get a little more complicated—because he'd be right and not right.

PRESQUE RÊVÉ

How like a plague do dreams spread what is not—
Might-haves and maybes, of life lived otherwise.
—'NONYMOUS

How could an outbreak of images lead to anything but a plague of dreams? If images do invade the air and spread from one world to another, then they are like vectors of an oneiric contagion rather than heralds of a poetic age. Bachelard was right in that respect. We are all made dreamers because the "flare up of being in the imagination" (1964a, xiv) can't help but solicit our attention and tug at our reflex to transform perception into conception. But for that same reason, Bachelard was wrong. A swarm of images does not a plague make, for attention is nothing apart from the "adventure in perception" (Bachelard 2002, 3) that has to be given time to progress from the bare fact of change it indicates. As Brian Massumi notes, "Attention is the base-state habit of perception" and little more than an automatism "tagging a change in the perceptual field as new and potentially important" (2015, 65). What matters, for taking action and for taking leave of perception's simple givenness—that is, for dreaming and for what is called experience—is the awareness that gathers itself and the tonalities of becoming around that tagged change. This means that attention qua attention is not a sufficient condition for reverie. Yet, because attention is what pulls an already-established awareness into its next potential perception, when sequenced rapidly over and over again and across a variety of sensory modalities (which is arguably the central way in which media-saturated societies conduct themselves) the perception of this next potential perception becomes the dominant way in which each dawning awareness takes account of itself. The perceived effect of perceiving over and over again perception's next potential perception is disorienting, but it's also *hyperorienting*. For every tag in the perceptual field places the percipient at the center of an event's just beginning to stir and always already infuses her with the sense of what's possibly about to come. Langer (1953) argues that artists experience something similar when they're in the middle of creating a work. Every compositional gesture made by an artist during the act of creation is guided by a commanding form, or what might be described as a sensitivity to the possible forms of expression afforded by a material worked by a person with just this technique in just this particular way. Attuned to this command, an artist can be said to be hyperoriented to the immediately ongoing potential ways that a work might (or might not) come to expression. But, strangely, this peculiar hyperorienting tendency found in the creative act is also found in dreams. In her discussion of film's likeness to dreaming, Langer observes:

> The most noteworthy formal characteristic of a dream is that the dreamer is always at the centre of it. Places shift, persons act and speak, or change or fade—facts emerge, situations grow, objects come into view with strange importance, ordinary things infinitely valuable or horrible, and they may be superseded by others that are

> related to them essentially by feeling, not by natural proximity. But the dreamer is always "there," his relation is, so to speak, equidistant from all events. Things may occur around him or unroll before his eyes; he may act or want to act, or suffer or contemplate; but the *immediacy* of everything in a dream is the same for him. (1953, 413)

So, if a proliferation of attention-seeking tags fixates awareness on the perception of the perception of the next potential perception, then maybe the images that "invade the air and spread from one world to another," one after the other after the other, make us *almost* dream. Such a world would be, like Bachelard's, a world spinning around us. But instead of bringing in news of the universe, this world would just be distracting.

DISTRACTION'S NEW CLOTHES

But is distraction really so bad? Or does it at least have a workable stand-in? Continuous partial attention and multitasking, for example, are two contemporary deputies. N. Katherine Hayles has proposed distraction as a new cognitive style that is characterized by our tendency toward "switching focus rapidly among different tasks, preferring multiple information streams, seeking a high level of stimulation, and having a low tolerance for boredom" (2007, 187). Elie During (2010), too, has suggested that distraction might be understood to describe the way attention has become a distributed affair coordinated by communication media that articulate a technologically specious present. Even my own theory of aesthetic failure (Priest 2013) sees distraction functioning as an expressive technique in experimental music, where listening away becomes productive of aesthetic experience. A more historical example of a depathologized distraction might be Walter Benjamin's take on it as simply an alternative mode of attention. In the early days of cinema and the acceleration of industrialized city life, Benjamin was already inventing an alibi for the attenuation of the contemplative life, arguing that urban living and mechanical reproduction promoted a form of awareness that was less concentrated and much more reliant on apperceptive skills. Modern living, he wrote, "requires no attention" (1968, 241) and involves cognitive, nervous, and somatic processes that often occur to the side of other activities and without mindful direction. These autonomic processes, which for him were exercised specifically and in novel ways by photography and cinema, do not properly designate an inability to concentrate but instead suggest a capacity for "openness to contingency and happenstance [and possibly] a penchant for the diffuse and dispersed" (Gilloch 2007, 123). In this way, distraction describes not an absentmindedness but a form of attention that shows itself in the way it brings the otherwise-occulted refrains of daily living to a more reflexive (if not entirely conscious) register of awareness. Interestingly, this semiconscious way of taking "in the smallest things, meaningful yet covert enough to find a hiding place in waking dreams" (Benjamin 1979, 243), makes Benjamin's distraction sound a lot like daydreaming.

And daydreaming isn't so bad, is it? Well, it depends on who you ask. Traditionally regarded as wasteful and insalubrious, daydreaming has recently begun to acquire a much healthier reputation, but not because something fundamental has changed about the way we do it. The makeover of daydreaming owes much of its contemporary rehabilitation not to the literary works of James Joyce, Virginia Woolf, and Marcel Proust, nor to the critical interventions of Sigmund Freud, William James, or Bachelard, but to the way brain-imaging technologies have shown the existence of a neural network that is active when the organ is said to be "at rest" and "untasked."[5] Although Jerome Singer had proposed as early as 1966 that daydreaming might be a constructive activity, and Eric Klinger in 1971 suggested that spontaneous or perceptually decoupled thought might form a baseline state of mental activity, it's largely been in response to the discovery at the turn of the twenty-first century of a so-called default mode network that daydreaming has been reimagined as not only a legitimate domain of study but an indispensable activity for the constitution and maintenance of what we recognize as a self. A host of studies since the confirmation of the default mode network have in the past fifteen years sought to show how mind-wandering is linked to creativity and improved productivity.[6] Yet, while these correlations between brain functions and mental states are being affirmed and leveraged in ways that appear to redeem daydreaming—and, in a sense, give distraction a brand-new set of neurodynamic and adaptive clothes—they provoke a host of other questions regarding the role that unguided thought plays in contemporary culture. For instance: How does the valorization of daydreaming intersect with the problematic emergence of distraction as an experiential norm? Does absentmindedness really contribute to mental well-being? Can reverie be an art? Who decides what thoughts count as unguided or spontaneous? Is there a politics of daydreaming? An ethics? And how is it that all this interest in daydreaming comes at a moment when we seem to have so much less time to do it? And yet, what happens when we do have too much time on our hands? Or, more startlingly: How come daydreaming's new wardrobe also includes pathological attire?

Everybody daydreams. Or, as William James was said to say, everyone from time to time is present-minded elsewhere.[7] James suggested:

> Most people probably fall several times a day into a fit of something like this: The eyes are fixed on vacancy, the sounds of the world melt into confused unity, the attention is dispersed so that the whole body is felt, as it were, at once, and the foreground of consciousness is filled, if by anything, by a sort of solemn sense of surrender to the empty passing of time. In the dim background of our mind we know meanwhile what we ought to be doing: getting up, dressing ourselves, answering the person who has spoken to us, trying to make the next step in our reasoning. . . . Every moment we expect the spell to break, for we know no reason why it should continue. But it does continue, pulse after pulse, and we float with it, until also without reason that we can discover an energy is given, something we know not what enables us to gather ourselves together, we wink our eyes, we shake our heads, the background-ideas become effective, and the wheels of life go round again. (1950, 404)

Half our thoughts, it turns out, turn us into daydreamers of a sort. But we always return from these inward turnings, if not a little refreshed, then at the very least somewhat reacquainted with that part of ourselves where might-haves and maybes are the dominant ontological class. But not everyone returns, apparently. For some, daydreaming isn't, as Bachelard proposed, "the gift of an hour which knows the plenitude of the soul" (1969, 64). For some, daydreaming is an addiction.

MALADAPTIVE DAYDREAMING

Now that ADHD (attention deficit hyperactivity disorder) and its subtypes have found a home in the *Diagnostic and Statistical Manual of Mental Disorders*, an "extensive fantasy activity that replaces human interaction and/or interferes with academic, interpersonal or vocational functioning" (Somer 2002, 199) is vying to become our culture's next great cognitive cock-up. In a 2002 study, Eli Somer gave this extensive fantasy activity the name "maladaptive daydreaming" (MD), to distinguish the chronic pursuit of highly structured imaginary refrains that are almost always accompanied by a stereotypic movement from the more fleeting pastime of woolgathering, as well as from other dissociative conditions like narcissistic and fantasy-prone personality disorders. The etiology of MD isn't clear, but there are studies on stereotypic movement disorder—repetitive, coordinated, and rhythmic behaviors—that show a correlation between such activities and fantasizing, suggesting that MD might begin in early childhood.[8] And while several of its symptoms resemble those of dissociative and obsessive-compulsive conditions, many MDers report a yearning or craving to daydream, a fact that suggests it's much closer to the kind of psychological addiction that chronic gamblers suffer.[9] That said, MD isn't yet a classified mental disorder, but it is a bona fide discursive construct that has given rise to not only several clinical studies and popular media articles but a host of online discussion forums.[10] So even though it took ADHD about seventy years to differentiate itself from simply being constantly "all wind and piss like a tanyard cat" (Joyce 2000, 425), and then another thirty to become a handy cultural index for a society whose expressions of thought look more like distraction than contemplation, because things move more swiftly these days, with luck (and more internet traffic) MD will develop a robust research history, earn a few pages in a future edition of the *Diagnostic and Statistical Manual*, invent a recommended form of treatment (one that includes both therapy and pharmacological intervention, of course), and thereby have a good shot at becoming the twenty-first century's favorite inner affliction.

But what if we're always already addicted to building castles in the sky? What if we're naturally excessive daydreamers—not literally but technically and speculatively? If we take the position that the carryings-on we call "mind" are not the happenings of the glassy essence that Shakespeare showed us angels make fun of but rather a way of talking about sheer appearances, of which only *some* are amenable to discipline and control, then excessive fantasizing can be seen as part of everyday living and everyday thinking.[11] But to do this, to be speculative and technical about it, we have to understand thinking as a semblance.

IT'S NOT WHAT YOU THINK THINKING IS

We might call thinking a semblance if we extend the definition of "semblance" to include in perception's remit not just sense impressions but abstractions. Langer's formulation of semblance admits just as much when she argues, "Everything has an aspect of appearance. Even so nonsensuous a thing as a fact or a possibility *appears* this way to one person and that way to another" (1953, 49). For her, a semblance is not just a mere image, and it's definitely not a mirror image. Although examples of images, she writes, tend to come from "the looking-glass world that gives us a visible copy of the things opposite the mirror without a tactual or other sensory replica of them" (48), they are more precisely abstractable patterns of experience that, in their abstraction, lend themselves to the kinds of schematic processes that go by the name "thinking."[12]

They go by the way of thinking because a process of abstraction is, in a sense, a process of dissociation. For Langer, this is what gives artworks, or pure appearances like rainbows, "a peculiar air of 'otherness'" (1953, 46). But, for Massumi, who expands on Langer's concept of semblance, this is also what gives everyday experience its qualitative "'uncanny' moreness" (2011, 46). For him, a semblance is "a kind of perception of the event of perception in the perception" (44). And this perception of perception is experienced not as a sensation, or even a perception as such, but as something that its event is *like*. The likening of an event is a way of taking direct account of an event's own potential, without recourse to any particular sensory input. Where the effect of this likening is made intense and used entirely for its own satisfaction, we call it "art." But where it's also intense, yet used for other purposes than its own enjoyment, we call it "thinking." Everyday experience is also composed of likenesses, but its techniques of existence are such that what is felt abstractly—a semblance—is lost in the use we make of its likeness to map forms of experience to conceptual structures. In other words, whereas an artwork's semblance is made to haunt its conditions of emergence in such a way that we can't help but think-feel it as a strange doubling of the event itself, an everyday semblance has a way of neglecting its conditions so that it can be taken as just thought.

Perhaps it's because an event never resembles its conditions of emergence that the event of the perception of the event of perception naturally takes a distance from itself and thereby lends its semblance to being taken as something other than what it is. What is called thinking or "mind" is in this way like a rainbow—"apart from its appearance it has no cohesion" (Langer 1953, 49). We talk about mind as though it were a substance, when in fact we are talking about semblances that are felt as thought. Art exploits the semblance of semblance, to aesthetic effect, while what we take to be thought exploits the dissemblance of semblance, to cognitive effect. Our glassy essence is, then, the product of a vitrescent complex, which means that all thinking needs therapy. Or maybe it just means that we need more metaphors.

TO WANT TO BE A METAPHOR

"I'm fine with metaphors, I just don't think that everything is one."

Have you ever heard anything so true? I don't mean correct. I mean something that's so well aimed and on the mark. A colleague and friend said this during a panel he and I were on back in 2017. I don't remember what exactly he was talking about when he said it—I was almost certainly ruminating about something while he was delivering his paper—but these words, their sentiment and step and the way they bring thought to rest in a sense they only seem to make, have stuck with me.

I wish I'd said that. In fact, I wish I'd've said a lot of things. I wish it had been me who asked, "Is it not first through the voice that one becomes animal?" (Deleuze and Guattari 1987, 4). Or, "I am rooted, but I flow" (Woolf 2004, 66) would have been good, too. I've said this: "The still body is still a body doing" (see *Earworm*, EW10), which is okay, I think. But I can't help but feel that it would have been so much better if it hadn't been me but someone else who'd said it.

Maybe it's because we borrow our desires and aims from others that I think this. Desire in this respect has nothing to do with a need or an appetite, and even less to do with wanting to get a fix on that which others think is wonderful or interesting. Instead, desire is about wanting to be *like* someone who has a desire; one who is, for instance, in love with experimental poetry, or utterly fascinated with Iranian cinema, or even someone who's deeply devoted to a path of asceticism. It's not the objects of desire that matter; things and people are not desire's target—instead, the affections (affectations?) that affirm one's existence are. Desire to be *like* someone is a desire to be existentially qualified. To have a desire is to *be* in some manner or another. From others, then, we learn not simply what to want—we learn to want to want to want something.

So maybe not everything is a metaphor, but maybe everything wants to be one.

It's catchy, no? "To want to be a metaphor" is nearly Shakespearean in tone. And who wouldn't want to be Shakespearean? To be catchy? Nowadays it seems that catchy is exactly what one desires to be. Or maybe it's all that one can hope to be. Which means that the question is no longer to be or not to be; instead, it's how to be said and said again. Like a rumor, whose value lies in its being passed along rather than its being true, going viral is what matters.

But the metaphor of contagion is itself oddly contagious. Because the concept of contagion has from its first uses been equally applicable to moral, affective, and physical processes, its mode of action lends itself to spreading in exactly the manner that it denotes.[13] The metaphor of virality that seems to seize the imagination of academics and media commentators alike every decade or so is as viral as a string of code that hijacks a cell's metabolic machinery. Cognitive, affective, and moral contagions are as literal as biological contagion is, then—or as metaphorical. It's all in the setup: microbes versus examples versus concept. So: a metaphor is a contagion is a metaphor, but it's also the case. Does this mean that a virus is a metaphor? Yes and no.

It's been suggested that the virus "has always functioned as a label for that which cannot be named otherwise, a remainder of the known world, and a reminder of nature's unintelligibility" (Van Loon 2002, 108). In other words, a virus is a kind of nonsense. Any invocation of it is, therefore, metaphorical. Yet, like all metaphors, when said again and again, it is said literally-truthfully. But why? Friedrich Nietzsche insists that our need to mobilize metaphors again and again stems not from a desire for the truth but from "a duty to lie according to a fixed convention, to lie with the herd and in a manner binding upon everyone" (2006, 117). But he also asserts that the truth of metaphors results from their simply getting worn out like a coin that loses its embossing. As such, the nonsense that a virus names over and over again wears itself out to become set in metaphorical stone. That's why language really is a virus. And that's why words can kill—or, maybe, kiss.

CHANGE IS EVERYTHING

In the 1998 novel *Pontypool Changes Everything*, Tony Burgess composes an outbreak narrative that takes the famous metaphor of language as a virus literally. The population of the small Ontario town of Pontypool becomes infected with the *idea* of a virus whose vector is the spoken word—or, more precisely, the *understanding* of spoken words. The symptoms of infection include, first, a form of acute aphasia, and then . . . cannibalistic zombie rage. The name given to the disease is Acquired Meta-Structural Pediculosis (AMPs), and its metaphysical transmission means that it is halted not by a vaccine but by a ban on communication. Supposedly, AMPs had its origins at the dawn of time, which is strangely placed in the middle of the book; however, this particular outbreak has its epicenter in an implosive metaphor that opens the novel:

> Down in the strange hooves of Pontypool's tanning horses scratches one of Ontario's thinnest winds. Cold as a needle and far too complicated to ever leave the ground, these picks of air snap at fetlocks, blackening the legs of horses. The anonymous wind gathers its speed in turns around a cannon bone and tears across the ice of a frozen pool. It feels the behaviour of more famous systems and is consumed by the complexity of its origins, breaking into mad daggers and splintering into the phantoms of horses. These horses, vacancies now, or maybe caskets, are places for the wind to rest. And when a wind rests, its heart stops and it is dead forever. The horses on the ice, built from the corpse of a breeze, skate towards each other, not breathing, but intelligent. They leap inside their crazy minds and begin to make plans. (13)

This opening is both a metaphor of contagion and a case of contagion. As literal hooves are figuratively abraded by a figuratively slim wind that figuratively shatters into a figurative team of ghost horses, the narrative infects itself with tropes that transform the literal diegesis into a metaphorical one, which becomes the literal ground for a new diegesis. By the time the wind dies down, when "its heart stops and it is dead forever," the spectral harem blusters on not as a descriptive device but as a subject of its own. Through this metaphor, increasingly literal undead horses "built from the corpse of a breeze" come together, and come to mind, to plot the plot of the rest of the novel.[14]

That's the novel. But there's the film, too, also written by Burgess but directed by Bruce McDonald. Eleven years after the novel (2008), Burgess mutates the virus into a screenplay. In the book the story focuses largely on the exploits of a mentally ill garbageman turned high school drama teacher, whose psychosis spills across the page *in* and *as* the unbridled figurative language that eats its own tail to undermine the veracity of its telling. The film instead features an AM radio shock jock named Grant Mazzy, who along with his producer, Sydney, and engineer, Laurel Ann, report from their snowed-in radio station on an infection that seems to be turning people into stammering zombies. Like the novel, the people of a small Ontario town named Pontypool experience a language-transmitted plague, and they basically suffer the same fate as their paperbound cousins—trouble with language and zombie rage. But in the film the infection presents itself not as aphasia but as a compulsion to repeat a word or a phrase—over and over and over again. Ultimately, this film plays out a masculinist hero fantasy in which the loathsome Mazzy saves not the day but the woman in distress.

An early scene shows the infection take hold when members from a community theater group staging *Lawrence of Arabia* visit Mazzy's show to sing a number from the play. At the end of the performance, one of the girls—in blackface and dressed as a stereotypical Muslim nomad—says to herself, "I can't remember how it ends. I can't remember how it ends." When Mazzy asks her, "How what ends?" she replies, "It just keeps starting over and over . . . and over and over . . . and it's not called 'The Lawrence and . . . the table' is it? No, not anymore. . . . no, no . . . praah, praah, praah, praah."

Later in the film, we see the sound engineer, Laurel Ann, become infected while she's speaking to Sydney, the producer, as she helps Sydney bandage a cut on her hand that she received a moment before: "I'm going to go see if Mister Mazzy is missing," says Laurel Ann. "Missing . . . missing . . . missing . . . I mean, Mr. Mazzy . . . Mr. Mazzy's missing, I mean, I mean . . . Mr. Mazzy . . . Mr. Mazzy's missing as in case . . . 'he's not here.'" Realizing that something is wrong, Laurel Ann confusedly walks away from Sydney. Immediately after this, we see, over Sydney's shoulder, a man squeezing himself through a window into the radio studio. This man approaches Sydney and shuffles her away from Laurel Ann, who is now standing frozen in her tracks, staring blankly into space and making the whistling sound of a boiling teakettle. When the mystery man (Dr. Mendez), Sydney, and Mazzy are safely locked in the sound booth, Laurel Ann comes to and resumes her confused refrain: "Mr. Mazzy is missing Mazzy . . . No! No, I'm Missy Mazzy and I have to. . . ."

As Laurel Ann approaches the sound booth, Dr. Mendez explains to Mazzy and Sydney: "Your friend is sick. I've seen a lot of this lately. She doesn't know it yet, but . . . she's hunting us."

Cut again to Laurel Ann: "I don't miss Mr. Mazzy. I'm not missing anymore."

(Eventually and inevitably, after trying to break into the sound booth, Laurel Ann succumbs to the virus in a scene that shows her choking on her own bloody vomit.)

As the film approaches its conclusion, Sydney and Mazzy find themselves in a storage room hiding from the townsfolk who were infected by words Mazzy broadcast earlier that day. We see Sydney sitting despondently on the floor, swilling shots of Glenfiddich directly from the bottle, while Mazzy struggles to understand the nature of the contamination. He considers something that Dr. Mendez told him and asks himself:

"Dr. Mendez . . . He said that understanding a word copies the virus. So how do you . . . how do you *not* understand a word? . . . How do you not understand something, something you understand automatically? How do you take, you know, a word . . . How do you make it . . . strange? . . . See, it's *not* understanding that disinfects it . . . If it disinfects it, then how . . . without distorting it, how do you do that?"

> SYDNEY, in her stupor, replies: "You kill the word that's killing you."
>
> MAZZY: "Oh, you kill the word that's killing you . . . That's good! That's good! You repeat it! Yeah, I remember as a kid, I used to, uh . . . I used to repeat words over and over and over again 'til they were incomprehensible?"

As Mazzy speculates on whether the repetition of words is an immune response, Sydney, drunk but clearly struggling to control herself, reiterates: "You have to kill . . ."

Ignoring her, Mazzy discards the idea that repetition sanitizes language, noting that people are still getting sick even after repeating words. (He notices, in other words, that by repeating a word you don't stop making sense, you just stop spreading it.)[15]

"So how do you make it . . . unrecognizable?" Mazzy asks.

> SYDNEY: "Kill . . . kill . . . kill . . . kill . . ."

Seeing that Sydney is now infected, Mazzy desperately tries to get her to stop speaking and then tells her: "Kill isn't kill. Kill isn't kill. Kill isn't kill!"

It sounds like Mazzy, too, is infected, but in fact he's scrambling for a way to make "kill" not mean "kill."

MAZZY: "Alright . . . 'Kill' is 'blue'! 'Kill' is 'wonderful'! 'Kill' is . . . 'Kill' is 'loving'! 'Kill' is the . . . 'Kill' is 'baby'! 'Kill' is the . . . 'Kill' is 'Manet's Garden'! . . . 'Kill' is, uh . . . 'beautiful morning'! . . . 'Kill' is 'everything you ever wanted'! . . . 'Kill' is . . . 'Kill' is 'kiss'!"

Suddenly, Sydney stops repeating the word "kill."

Noticing the pause, Mazzy continues: "'Kill' is, uh. . . . . . 'Kill' is . . . 'Kill' is 'kiss' . . . 'Kill' is 'kiss.' 'Kill' is 'kiss'! Is that it? 'Kill' is 'kiss'? 'Kill' is 'kiss.' 'Kill' is 'kiss.' 'Kill . . . is . . . 'kiss.' 'Kill' is 'kiss.' 'Kill' is 'kiss'? 'Kill' is 'kiss.' What is 'kill'?"

SYDNEY: "'Kiss'—(whispered . . .) 'Kill me.'"

KISSING ME SOFTLY WITH THIS SONG

Obviously, you can't literally kill a word. And you can't really change the meaning of a word just by saying that it means something else; language doesn't work that way. I'm with Ludwig Wittgenstein on this: the meaning of a word lies in its being part of an activity, or of a form of life. It's in the placement, too—in the syntax—that words mean, but only partly. Mostly they mean because of the way they're played in a language game, which is a shared set of semiotic rules that make it possible to establish the conditions that make signification possible. Now . . . this idea of a game and play makes me wonder what would have happened if Mazzy had *sung* the phrase "kill is kiss," if he had played language less like a game and more like the instrument that it is. Saying "kill is kiss" over and over again is not unlike singing a song: abstracting from vocal tones and speech impulses an audible form that bears a striking resemblance to the way that feelings go. Birds know this. Whales, too. Even human infants recognize the way that repeated words—"There, there . . ." "Now, now . . ."—cradle a song. Maybe, as a song, "kill is kiss" would have contained the contagion coursing through language in an event that, like an artwork's semblance, goes nowhere. Because isn't it precisely the way of aesthetic events to suspend perception in its own activity, to abstract seeing or hearing—thinking even—from the practical contexts that bind them to action or even being understood? In other words—wouldn't a song make what is felt as a thought felt as feeling?

But maybe singing "kill is kiss" would just metastasize the virus and raise the contagion to a register articulated less by a synthesis of discrete elements and more by "forms of growth and of attenuation, flowing and stowing, conflict and resolution, speed, arrest, terrific excitement, calm, or subtle activation and dreamy lapses" (Langer 1953, 27). This seems perfectly plausible, if by kissing Sydney with a song instead of a repeating word Mazzy would be spreading something of the word's poetry to the stuff of music, the stuff that, "bear[ing] a close logical similarity to the forms of human feeling" (27), makes it felt as a thought she can't help but hear as a feeling being done to her by her own brain. In this way, Mazzy would infect Sydney with just the *semblance* of a virus. But would this mean that she suffers only the semblance of a disease and ultimately meets only the semblance of a death? In other words, would musical contagion just be a metaphor? If so, then a metaphor of what? What's the vehicle? What's the tenor?

Or maybe I've mixed things up. Maybe it's *this* musical metaphor that's contagious, the one I've been floating here that says songs sung softly can kiss me. Or at least I want it to be. Or maybe I want to want it to be, to be. To be or not, I don't mean to be, like that to be said and be said again is what I mean to say, I mean, to be, not to be, or not, I mean, a metaphor, like laughter is contagious. Which is not a metaphor. Or at least it's not clearly not a metaphor because, as noted earlier, contagion's equal sense as material cause and figurative application "unsettles clear distinctions between the literal and the metaphorical." This means that contagion, too, is not clearly not a metaphor, or clearly not *not* a metaphor, for that matter. But it really doesn't matter, does it, so long as what comes next just comes next—until it doesn't.

Notes

INTRODUCTION: EVENT

1 On musical disposition, see Beaman and Williams (2010). On musical features and recency effects, see Jakubowski et al. (2017). On cortical thickness, see Farrugia et al. (2015).

2 See *Earworm*, the flip side of this book.

3 See Brian Kane's (2015) insightful and critical essay that redescribes the so-called ontological turn in sound studies as a form of niche scholarship that generalizes from local metaphysical commitments a broader onto-aesthetic perspective that claims to address "universals concerning the nature of sound, the body, and media" (3).

4 See Somer (2002) as well as Freeman, Soltanifar, and Baer (2010); and Robinson, et al. (2014).

CHAPTER 1. WHAT IT'S LIKE TO THINK LIKE WHAT IT'S LIKE TO THINK LIKE WHAT IT'S LIKE

1 See chapter 2 of *Earworm*.

2 There are actually a number of turkey circles that can be viewed online, but here's the link to the one that I'm thinking about: Eric Campbell, "Turkeys Circle a Dead Cat," video, 0:24, YouTube, March 3, 2017, https://www.youtube.com/watch?v=vbnfCsAIops.

3 More accurately, Langer (1972, 45–102) would say that animals are not motivated by a series of conceptually framed purposes and means as much as they are motivated by a desire to consummate the overall tension of acts that arise intraorganically from situation to situation.

4 I want to be clear that I am sensitive to the fact that, as Derrida (2008) argues, there is no such thing as "animal," but only "giraffe," "wasp," "worm" . . . "virus," etcetera. (And of course within each of those categories there are species of giraffe, wasp, worm, and then individuals, and so on.) Homo sapiens are animals, too, and their appellation "human" is as much a construct as "animal."

That said, I don't think the term "animal" is a necessarily diminishing category, as some might suggest it is, and in this regard I use it respectfully as a way to acknowledge a difference in techniques of existence rather than a difference in status of being. For a sustained and thought-provoking mediation on this issue of writing (about) animals see David Brooks's *Animal Dreaming* (2021).

5 It's important to note that there is an ambiguity in Langer's concept of the art symbol as a symbol of feeling. On the one hand, the art symbol acquires its meaning through its correspondence with patterns of sentience while, on the other, its meaning (import) is a function of the immanent relation of its parts to an organic whole. Although accused by critics of simply misunderstanding the terms of symbolism and semantics (see Nagel 1943), it's arguable that the ambiguity in Langer's sense of the art symbol is a result of the way she understands symbol making to be an embodied process and, thus, a process in which the correspondence of logical form and the internal structure of form can't be easily separated. For a critical interrogation of Langer's (mis)use of the concept of symbol, see Auxier (1997). And for a comprehensive account of the influences that led to Langer's understanding of symbolism, see Chaplin (2021).

6 "Technique of existence" is an expression that Massumi uses to describe a way of doing something that "event-fully effects a fusional mutual inclusion of a heterogeneity of factors in a signature species of semblance" (2011, 143). Anything that exists can be said to possess a technique of existence insofar as a technique of existence is a necessary condition for existence. However, Massumi treats the arts as exemplary techniques of existence, for their execution brings about an abstraction (semblance) that makes the qualitative-relational order of their occasion emphatic.

CHAPTER 2. BEATING A DEAD BEETLE

1 For an insightful study on obsessive-compulsive disorder, Wittgenstein, and performance studies, see Golub (2014).

2 I'm citing the 1958 version by G. E. M. Anscombe here because the translation of §464 is so much better than in the 2009 version, which reads, "What I want to teach is: to pass from unobvious nonsense to obvious nonsense" (141[e]).

3 Gilles Deleuze is well known for insisting that philosophy concerns the invention of concepts. His work, especially his texts that don't focus on a particular thinker, can be seen as nothing if not deliriously devoted to just that. However, as far as I can tell, he doesn't take what he's doing to be a game or play. Although sentences like the one below give every indication that his philosophy is satisfying its ludic impulse, there's a distinct lack of humour, comedy, or even irony that's endemic to the kind of paradox-producing activity Massumi links to Deleuze's own concept of becoming-animal (see Massumi 2014, "Supplement 1"):

> Hence the reversals which constitute Alice's adventures: the reversal of becoming larger and becoming smaller—"which way, which way?"—asks Alice, sensing that it is always in both directions at the same time, so that for once she stays the same, through an optical illusion; the reversal of the day before and the day after, the present always being eluded—"jam tomorrow and jam yesterday—but never jam to-day"; the reversal of more and less: five nights are five times hotter than a single one, "but they must be five times as cold for the same reason"; the reversal of active and passive: "do cats eat bats?" is as good as "do bats eat cats?"; the reversal of cause and effect: to be punished before having committed a fault, to cry before having pricked oneself, to serve before having divided up the servings. (Deleuze 1990, 3)

This is not, however, to say that Deleuze isn't playing philosophy. Clearly he is, especially when he does it with Félix Guattari. The problem (which is less a problem than a matter of emphasis) is that his delivery is a little off, such that his material attracts interpretation rather than laughter and the latter's concomitant affirmation of the force of existence. Then again, the irony that a life-affirming philosophical game should be taken so seriously may itself be Deleuze's way of playing philosophy. But if so, who's playing along? Who's laughing? I don't think the horde of academicians and artists who celebrate in their essays and artist statements the rhizomatic proliferation of anorganic becomings are laughing. And I don't think they're playing along, either. It's more like they're trying to explain a joke. (No, actually it's worse. It's as if they're trying to explain a joke that they haven't actually gotten. Maybe Andrew Culp is playing along. His work in *Dark Deleuze* [2016] certainly shows that he understands the rules of Deleuze's game, if not how to actually play it. I think I'm laughing. But then again, maybe I'm only laughing at my own jokes . . .)

CHAPTER 3. IMPRACTICAL ENTHUSIASM

1 The act concept is Susanne Langer's adaptation of Alfred North Whitehead's "event" to her own biologically grounded theory of mind. Where the latter takes "the event as the ultimate unit of natural occurrence" (Whitehead 1985, 103), Langer sees the act as a "formal unit, or modulus, of living processes" (1967, 288). The act's phase structure underlines how it is "characteristic of living things, though not absolutely peculiar to them" (261). Unlike simple natural events, such as a chemical reaction or the radioactive decay of atoms, which expire when their process has run its course, an act "develop[s] into a self-continuing system of actions proliferating and differentiating in more and more centralized and interdependent ways" (314). Although Whitehead treats events in a similar way, calling the concrescence of actual occasions a process of growing together, for Langer, growing together belongs principally to *living forms*, and even though act-like phenomena, such as the rising and

falling of ocean waves, seem like living forms, they are not. Langer's "act" can be understood, then, as her attempt to create from "the mythical import of [Whitehead's] system which in itself is fantastic" (Langer 1930, 220) a concept adequate to her biological theory of mind. In different, but perhaps more familiar, Deleuzean terms, the act concept might be said to describe the biological rather than physical, chemical, meteorological, or geological refrain of events. For more on the act concept's relationship to Whitehead's metaphysics, see Dryden (1997).

2 Langer conceptualizes rhythm as a force of transformation *and* continuity. In this respect, she sees rhythm as a differential synthesis of acts characterized by "the alternation of tension building up to a crisis, and ebbing away in a graduated course of relaxation whereby a new build-up of tension is prepared and driven to the next crisis, which necessitates the next cadence" (1967, 324). For her, as well as for others like Gaston Bachelard, Alfred North Whitehead, and John Dewey, this sense of rhythm does not specifically denote a periodic sequence so much as a dialectical interdependence between acts that makes them hang together. In other words, repetition is not a necessary element of rhythm. To illustrate this, Langer goes so far as to describe the acts of a cat *running* across a floor and *leaping* onto a table as forming a rhythmic sequence. She writes, "The leap is as rhythmic as the repeated loping movements, although it is a unique element. It need not even terminate the series; if the animal goes on, leaping down again and bounding away, the unrepeated movements may have broken its course, but not the rhythm of its over-all act" (325). As noted, this expanded sense of rhythm is not held by Langer alone. However, it's central to her work in a way that it wasn't for other philosophers of her time, and it is a crucial conceptual element that links her theory of art to her philosophy of mind. More radically, Langer's take on vital rhythm as the symbolically expressed import of an artwork makes mind as the expressed of organic acts into something resembling an aesthetic experience.

3 This is Langer's paraphrase of D'Arcy Thompson's distinction between mere chemical reactions and organic acts. See Langer's "The Great Shift" (1971). See also Thompson's *On Growth and Form* (1992).

4 Peirce invokes the figure of a Strange Intruder in one of the drafts of his 1903 Harvard lectures on pragmatism as a way to articulate how the immediacy of feeling or "pure presentness" describes his concept of firstness and the sense in which this firstness is not something in the mind of a subject but something of the field of experience that constitutes a subject (Peirce 1997, 160). Interestingly, in explaining her concept of semblance, Langer (1953, 50) uses the term "strange guest" to describe the way in which the direct and immediate appearance of an aesthetic quality intrudes into the event that an artwork expresses. Langer's strange guest would seem incompatible with Peirce's Strange Intruder, insofar as the former appears to accept the preexistence of a subject on whom a semblance's characteristic strangeness is visited. However,

if it's understood that a semblance describes a quality of significance from which a perceiving subject is abstracted and whose being is unfolded, then this strangeness is as much an intruder as a guest.

5 Noam Chomsky (1957) composed this now-(in)famous sentence to show a distinction between syntax and semantics and to argue that meaning is not a basis for language's structural potentials. I have little to add to this debate except to point out that sense and meaning are not the same thing. In this respect I follow Gilles Deleuze's argument (1990) that sense is a dimension of propositions separate from denotation or signification. Because of this distinction it can be said that while colorless green ideas sleep furiously might not mean anything, it nevertheless makes sense, a sense that we might find more immediately expressed in the domain of poetry.

6 I poached this sentence from David Markson's *Wittgenstein's Mistress* (1988). You'll find it on page 126.

7 GronLaser, "Hedgehog Gone Crazy! (Running in Circles)," video, 0:15, YouTube, May 24, 2012, https://www.youtube.com/watch?v=UMKd_ZTMLfU.

8 Langer understands nonhuman animals to live in and experience only a world of actionable values. For her, this means that "all the qualities of form, color, shape, sound, warmth, and even smell, by which we would naturally expect [animals] to recognize things, enter into their perceptual acts only as they enter into their overt behavior as values for action" (1972, 55). Like us, nonhuman animals dwell within a world full of smells, colors, shapes, and so on; however, unlike us, they experience these qualities as lures for the completion or continuation of acts in progress rather than as ideas to be thought. The world they perceive is in effect and in value an extension of their organism, a domain of, as Raymond Ruyer (1957) puts it, drawing as Langer does from Ernst Cassirer and Jakob von Uexküll, psychobiological valences. For Langer, these lures for action constitute an animal's psychic domain and have the unequivocal status of mentality. But these lures are not felt as thought. Although they have value, this value is bound to various positive or negative reactions that they evoke or express. Their value is indissociably linked and restricted to such existential affairs as whether a sound or movement is something to be undergone or dealt with. The cockroach may value its circumambulation for the way it continues and affirms the vital rhythm of those acts induced by a constellation of other acts in progress, but it will never, according to Langer, value the geometric shape of its circular crawl for the uses to which it can be put as a carrier of significance and a vehicle for the creation of concepts such as radius, circumference, and diameter, or, even more abstractly, roundness, wholeness, eternity, or perfection. Nonhuman animals don't have the nervous apparatus to *transform* their values into symbols, into "*vehicles for the conception of objects*" (Langer 1942, 60–61). Because they don't feel or experience their values as *mediated* in this way, those values are not felt as thought. Only because human animals recognize and *use* the

images and ideas that their cerebral organ produces in excess as a means of abstracting—or, rather, of expressing and making conceivable—values that have no sensory correlate or existential obligation do they feel their nervous or vital activities *as thought*. Some may argue that since certain nonhuman animals do show symbolic capacities and can arguably experience values that surpass the practical demands of an existential situation, they, too, can think. Maybe so, but given that the symbolic use of gestures by apes and bees—and even the counting of prey by spiders, which indicates a form of symbolic abstraction—is extremely restricted and constrained, their thinking will be exceedingly narrow. (See Cross and Jackson [2017], as well as Japyassú and Laland [2017]). Despite this difference, Langer is in no way endorsing a hierarchy of being. Humans are biologically organized, as any other animal is. It just happens that they're biologically organized in such a way that they've developed a need—as unreflectively felt as hunger is—to symbolize, to extract an expressive value from forms of experience. Ritual, art, language, and even reason are paradigmatic forms in which this need for expression manifests, and as Langer argues, any practical purpose they serve is an *effect* rather than a cause of their growth and development. This emphasis on the impractical roots of human expression is one of Langer's most radical contributions to the study of the origins of language and mind and makes aesthetic experience a foundational register of life rather than a happy side effect. Ironically, while Langer developed this heretical thesis to overturn the zoologically conceived inventory of human needs, from a certain perspective it actually brings humanity and animality into what Brian Massumi calls a "zone of indiscernibility" (2014). Following Gregory Bateson's (1972) analysis of play as enacting a violation of the logical principles underwriting communication, Massumi argues that when animals do something that does not denote what it would otherwise denote, they draw expressive value from their actions in a way that approaches what humans do when they ritualize, tell stories, make art, or prove theorems. However, because animals can only *enact* this form of abstraction, they can't decouple the expressive value from the existential value of the gesture or action through which it's conveyed. That they can nevertheless experience this qualitative difference suggests to Massumi that animals can participate directly and enthusiastically, if not discernibly, in a zone of thought otherwise considered the sole domain of the human animal. Humans, too, participate in this zone of indiscernibility, of course. But according to Massumi, because this zone is characterized by a logic of mutual inclusion in which a difference that makes a difference is experienced as belonging equally to all of the terms and categories that it separates, humans are not activated by it in the way that animals are. For humans, a logic of mutual inclusion entails paradoxes, and paradoxes, Massumi suggests, are aggravating more than they are animating. However, valencing the experience of indiscernibility in this way is probably unhelpful, because in a ritual or an artwork the semblance and the import that its appearance expresses are indiscernible in the same way that a nip and a bite are, yet humans don't necessarily experience "paradoxes of mutual inclusion as a breakdown of their capacity to think" (Massumi 2014, 7). In fact, it could be argued that humans are as activated and as affirming of paradox in rituals and art as animals are when they play. What is the experience of "getting lost" in a novel or "swept away" by a saxophone solo but the lived experience of a paradox? That aside, the important point for Massumi is that in play the supposedly human need to symbolize, to draw expressive value from experience and more fully deploy its life capacities (8), is, at least to some degree, shared by nonhuman animals, and thus, if only in a narrow or preparatory way, so is the capacity to think. Although Massumi's argument might appear to weaken Langer's claim that an expressive need is a characteristically human one, it actually strengthens it, because animal play suggests that the capacity for abstraction that defines symbol making and symbol use is an *animal* capacity and that this capacity is peculiar to the creature that calls itself "human" only because it is a basic and *primary* need. To call symbolization or expression a *human need* is therefore to name the way in which a generic animal power is *integral* to rather than merely contingent on the individuation of the species.

9 ohhhsnaaap, "Mouse Running in Circles," video, 1:33, YouTube, August 5, 2009, https://www.youtube.com/watch?v=ND8jYZ5p9qo. A person in the comment section of this video suggested that the mouse is not diseased or under the control of a parasite, did not have a stroke, but has simply become, or is in the process of becoming, addicted to dizziness. At the time I wrote this footnote, I couldn't find any empirical studies suggesting that this might be the case. Nevertheless, I want to consider this possibility because it runs interference with the knee-jerk conclusion that this creature's behavior is necessarily expressive of a disorder. Of course, I don't know that this mouse *isn't* ill, but I also don't know that it is. Roger Caillois (2001) singled out games of vertigo as a desirable human pursuit, but perhaps animals shouldn't be exempt from this order of activity. This video of a gorilla spinning in circles is convincing: KennyCamacho1, "Spinning Gorilla," video, 0:13, YouTube, September 4, 2009, https://www.youtube.com/watch?v=uBxRLw_YuSw. And so is this one: Chris Maddern, "Gorilla Spinning at Sydney Zoo," video, 1:34, YouTube, September 17, 2009, https://www.youtube.com/watch?v=yktjuY_piLQ. For the record, it's not lost on me that both of these videos show apes making themselves dizzy *in a zoo*.

10 Lyle Montgomery, "Cat Going in Circles," video, 1:55, YouTube, September 25, 2010, https://www.youtube.com/watch?v=f7QSoA3URrQ.

11 "Extra-being" is a concept of Gilles Deleuze's that competes with "the refrain" for his most profound and most obscure. He writes about extra-being most directly in *The Logic of Sense* (1990), where he describes it at times as an "effect," a "problem," an "*aliquid*," an "aspect of sense," the "outer-surface of

Being," and, my favorite, "?-being." Notwithstanding this flock of terms, for Deleuze, extra-being is in essence what a verb or predicate expresses. "Cutting," for instance, is not exactly a thing but a term that expresses a relationship between things—the tip of my finger and the blade of a mandoline, for instance. In this way, cutting is more like an event but only "on the condition that the event is not confused with its spatio-temporal realization in a state of affairs" (22). For Deleuze, the being of cutting is "an attribute which is said of the thing[s]" (21). But as an attribute, it doesn't "merge with the propositions which express it . . . the state of affairs to which it is attributed, or with the things and qualities which realize it" (81). Extra-being, then, is what is sayable about things in some set of circumstances and entails all that has been, will be, and, importantly, *could* be said of anything, including, strangely, those things that could be said to *not* be said of something. Another way to think about this that is more in line with Langer's theory of symbols, a theory that informs so much of this work, is to understand extra-being as what she calls "logical form." For Langer, everything—"propositions, geometric figures, musical compositions, or any other matter" (1930, 87)—has an aspect of appearance, by which she means "*the way its parts are put together*" (87). How something is put together is its form, and this refers essentially to a being of relation, a structure rather than a substance. In this respect, form inheres in structural relations that are logical to the extent that they can be "variously exemplified" (130). For example, a melody is a sequence of tonal relations—a form—that can be exemplified using not only different instruments but different manners, different expressive techniques. Similarly, and more radically, a cockroach is a form of existence that can be variously exemplified (expressed) not just by the creeping brown thing that scuttles away when you turn on your kitchen light but by a weird story written by a German-speaking Czech Jew. In the latter, the logical form of a cockroach is not so much distorted as it is exemplified in a discursive mode. And that it bears no sensuous similarity to the insect on your floor or in your box of cereal doesn't matter, because logical form is not reducible to a sensible order. Although Langer speaks of analogy as logical form's primary mode of expression, analogy by formal relations is not sensibly verifiable; form is an abstraction, and abstractions are not confirmed or substantiated so much as they are thought. The implication of this is that the expression of logical form is the thought of extra-being. (For more on nonsensuous similarity, see Massumi 2011, especially chap. 4.)

CHAPTER 4. EX POST FACTO EX ANTE (OR, IT'S ALL IN THE SETUP . . .)

1 This condition is called "maladaptive daydreaming." More in the next chapter. For a preview, see Jayne Bigelsen and Tina Kelley's essay "When Daydreaming Replaces Real Life" (2015).

2 Leading up to his studies on the imagination, Bachelard tried to psychoanalyze fire. But it's not what you think. In this work he wasn't trying to understand the psychology of fire so much as how our fascination with an object distorts the processes of induction (Bachelard 1964b, 5). It's also important to note that Bachelard never tried to diminish the force of what he called "the material imagination" and in fact turned his attention later in life to uncovering the profundity of how our encounters with elemental forces not only mediate our understanding of the world but let us live it more intensely and poetically.

3 Apparently, "thinking off" goes back to the 1960s or 1970s and was developed either as a form of safe sex or as a way for persons with spinal injuries to experience something like an orgasm. Or maybe both. Dr. Gina Ogden's *Women Who Love Sex* (2007) contains a fascinating chapter on thinking off that describes her own laboratory-based research, a reflection on the lack of literature in the field about this technique, and speculations on the relationship between female sexuality and its sociopolitical representations. You can also find how-to guides by doing a search on your favorite search engine.

4 *Ludic Dreaming* (Cechetto et al. 2017) is a book that I cowrote with David Cecchetto, Marc Couroux, and Ted Hiebert as the experimental theory group The Occulture.

5 "Infra-ordinary" and "endotic" are neologisms introduced by Perec (1989) to describe the everyday in its most unspectacular and overlooked. The aim for him was to perform a kind of anthropology of that which has not yet entered the fields of significance or insignificance.

6 Gilles Deleuze and Félix Guattari said this: "The milieus are open to chaos, which threatens them with exhaustion or intrusion. Rhythm is the milieus' answer to chaos" (1987, 313).

7 Leckie's *Ancillary Justice* (2013) is a speculative fiction that explores, among other things (such as the conventions of gender), how artificial intelligence could manifest and function in ways that challenge our current paradigms of consciousness and identity. Like all great speculative fiction, *Ancillary Justice* can be taken as a form of thought experiment that, as Steven Shaviro notes, "instead of approaching its issues abstractly, as philosophy does, or breaking them down into empirically testable propositions, as physical science does . . . *embodies* these issues in characters and narratives" (2016, 8–9). Thought experiments of this kind entail a method that is "emotional and situational, rather than rational and universalizing," and that, rather than aiming to prove or ground an argument, aims "to work through the weirdest and most extreme ramifications of these scenarios, and to imagine *what it would be like* if they were true" (9). If you haven't figured it out by now, this is basically what I've been up to here—although I'm not sure that I'm working through the ramifications of anything but the sheer fallout of experimenting with thought.

8 Unabashedly taken from the first lines of Friedrich Nietzsche's *Human, All Too Human* (1996).

9 I was asked by a friend and colleague, Why the Latin? My answer is that it has a rhythm to it that stuck with me as I was composing this piece. Given the nature of this writing and its concern with rhythm, I kept it as a way to honour that part of my thinking that was impelled more by rhythm than sense. But I think I also kept it because it seems to exemplify the way meaning happens only at the conclusion of a sentence or gesture, where, like a melody, it gives the impression that it ought to have meant something all along.

10 I didn't write these clown jokes. I don't know who did. But they make me laugh, every time.

CHAPTER 5. DO EARWORMS HAVE DAYDREAMS?

1 See Antrobus, Singer, and Greenberg (1966); Kunzendorf, Brown, and McGee (1983); McVay, Kane, and Kwapil (2009); Mikulincer et al. (1990); Ottaviani, Shapiro, and Couyoumdjian (2013); and Pritzl (2003).

2 Chung and Cheung (2008); Harvey and Payne (2002); Lund et al. (2010); Ottaviani and Couyoumdjian (2013); Verlander, Benedict, and Hanson (1999); and Zoccola, Dickerson, and Lam (2009).

3 In addition to its splendid prose and general erudition, Connor's (2008) "Thinking Things" paints a compelling portrait of thinking as an activity that "must lose itself in objects, be unthinkable except through substitution, surrogacy and standing-in." This approaches what I propose a little later in this chapter about thought as an activity of abstraction that can't, apart from what we call "art" or illusion, take itself as such.

4 For an example of such a musical work, see my piece *the brown study* (2006–7). A recording of a performance and the score can be found on the "Sounds" page of my website, http://www.strangemonk.com. For a hexegetical reading of this work, see Marc Couroux's 2016 essay "The Egregor That Was, Is and Will Be the Brown Study (Speculative Relayism)."

5 It has been argued that the task-negative expression of the default mode network is fallacious and derives from a study that drew its results from a method in which "two distinct and dissociable functional-anatomic networks" were "anti-correlated," one of which, the executive attention network, is notably active during focused and outwardly directed attentional tasks. Although the default network has been shown to correlate with a host of internally directed tasks like past recollection, future planning, and emotional processing, its characterization as "task-negative" misconstrues its "functional role in active task conditions" (Spreng 2012).

6 See Baird, Smallwood, and Schooler (2011); Baird et al. (2012); McMillan, Kaufman, and Singer (2013); Schooler at el. (2011); and Zedelius and Schooler (2016).

7 In his biography of James, Jacques Barzun opens with an anecdote that sees the philosopher strolling with two students after his class on experimental psychology. As they amble together through Harvard Yard, one of the students notices a figure approaching them. "His long white beard blowing, cane swinging, he seems in a world of his own, talking to himself, or else to some invisible listener." When this student comments on the figure as being "the epitome of the absentminded professor," James replies, "What you really mean is that he is present-minded somewhere else" (Barzun 2002, 6).

8 See Freeman, Soltanifar, and Baer (2010); and Robinson et al. (2014).

9 The compulsive nature and altered state of consciousness that characterizes MDers' absorption, as well as the insulating effects such absorption brings, resonate with a state that Natasha Dow Schüll (2013) calls the "machine zone." In her study on machine-based gambling, Schüll found gamblers were interested less in the thrill of risk or the hope of winning and more in establishing a sense of continuity that would keep "worldly contingencies in a kind of abeyance" (13). This sense of continuity, she suggests, is achieved when the coupling of humans and machines develops "distinctive procedural and phenomenological routines" to produce "a unique 'cycle of energy and concentration' and a corresponding cycle of affective peaks and dips" (18). In a game like poker, which entails intersubjective feedback, these routines can place a gambler in an extremely heightened sense of suspense that swings through intense highs and lows. However, because it's usually conducted alone (as is MD), machine gambling doesn't have an intersubjective dimension through which intensities can circuit, the effect of which is not a heightened state of suspense but a steady, trancelike condition that she names the "machine zone." Although her study focused largely on the culture of slot machine gambling, Schüll notes that the procedural routines and behavioral refrains formed by the use of interactive gadgetry establishes a similar type of short circuit, which acts upon itself to promote its steady and low-intensity perpetuation. Schüll calls these short circuits "ludic loops" and suggests that they are found everywhere. Apart from a master's thesis that examines the relationship between MD and the use of media (see Uslu 2015), there is no research that links obsessive daydreaming to the gambling-like design features of certain technologies that foster the production of ludic loops. That said, because ludic loops share a set of symptoms with MD, it's not inconceivable that they could both be understood as contemporary exploits that capture something of the machinic nature of organisms.

10 The search I just conducted with Google's engine yields 438,000 hits. As of June 2021, two of the more prominent MD sites, one on Reddit (https://www.reddit.com/r/MaladaptiveDreaming) and another titled "Wild Minds Network" (wildminds.ning.com), boast 61,000 and 17,562 members, respectively.

11. William Shakespeare, *Measure for Measure*, 2.3.11.117–23:

But man, proud man

Dressed in a little brief authority
Most ignorant of what he's most assured—
His glassy essence—like an angry ape,
Plays such fantastic tricks before high Heaven
As makes the angels weep—who, with our spleens,
Would all laugh themselves mortal.

12 The concept of image schema developed by Mark Johnson resembles Langer's theory of symbolic projection. Basically, what Johnson calls "image schema"—meaningful cognitive structures that emerge "at the level of our bodily movements through space, our manipulations of objects, and our perceptual interactions" (1987, 29)—is what Langer calls "logical form." There's some advantage to Johnson's formulation over Langer's, chiefly because the expression "logical form" lends itself to a confusion between perceptual and conceptual patterning whereas "image schema" does not. In a somewhat snarky footnote, Langer acknowledges this confusion when she asserts against the eminent literary critic I. A. Richards that while *he* may not know what people mean when they say "logical form," *she* does, and he can find a simple but systematic accounting of it in an early work of hers (Langer 1953, 51n3). For a comparison of Langer's and Johnson's views, see Chaplin (2016).

13 In *Contagious Metaphor*, Peta Mitchell (2014) argues that "contagion is a limit case for metaphorical language" (5) because the "history [and] the etymology of contagion unsettles clear distinctions between the physical, the medical, the cultural and the affective" (6). This essential instability between the term's literal and metaphorical levels is what makes it easily transmissible to all manner of discourses. However, the fitness of the expression to such a wide range of phenomena is also what unsettles any epistemological claims made under the sign of contagion, for the performance of its indiscriminate application discloses the permeability of those bodies we call "knowledge." See also Marc Guillaume: "Returning to the abstract model of epidemia, it becomes evident that this model can be applied to phenomena that have nothing to do with disease: the circulation of objects, money, customs, or the propagation of affects and information. Fashion, the circulation of violence and even rumours, those contagions passing from mouth to ear, are all epidemics" (1987, 59).

14 This take on the opening lines of *Pontypool Changes Everything* is filched from Jonathan Ball's preface to Burgess's *The Bewdley Mayhem* (2014).

15 Mazzy may have been wrong about the repetition of words not being an immunological response. Repeating a word is the brain trying to modulate the process of symbolic transformation by accelerating the rate of its encounter with material reality. As Mazzy notes, repeating words makes them strange; it makes them strange because their symbolic uptake is short-circuited, and this short circuit grounds the word in its material substrate—vibrations and the

constriction of throat muscles—which offers new dynamic forms for new articulations. The virus doesn't cause the repetition of words, however, so much as the repetition is a symptom of an infection that has already taken hold of the person. But if the virus doesn't cause the repetition, then its symptomatic expression has a double indication. On the one hand, it indexes the malfunctioning of discursive thought, while, on the other, it shows, as a fever does with body temperature, the brain's attempt to transform its own process of symbolic transformation of experience.

Works Cited

Antrobus, John S., J. Singer, and S. Greenberg. 1966. "Studies in the Stream of Consciousness: Experimental Enhancement and Suppression of Spontaneous Cognitive Processes." *Perceptual and Motor Skills* 23 (2): 399–417.

Auxier, Randall. 1997. "Susanne Langer on Symbols and Analogy: A Case of Misplaced Concreteness?" *Process Studies* 26 (1): 86–106.

Bachelard, Gaston. 1964a. *The Poetics of Space*. Translated by Maria Jolas. Boston: Beacon.

Bachelard, Gaston. 1964b. *The Psychoanalysis of Fire*. Boston: Beacon.

Bachelard, Gaston. 1969. *The Poetics of Reverie*. Translated by Daniel Russell. Boston: Beacon.

Bachelard, Gaston. 1988a. *Air and Dreams: An Essay on the Imagination of Movement*. Translated by Edith Farrell and C. Frederick Farrell. Dallas: Dallas Institute of Humanities and Culture.

Bachelard, Gaston. 1988b. *The Flame of a Candle*. Translated by Joni Caldwell. Dallas: Dallas Institute of Humanities and Culture.

Bachelard, Gaston. 1994. *Water and Dreams: An Essay on the Imagination of Matter*. Translated by Edith Farrell. Dallas: Dallas Institute of Humanities and Culture.

Bachelard, Gaston. 2000. *The Dialectics of Duration*. Translated by Mary McAllester Jones. Manchester: Clinamen.

Bachelard, Gaston. 2002. *Earth and Reveries of Will: An Essay on the Imagination of Matter*. Translated by Kenneth Haltman. Dallas: Dallas Institute Humanities and Culture.

Baird, Benjamin, Jonathan Smallwood, Michael Mrazek, Julia Kam, Michael Franklin, and Jonathan Schooler. 2012. "Inspired by Distraction: Mind Wandering Facilitates Creative Incubation." *Psychological Science* 23 (10): 1117–22.

Baird, Benjamin, Jonathan Smallwood, and Jonathan W. Schooler. 2011. "Back to the Future: Autobiographical Planning and the Functionality of Mind-Wandering." *Consciousness and Cognition* 20 (4): 1604–11.

Ball, Jonathan. 2014. Preface to *The Bewdley Mayhem: Hellmouths of Bewdley, Pontypool Changes Everything, Caesarea*, by Tony Burgess, ix–xix.

Barzun, Jacques. 2002. *A Stroll with William James*. Chicago: University of Chicago Press.

Bateson, Gregory. 1972. *Steps to an Ecology of Mind*. Northvale, NJ: Jason Aronson.

Beaman, C. Philip, and Timothy Williams. 2010. "Earworms (Stuck Song Syndrome): Towards a Natural History of Intrusive Thoughts." *British Journal of Psychology* 101 (4): 637–53.

Beckett, Samuel. 1995. *The Complete Short Prose of Samuel Beckett, 1929–1989*. Edited by S. E. Gontarski. New York: Grove.

Benjamin, Walter. 1968. *Illuminations: Essays and Reflections*. Translated by Harry Zohn. New York: Schocken Books.

Benjamin, Walter. 1979. *One-Way Street and Other Writings*. Translated by Edmund Jephcott and Kingsley Shorter. London: Verso.

Bigelsen, Jayne, and Tina Kelley. 2015. "When Daydreaming Replaces Real Life." *Atlantic*, April 29. https://www.theatlantic.com/health/archive/2015/04/when-daydreaming-replaces-real-life/391319/.

Brooks, David. 2021. *Animal Dreaming*. Sydney: Sydney University Press.

Burgess, Tony. 1998. *Pontypool Changes Everything*. Toronto: ECW Press.

Burgess, Tony. 2014. *The Bewdley Mayhem: Hellmouths of Bewdley, Pontypool Changes Everything, Caesarea*. Toronto: Misfit/ECW Press.

Caillois, Roger. 2001. *Man, Play and Games*. Urbana: University of Illinois Press.

Cecchetto, David, Marc Couroux, Ted Hiebert, and Eldritch Priest. 2017. *Ludic Dreaming: How to Listen Away from Contemporary Technoculture*. London: Bloomsbury Academic.

Chaplin, Adrianne Dengerink. 2016. "Feeling the Body in Art: Embodied Cognition and Aesthetics in Mark Johnson and Susanne K. Langer." *Sztuka i Filozofia/Art and Philosophy* 48:5–11.

Chaplin, Adrienne Dengerink. 2021. *The Philosophy of Susanne Langer: Embodied Meaning in Logic, Art and Feeling*. London: Bloomsbury Academic.

Chomsky, Noam. 1957. *Syntactic Structures*. The Hague: Mouton.

Chung, Ka-Fai, and M.-M. Cheung. 2008. "Sleep-Wake Patterns and Sleep Disturbance among Hong Kong Chinese Adolescents." *Sleep* 31 (2): 185–94.

Coetzee, J. M. 2001. *The Lives of Animals*. Princeton, NJ: Princeton University Press.

Connor, Steven. 2008. "Thinking Things." Steven Connor website. http://stevenconnor.com/thinkingthings.html.

Coppola, Francis Ford, dir. 1974. *The Conversation*. Hollywood: Paramount Pictures.

Couroux, Marc. 2016. "The Egregor That Was, Is and Will Be the Brown Study (Speculative Relayism)." In *Phono-Fictions and Other Felt Thoughts*, edited by David Cecchetto, 185–217. Seattle: Noxious Sector.

Cross, Fiona R., and Robert R. Jackson. 2017. "Representation of Different Exact Numbers of Prey by a Spider-Eating Predator." *Interface Focus* 7 (3): Article 20160035.

Culp, Andrew. 2016. *Dark Deleuze*. Minneapolis: University of Minnesota Press.

Deleuze, Gilles. 1990. *The Logic of Sense*. Translated by Mark Lester. New York: Columbia University Press.

Deleuze, Gilles. 1994. *Difference and Repetition*. Translated by Paul Patton. New York: Columbia University Press.

Deleuze, Gilles, and Félix Guattari. 1983. *Anti-Oedipus: Capitalism and Schizophrenia*. Minneapolis: University of Minnesota Press.

Deleuze, Gilles, and Félix Guattari. 1987. *A Thousand Plateaus: Capitalism and Schizophrenia*. Translated by Brian Massumi. Minneapolis: University of Minnesota Press.

Dennett, Daniel. 2014. *Intuition Pumps and Other Tools for Thinking*. London: Penguin.

Derrida, Jacques. 2008. *The Animal That Therefore I Am*. Edited by Marie-Louise Mallet. Translated by David Wills. New York: Fordham University Press.

Dryden, Donald. 1997. "Whitehead's Influence on Susanne Langer's Conception of Living Form." *Process Studies* 26 (1–2): 62–85.

During, Elie. 2010. "Loose Coexistence : Technologies of Attention in the Post-Metropoli." In *Cognitive Architecture: from Bio-politics to Noo-politics*, edited by Deborah Hauptmann and Warren Neidich, 267–82. Rotterdam: 010 Publishers.

Farrugia, Nicholas, Kelly Jakubowski, Rhodri Cusack, and Lauren Stewart. 2015. "Tunes Stuck in Your Brain: The Frequency and Affective Evaluation of Involuntary Musical Imagery Correlate with Cortical Structure." *Consciousness and Cognition* 35:66–77.

Freeman, Roger D., Atefeh Soltanifar, and Susan Baer. 2010. "Stereotypic Movement Disorder: Easily Missed." *Developmental Medicine and Child Neurology* 52 (8): 733–38.

Gilloch, Graham. 2007. "Urban Optics: Film, Phantasmagoria and the City in Benjamin and Kracauer." *New Formations* 61 (2): 115–37.

Golub, Spenser. 2014. *Incapacity: Wittgenstein, Anxiety, and Performance Behavior*. Chicago: Northwestern University Press.

Guillaume, Marc. 1987. "The Metamorphoses of Epidemia." In *Zone 1|2: The Contemporary City*, edited by Michel Ferher and Sanford Kwinter, 59–69. New York: Zone Books.

Harvey, Allison G., and Suzanna Payne. 2002. "The Management of Unwanted Pre-sleep Thoughts in Insomnia: Distraction with Imagery versus General Distraction." *Behaviour Research and Therapy* 40 (3): 267–77.

Hayles, N. Katherine. 2007. "Hyper and Deep Attention: The Generational Divide in Cognitive Modes." *Profession* 2007 (1): 187–99.

Hayot, Eric. 2014. *The Elements of Academic Style: Writing for the Humanities*. New York: Columbia University Press.

Hughes, Ted. 2016a. "The Jaguar." In *A Ted Hughes Bestiary: Poems*, edited by Alice Oswald, 4. New York: Farrar, Straus and Giroux.

Hughes, Ted. 2016b. "A Second Glance at a Jaguar." In *A Ted Hughes Bestiary: Poems*, edited by Alice Oswald, 29–30. New York: Farrar, Straus and Giroux.

Jakubowski, Kelly, Sebastian Finkel, Lauren Stewart, and Daniel Müllensiefen. 2017. "Dissecting an Earworm: Melodic Features and Song Popularity Predict Involuntary Musical Imagery." *Psychology of Aesthetics, Creativity, and the Arts* 11 (2): 122–35.

James, William. 1950. *The Principles of Psychology*. New York: Dover.

James, William. 1996. *Essays in Radical Empiricism*. Lincoln: University of Nebraska Press.

James, William. 2000. *Pragmatism and Other Writings*. Edited by Giles Gunn. New York: Penguin Classics.

Japyassú, Hilton F., and Kevin N. Laland. 2017. "Extended Spider Cognition." *Animal Cognition* 20 (3): 375–95.

Johnson, Mark. 1987. *The Body in the Mind: The Bodily Basis of Meaning, Imagination, and Reason*. Chicago: University of Chicago Press.

Joyce, James. 2000. *Ulysses*. London: Penguin Classic.

Kafka, Franz. 1995. *The Metamorphosis and Other Stories*. New York: Schocken.

Kane, Brian. 2015. "Sound Studies without Auditory Culture: A Critique of the Ontological Turn." *Sound Studies* 1 (1): 2–21. https://doi.org/10.1080/20551940.2015.1079063.

Kierkegaard, Søren. 2008. *Kierkegaard's Journals and Notebooks*. Vol. 2, *Journals EE–KK*. Edited by Niels Jørgen Cappelørn, Alastair Hannay, David J. Kangas, Bruce H. Kirmmse, Vanessa Rumble, K. Brian Söderquist, and George Pattison. Princeton, NJ: Princeton University Press.

Killingsworth, Matthew A., and Daniel T. Gilbert. 2010. "A Wandering Mind Is an Unhappy Mind." *Science* 330 (6006): 932. https://doi.org/10.1126/science.1192439.

Klinger, Eric. 1971. *Structure and Functions of Fantasy*. Chichester, UK: Wiley Interscience.

Köhler, Wolfgang. 1925. *The Mentality of Apes*. Translated by Ella Winter. London: Kegan Paul, Trench.

Kunzendorf, Robert, Cynthia Brown, and Darlene McGee. 1983. "Hypnotizability: Correlations with Daydreaming and Sleeping." *Psychological Reports* 53 (2): 406.

Langer, Susanne K. 1930. *The Practice of Philosophy*. New York: Holt.

Langer, Susanne K. 1942. *Philosophy in a New Key: A Study in the Symbolism of Reason, Rite, and Art*. 3rd ed. Cambridge, MA: Harvard University Press.

Langer, Susanne K. 1953. *Feeling and Form*. New York: Charles Scribner's Sons.

Langer, Susanne K. 1967. *Mind: An Essay on Human Feeling*. Vol. 1. Baltimore: Johns Hopkins University Press.

Langer, Susanne K. 1971. "The Great Shift: From Instinct to Intuition." In *Man and Beast: Comparative Social Behavior*, edited by J. F. Eisenberg and Wilton Dillon, 315–29. Washington, DC: Smithsonian Institution Press.

Langer, Susanne K. 1972. *Mind: An Essay on Human Feeling*. Vol. 2. Baltimore: Johns Hopkins University Press.

Leckie, Ann. 2013. *Ancillary Justice*. New York: Orbit. Epub.

Lund, Hannah G., Brian D. Reider, Annie Whiting, and J. Roxanne Prichard. 2010. "Sleep Patterns and Predictors of Disturbed Sleep in a Large Population of College Students." *Journal of Adolescent Health: Official Publication of the Society for Adolescent Medicine* 46 (2): 124–32.

Malcolm, Norman. 2001. *Ludwig Wittgenstein: A Memoir*. Oxford: Clarendon.

Markson, David. 1988. *Wittgenstein's Mistress*. Normal, IL: Dalkey Archive Press.

Massumi, Brian. 2011. *Semblance and Event: Activist Philosophy and the Occurrent Arts*. Cambridge, MA: MIT Press.

Massumi, Brian. 2014. *What Animals Teach Us about Politics*. Durham, NC: Duke University Press.

Massumi, Brian. 2015. *Ontopower: War, Powers, and the State of Perception*. Durham, NC: Duke University Press.

McDonald, Bruce, dir. 2008. *Pontypool*. Toronto: Ponty Up Pictures.

McMillan, Rebecca, Scott Kaufman, and Jerome Singer. 2013. "Ode to Positive Constructive Daydreaming." *Frontiers in Psychology* 4: Article 626.

McVay, Jennifer C., Michael J. Kane, and Thomas Kwapil. 2009. "Tracking the Train of Thought from the Laboratory into Everyday Life: An Experience-Sampling Study of Mind Wandering across Controlled and Ecological Contexts." *Psychonomic Bulletin and Review* 16 (5): 857–63.

Mikulincer, Mario, Harvey Babkoff, Tamir Caspy, and Hillel Weiss. 1990. "The Impact of Cognitive Interference on Performance during Prolonged Sleep Loss." *Psychological Research* 52 (1): 80–86.

Mitchell, Peta. 2014. *Contagious Metaphor*. London: Bloomsbury Academic.

Nagel, Thomas. 1974. "What Is It Like to Be a Bat?" *Philosophical Review* 83 (4): 435–50.

Nietzsche, Friedrich. 1996. *Human, All Too Human: A Book for Free Spirits*. Translated by R. J. Hollingdale. 2nd ed. Cambridge: Cambridge University Press.

Nietzsche, Friedrich. 2006. "On Truth and Lies in a Nonmoral Sense." In *The Nietzsche Reader*, edited by Keith Ansell Pearson and Duncan Large, 114–23. Malden, MA: Wiley-Blackwell.

Nagel, Ernest, 1943. "Review of Susanne K. Langer, *Philosophy in a New Key*." *Journal of Philosophy* 40 (12): 323–29.

Ogden, Gina. 2007. *Women Who Love Sex: Ordinary Women Describe Their Paths to Pleasure, Intimacy, and Ecstasy*. Boston: Trumpeter.

Ottaviani, Cristina, and Alessandro Couyoumdjian. 2013. "Pros and Cons of a Wandering Mind: A Prospective Study." *Frontiers in Psychology* 4: Article 524.

Ottaviani, Cristina, David Shapiro, and Alessandro Couyoumdjian. 2013. "Flexibility as the Key for Somatic Health: From Mind Wandering to Perseverative Cognition." *Biological Psychology* 94 (1): 38–43.

Peirce, Charles Sanders. 1997. *Pragmatism as a Principle and Method of Right Thinking: The 1903 Harvard Lectures on Pragmatism*. Edited by Patricia Ann Turrisi. Albany: State University of New York Press.

Perec, Georges. 1989. *L'infra-ordinaire*. Paris: Seuil.

Potenza, Alessandra, and Rachel Becker. 2017. "Why Exactly Are These Turkeys Circling a Dead Cat?" *The Verge*, March 2. https://www.theverge.com/2017/3/2/14792602/turkeys-circling-dead-cat-animal-behavior-twitter-video

Priest, Eldritch. 2013. *Boring Formless Nonsense: Experimental Music and the Aesthetics of Failure*. London: Bloomsbury Academic.

Pritzl, T. Jane. 2003. "The Effect of Experimentally Enhanced Daydreaming on an Electroencephalographic Measure of Sleepiness." PhD diss., North Carolina State University. http://www.lib.ncsu.edu/resolver/1840.16/3833.

Robinson, Sally, Martin Woods, Francesco Cardona, Valentina Baglioni, and Tammy Hedderly. 2014. "Intense Imagery Movements: A Common and Distinct Paediatric Subgroup of Motor Stereotypies." *Developmental Medicine and Child Neurology* 56 (12): 1212–18.

Ruyer, Raymond. 1957. "The Vital Domain of Animals and the Religious World of Man." *Diogenes* 5 (18): 35–46.

Schooler, Jonathan W., Jonathan Smallwood, Kalina Christoff, Todd Handy, Erik Reichle, and Michael Sayette. 2011. "Meta-awareness, Perceptual Decoupling and the Wandering Mind." *Trends in Cognitive Sciences* 15 (7): 319–26.

Schüll, Natasha Dow. 2014. *Addiction by Design: Machine Gambling in Las Vegas*. Princeton, NJ: Princeton University Press.

Shakespeare, William. 2010. *Measure for Measure*. Edited by Jonathan Bate and Eric Rasmussen. New York: Modern Library.

Shaviro, Steven. 2016. *Discognition*. London: Repeater.

Singer, Jerome L. 1966. *Daydreaming: An Introduction to the Experimental Study of Inner Experience*. New York: Random House.

Somer, Eli. 2002. "Maladaptive Daydreaming: A Qualitative Inquiry." *Journal of Contemporary Psychotherapy* 32 (2): 197–212.

Spreng, Nathan. 2012. "The Fallacy of a 'Task-Negative' Network." *Frontiers in Psychology* 3: Article 145.

Stiegler, Bernard. 1998. *Technics and Time*. Vol. 1, *The Fault of Epimetheus*. Translated by Richard Beardsworth and George Collins. Stanford, CA: Stanford University Press.

Thompson, D'Arcy. 1992. *On Growth and Form: The Complete Revised Edition*. New York: Dover.

Uslu, Handan. 2015. "Understanding the Relationship between Media Use and Maladaptive Daydreaming." Master's thesis, Georgetown University.

Van Loon, Joost. 2002. "A Contagious Living Fluid: Objectification and Assemblage in the History of Virology." *Theory, Culture and Society* 19 (5–6): 107–24.

Verlander, Lorrie A., James O. Benedict, and David P. Hanson. 1999. "Stress and Sleep Patterns of College Students." *Perceptual and Motor Skills* 88 (3, pt. 1): 893–98.

Wallace, David Foster. 2007. "Consider the Lobster." In *Consider the Lobster and Other Essays*, 235–53. New York: Back Bay Books.

Whitehead, Alfred North. 1978. *Process and Reality*. New York: Free Press.

Whitehead, Alfred North. 1985. *Science and the Modern World*. London: Free Association Books.

Wittgenstein, Ludwig. 1958. *Philosophical Investigations*. Translated by G. E. M. Anscombe. Oxford: Basil Blackwell.

Wittgenstein, Ludwig. 2001. *Tractatus Logico-Philosophicus*. Translated by D. F. Pears and B. F. McGuinness. 2nd ed. London: Routledge.

Wittgenstein, Ludwig. 2009. *Philosophical Investigations*. Edited by P. M. S. Hacker and Joachim Schulte. Translated by G. E. M. Anscombe, P. M. S. Hacker, and Joachim Schulte. 4th ed. Malden, MA: Wiley-Blackwell.

Woolf, Virginia. 1981. *The Letters of Virginia Woolf.* Vol. 4. Edited by Nigel Nicolson and Joanne Trautmann. New York: Mariner Books.

Woolf, Virginia. 2004. *The Waves*. London: Vintage.

Zedelius, Claire M., and Jonathan Schooler. 2016. "The Richness of Inner Experience: Relating Styles of Daydreaming to Creative Processes." *Frontiers in Psychology* 6: Article 2063. https://doi.org/10.3389/fpsyg.2015.02063.

Zoccola, Peggy M., Sally Dickerson, and Suman Lam. 2009. "Rumination Predicts Longer Sleep Onset Latency after an Acute Psychosocial Stressor." *Psychosomatic Medicine* 71 (7): 771–75.

Index

abstraction: and (nonhuman) animals, 16–17; and audio technologies, 2, 8; and dissociation, 56; and earworms, 8–9; and experience, 13–14, 56; and feeling, 15; and humanity, 8, 14; lived, 10, 16, 47; and living body, 11; and mind, 13; and music, 8; and play, 17; and rhythm, 41; and semblance, 56; and symbolism, 15–16; and thought, 1–2; and value, 8; and waves, 6, 41

act(ion), 30–33, 69n8; and bodies, 31; as contagious, 31–32; vs. event, 67n1; vs. perception, 35; and rhythm, 31; as sole motivation, 35, 65n3; and thought, 33, 42

ADHD, 6, 54–55

agency: of the wandering mind, 44

antimetabole: as a great word (to repeat), 32

attention: and distraction, 6, 47–48, 52–54; and imagination, 50–51; and reverie, 51

audio technologies: and abstraction, 2, 8; and earworms, 2

Bachelard, Gaston, 53; on daydreams/reveries, 6, 46, 50; on fire and psychoanalysis, 40, 73n2; on melody, 43; on the news, 49, 52; on the objective study of imagination, 45; and rhythm, 68n2

backwardness: and behavior, 20; and music, 3; and truth, 43

Bateson, Gregory: on the paradox of play, 16–17, 69n8. *See also* play

Beckett, Samuel, 46

Benjamin, Walter: on distraction, 52–53

body: and abstraction, 11; and acts, 31; still (as still a body doing), 57

boring: descriptions, 30–31; low tolerance for the, 52; questions, 19

brain: default mode network, 53, 74n5; and earworm, 1

Burgess, Tony: *Pontypool Changes Everything*, 58–63

Caillois, Roger: on games of vertigo, 27, 71n9. *See also* play

cartography, enactive, 48

Chomsky, Noam: on syntax vs. semantics, 33, 69n5

circling: of cockroaches, 30–31, 34–35, 69n8; of hedgehogs, 34; of mice, 71n9; of turkeys (around a dead cat), 9, 65n2; of the world (around Bachelard), 50, 52. *See also* enthusiasms

Coetzee, J. M., 4, 19–21; *Elizabeth Costello*, 4, 9–11, 19–21. *See also* what it would be like / what it's like

compulsion: and daydreaming, 6, 39, 46, 54–55, 75n9; and language, 26; to repeat, 60–61; and ritual, 15

Connor, Steven: on mixing usages, 46

contagious: acts, 31–32; (day)dreams, 46, 50; laughter, 63; as metaphor, 58–59, 63, 76n13. *See also* virality

Coppola, Francis Ford: *The Conversation*, 30

Culp, Andrew: on Deleuze's game, 66n3

daydreams/reveries, 32–33, 37, 45–63; as contagious, 46, 50; and earworms, 1, 8; exiting, 39; and hyperorientation, 51–52; and imagination, 6, 50; vs. insomnia, 45; as labor, 6; maladaptive daydreaming, 6, 39, 54–55, 75n9; and music, 46–48; as obsession, 6; as positive/practical, 15, 53; and the self, 6
death: and breezes, 59; and bugs, 29–30, 33; and circling turkeys, 9, 65n2; and earworms, 8; semblance of a, 63; thinking our way into, 9–10, 19; of wind, 59
Deleuze, Gilles, 6; on becoming-animal, 57, 66n3; on "contemplation," 19; on extra-being, 71n11; and play, 66n3; on practicality being a matter of degree, 15; on a refrain, 29; on rhythm, 73n7; on sense, 69n5; on truth, 34
Dennett, Daniel: on thought experiments, 2. *See also* thinking
Derrida, Jacques: on "animal," 65n4
desire: as the desire of others' desire, 57; and musical events, 46
Dewey, John: and rhythm, 68n2
discursivity, 20–21
distraction: and attention, 6, 47–48, 52–54; vs. contemplation, 55; continuous, 6; as expressive, 46; as positive, 48, 52–54; and thought, 7; world as, 52. *See also* mind: wandering
Duke University Press, 21
During, Elie: on distraction, 52. *See also* distraction

earworms: and abstraction, 8–9; and (nonhuman) animals, 4, 9, 21, 28–29; and audio technologies, 2; and brain, 1; and daydreams, 1, 8; and death, 8; as funny, 3; and memory, 1, 9; as practical, 15; and repetition, 1, 5, 22; as technical, 8; and thought, 9; as unpredictable, 1
enthusiasms, 5; as appearance, 31; excess felt as, 17; impractical, 14–18, 15, 30–38. *See also* circling; mind
event: vs. act, 67n1; as dependent on initial conditions, 2; fact vs., 42; mind as, 12
expression: and creativity, 9; vs. description, 25; vs. fact, 22; and gesture, 15–17; of ideas, 14–15; vs. practicality, 14–15; of reality, 46; and sense, 34; symbolic, 14; and thought, 20–22; and what it's like, 11; and writing, 37

feeling: and abstraction, 15; as doing, 12; immediacy of, 68n3; and mind, 12–14; and music, 63, 66n5; and play, 17; and rhythm, 12; symbol of, 18; and thought, 8, 13, 19–21, 69n8
fire: and psychoanalysis, 6, 42, 73n2; study of, 45
Freud, Sigmund, 53; on ritual, 15. *See also* ritual
frisson, 6, 40–41
function: vs. quality, 4, 16

Guattari, Félix: on becoming-animal, 57; and play, 66n3; on practicality being a matter of degree, 15; on a refrain, 29; on rhythm, 73n7
Guillaume, Marc: on the model of epidemia, 76n12. *See also* contagious; virality

Hayles, N. Katherine: on distraction as a new cognitive style, 52
Hayot, Eric: on writing, 3
Hughes, Ted, 11, 19–20

imagery: and daydreams, 6, 50; and humanity, 69n8; and the real, 50; repetition of, 7; study of, 45
imagination: and attention, 50–51; and daydreams, 6; study of, 45
intimacy, species, 8

James, William, 39, 53; on absentmindedness, 75n7; on the "blooming, buzzing confusion" of the world, 13; on daydreaming, 54; on truth, 42
Johnson, Mark: on image schema, 76n12
jokes, 6, 22–23, 29, 35, 38–40, 43, 66n3
Joyce, James, 53; *Ulysses*, 10–11, 19

Kafka, Franz, 5, 35, 71n11. *See also* circling; transformation
Kane, Brian: on the ontological turn in sound studies, 65n3
Kierkegaard, Søren: on life understood backward, 43
Klinger, Eric: on perceptually decoupled thought, 53
knowledge: and epistemology, 23, 32–34; of a lack of capacity for knowledge, 9; of what one is doing, 43. *See also* truth
Köhler, Wolfgang, 19–20. *See also* Coetzee, J. M.

Langer, Susanne, 11–22, 30–32; on acts, 5, 15–16, 30–32, 35, 67n1, 69n8; on animals, 65n3, 69n8; on art, 18, 56, 66n5; on artists (in the middle of a work), 51; on dreams, 51–52; *Feeling and Form*, 11, 15, 18; on the mind, 12–13, 56–57; *Philosophy in a New Key*, 11, 18; on practicality, 14; on rhythm, 68n2; on semblance, 11, 18–19, 47, 56, 68n4; on structure, 71n11; on symbols, 4, 11, 13–17, 20–21, 66n5, 69n8, 76n12; on thought, 20
language, 23–28, 69n5; and compulsion, 26; dizzying of, 5, 27–28; and experience, 4–5; games, 4–5, 26–28, 62; idioms, 32; limits of, 25–26; and manner of use, 21–22, 25–26; and music, 62–63; of noise, 40; and philosophy, 5, 23–28; pragmatism of, 5; private, 24–25; semantic saturation, 61, 76n15; sharing of, 4–5; as slippery, 32–33; as virus, 3, 7, 58–63
Leckie, Ann: *Ancillary Justice*, 42, 73n7

Mahler, Gustav: Symphony No. 3, 47
Markson, David: *Wittgenstein's Mistress*, 22
Massumi, Brian: on animal play, 17–18, 48, 69n8; on attention, 51; on the being of analogy, 4, 19; on paradoxes, 69n8; on semblance, 56; on techniques/technologies of existence, 9, 66n6
McDonald, Bruce: *Pontypool*, 59–60. *See also* Burgess, Tony: *Pontypool Changes Everything*
memory: and earworms, 1, 9; and musical events, 46
metaphor, 57–59, 63, 76n13
mimes: as event artists, 5; as truthful liars, 3, 34, 37–38. *See also* mimicry
mimicry: and admiration, 45. *See also* mimes
mind, 11–17, 25, 55–57; and daydreams, 46; as event, 12; wandering, 44, 47–49, 53. *See also* distraction
Mitchell, Peta: on contagion and metaphor, 76n13. *See also* contagious; metaphor
multitasking, 52. *See also* attention; distraction
music: and abstraction, 8; background, 1; backward, 3; and daydreams, 46–48; and feeling, 63; and language, 62–63; as technology of existence, 9; and truth, 43; unplayingly played, 6, 46–48

Nagel, Thomas, 9. *See also* what it would be like / what it's like
news, the: as essential to Bachelard, 49–50
Nietzsche, Friedrich: on metaphors and lying, 58

obsession: and daydreams, 6; as excessive enthusiasm, 30; and language, 26; obsessive-compulsive conditions, 55; and sticking together, 9

Peirce, Charles Sanders: on anonymous thinking, 33, 68n4
Perec, Georges: on the exceptionally unexceptional, 41, 73n5
philosophy: as a funhouse of thought, 24; and jokes, 6, 23, 29, 66n3; and language, 5, 23–28; and play, 66n3
play, 16–18; animal, 48, 69n8; and communication, 16, 69n8; and feeling, 17; vs. humor, 66n3; and panic, 27. *See also* language: games
poetry: and daydreams, 46; and fire, 40, 45; and music, 63; and thinking, 11, 19–21
practicality, 13–20. *See also* enthusiasms
Proust, Marcel, 53

repetition: and behavioral disorder, 55; and compulsion, 60–61; and daydreaming, 46; and earworms, 1, 5, 22; of image, 7; and language, 60–63, 76n15; of a name (or "this"), 25, 27; of perceiving perception's next potential perception, 51; and rhythm, 2, 68n2; and song, 62
reveries. *See* daydreams/reveries
revision: of thought, 22
rhythm: and abstraction, 41; and act, 31; and chaos, 73n7; and continuity, 68n2; and the expression of livingness, 11; and feeling, 12; and frisson, 40–41; of Latin, 74n9; and repetition, 2, 68n2; and sense, 41; of thinking, 41; writing to a, 41
Richter, Max: *Sleep*, 47
ritual, 15, 17, 69n8
rumor, 6, 40, 58

Schüll, Natasha Dow: on the "machine zone," 75n9
semblance, 11, 18–19, 47, 56–57, 63, 68n4
Shakespeare, William: on our "glassy essence," 55, 75n11
Shaviro, Steven: on science fiction and thought experiments, 2, 73n7
silence: as information, 49
Singer, Jerome: on daydreaming as a constructive activity, 53
sleep: insomnia, 44–45; and mind-wandering, 44; and music-listening, 47
slowness: and daydream music, 47, 49. *See also* music; daydreams/reveries
Somer, Eli: on "maladaptive daydreaming," 55
stuckness: in the act, 32; of earworms, 1, 6, 22–24; together (of turkey rafters), 9
style: vs. (model of) being, 37; of one's own (idiosyncrasies), 48
symbol: and abstraction, 15–16; and animals, 69n8; vs. being, 4; of feeling, 18–19; and humanity, 43; and thought, 20

technologies/techniques of existence, 9, 22, 65n4, 66n6
temporality: and lies, 43; the present, 35, 68n4; surrender to the passage of time, 54
thinking: absence of (during orgasm), 40; and abstraction, 1–2; and act, 33, 42; anonymous, 33; vs. art, 56; into the being of another, 4, 9–22, 36–37; and the default mode network, 74n5; and distraction, 7; and (nothing) doing, 41; and earworms, 9; and expression, 20–22; and feeling, 8, 13, 19–21, 69n8; and hearing, 25; and jokes, 6; and objects, 46; perceptually decoupled, 53; as semblance, 55–56; sympathetic, 11; about thinking, 9, 24; thinking off, 40, 73n3; thought experiments, 2, 4, 73n7; what counts as, 20–21, 45; and writing, 3
transformation, 5, 11, 13–18, 35–38, 76n15. *See also* what it would be like / what it's like
truth, 32–35, 40–43, 57–58. *See also* knowledge

value: and abstraction, 8; of circumambulation, 69n8; of ideas (depending on who owns them), 7, 57; of a joke, 38; and truth, 33–34
virality, 58–63, 76n15. *See also* contagious

waiting: and activity of the mind, 47
Wallace, David Foster: "Consider the Lobster," 29
what it would be like/what it's like, 1–2, 8–11, 16, 18–19, 23, 36–37, 56–57, 73n7. *See also* Coetzee, J. M.; transformation
Whitehead, Alfred North: on the event, 67n1; on feeling, 12; and rhythm, 68n2. *See also* Langer, Susanne
Wittgenstein, Ludwig, 30; on interior experience, 4, 24; on philosophy and jokes, 6, 23; on language, 24–28, 62; on the strangeness of mental processes, 23
Woolf, Virginia, 53; on flowing, 57; *The Waves*, 41; on writing to a rhythm (rather than a plot), 41
writing: and expression, 37; and rhythm, 41; and thinking, 3

www.ingramcontent.com/pod-product-compliance
Lightning Source LLC
LaVergne TN
LVHW010615100826
845148LV00014B/2982
* 9 7 8 1 4 7 8 0 1 7 9 8 1 *